James Hogg

De Quincey and his friends

Personal recollections, souvenirs and anecdotes of Thomas De Quincey, his friends

and associates

James Hogg

De Quincey and his friends
Personal recollections, souvenirs and anecdotes of Thomas De Quincey, his friends and associates

ISBN/EAN: 9783742882509

Manufactured in Europe, USA, Canada, Australia, Japa

Cover: Foto ©Thomas Meinert / pixelio.de

Manufactured and distributed by brebook publishing software (www.brebook.com)

James Hogg

De Quincey and his friends

DE QUINCEY

AND

HIS FRIENDS

PERSONAL RECOLLECTIONS, SOUVENIRS

AND ANECDOTES

OF

THOMAS DE QUINCEY

HIS FRIENDS AND ASSOCIATES

WRITTEN AND COLLECTED BY

JAMES HOGG

EDITOR OF DE QUINCEY'S "UNCOLLECTED WRITINGS"

LONDON

SAMPSON LOW, MARSTON AND COMPANY
LIMITED

St. Dunstan's House

FETTER LANE, FLEET STREET, E.C.

1895

CONTENTS.

PREFACE.

FOR many years, in the throng of a busy life, I have indulged the hope that I might, some day, be able to draw together the scattered souvenirs and anecdotes of THOMAS DE QUINCEY—adding such personal recollections of my own as memory still kept fresh.

It appeared to me that by doing so some service would be done to literature and some good use made of the unequalled opportunities I enjoyed during years of intimate and continuous intercourse with the author.

Now that the long-lost letters and papers, fragments of the "Suspiria," &c., have at last seen the light, and I have attained my sixty-sixth year, with sufficient leisure at command, I attempt the task.

It is my grateful duty to record the various cordial, kindly aids which I have received, and which, I trust, will make this volume a welcome addition to DE QUINCEY literature—worthy to stand on the shelf alongside those "Collected Works" of the author which my father, my brother, and myself were first privileged to set before the public.

To the able co-operation of my colleague, DR. A. H. JAPP, who so worthily fulfilled his office as the author's biographer, as well as editor of the "Posthumous Works," I owe the concise review, kindly undertaken at my request, of DE QUINCEY'S FRIENDS AND ASSO-

CIATES. We have here the salient points of a long and chequered career picturesquely set forth with that accurate knowledge of facts which the writer's previous work had made familiar. In this section due prominence is given to points which have been made plain by the "Memorials" and "Posthumous Works"—thus disposing of certain erroneous notions and unwarrantable assumptions which crept into print. Some rash writers thrust themselves forward to air fancies concerning DE QUINCEY'S "Autobiographic Sketches" in absolute personal ignorance of the author, and with very imperfect knowledge of matters which they essayed to handle.

To MR. JOHN RITCHIE FINDLAY (of *The Scotsman*) I have to express my special thanks for permission to incorporate his "Personal Recollections," now long out of print. Mr. Findlay was one of the few persons whom DE QUINCEY was always pleased to see, and whose society he thoroughly enjoyed. These "Recollections," therefore, are penned by one whose acquaintance with the author and his family afforded him ample means of observation, and whose sympathetic feeling is evident in these interesting notes.

To MESSRS. WILLIAM BLACKWOOD & SONS I am indebted for their kind allowance of the work of another old and esteemed friend of DE QUINCEY, the late JOHN HILL BURTON, *Queen's Historiographer for Scotland*, author of "The Book Hunter."

In the *bizarre* chapter about "PAPAVERIUS," which I am permitted to reproduce from the well-known "Book Hunter," we have an odd view of DE QUINCEY which is very amusing, although the author becomes rather inventive here and there.

While Dr. Japp's survey covers the whole career, the miscellaneous material of the volume may be considered as relating roughly to three principal periods:—

1. THE "CONFESSIONS" PERIOD.
2. THE GLASGOW PERIOD.
3. THE EDINBURGH PERIOD.

To the first of these belongs the interesting Notes of Conversations by RICHARD WOODHOUSE—happily preserved by DR. GARNETT (of the British Museum), in his admirable edition of "The Confessions" (Parchment Library), before the original MS. perished in a fire on the premises of MESSRS. KEGAN PAUL & CO. To that firm I have to express my thanks for their kind concurrence in the use of RICHARD WOODHOUSE'S valuable notes.

To these I am able to add a new pendant—a relic of Oxford days which I lately recovered from the papers of the late DR. GOODENOUGH, of Christ Church, who was one of DE QUINCEY'S examiners when he was at Worcester College.

This Latin composition appears to be the only Academic piece extant. Whether it is the "Declamation" referred to by WOODHOUSE as having brought fame to DE QUINCEY, or merely a college exercise, it is, at all events, one of the elements which led DR. GOODENOUGH to refer, so emphatically, as we find he did, to the extraordinary promise given by the student's written work, before that sudden and unaccountable disappearance the day before the *vivâ voce* examination came on. For the English rendering of this Latin composition I am indebted to DR. GARNETT.

The two pathetic letters to MR. HESSEY, of TAYLOR and HESSEY (Proprietors of the *London Magazine*), reporting the opium "wrestles," I received from

MR. DAVEY, the well-known autograph dealer of Great Russell Street. The originals were in his hands.

In the second or GLASGOW period, I have the kind aid of MR. COLIN RAE-BROWN, who has contributed his well-remembered recollections of that time.

In the third or EDINBURGH period I am indebted to the REV. FRANCIS JACOX for his interesting " Recollections." MR. JAMES PAYN, the distinguished novelist and veteran editor, also permits me to include some genial notes from his " Literary Memories."

In the same group is a characteristic passage from the pen of the late JAMES G. BERTRAM—long engaged with the proprietor of *Tait's Magazine*, to which DE QUINCEY was a contributor. This I am able to reprint by the courtesy of MESSRS. A. CONSTABLE & CO.

All the foregoing belong to the class of Personal and Anecdotic Memories. Two other papers do not :—

1. The essay on " The Genius of De Quincey," for which I owe thanks to DR. SHADWORTH H. HODGSON, a relative of the DE QUINCEY family. It is from his volume of " Outcast Essays," and presents in a fair and suggestive form an estimate of DE QUINCEY as a scholar, a critic, and a great master of English style.

2. The ballad of " De Quincey's Revenge," a legend of the Crusades. This strong and graceful composition by DR. MOIR (" Delta "), now half-forgotten, seems to be a thing which it is desirable to put on record in DE QUINCEY literature. The copious antiquarian notes shed light on the ancient Scottish standing of the DE QUINCEY family, previous to the confiscation of their estates in the time of Bruce.

Coming now to my own recollections—"Days and Nights with DE QUINCEY," which first appeared in *Harper's Magazine*, I can only deplore the utter loss of a world of charming thoughts, anecdotes, and criticisms which I might have "made a note of"—if, like Captain Cuttle, I had begun soon enough and fallen regularly into the habit. But it was not so—the more's the pity!

I have ventured at the end of my revised and expanded Notes to tell the story, for the first time, of a curious incident in the history of "The Confessions."

Being the only one of the chief actors now alive, I judge that I may at this time of day, without offence to any person, let the public know the very real danger which suddenly threatened the whole project of the "Collected Works," and with them any likelihood of the author persevering in the revision of his writings.

The four unpublished letters of a humorous character now brought forward were addressed to me by the author. They will, I am sure, give pleasure to many readers.

Finally, I must touch on a graver subject. The remarkable essay, "On the Supposed Scriptural Expression for Eternity," I have introduced for two reasons: (1.) It was written specially for me, as the outcome of many conversations with the author on the solemn question of Future Punishment. (2.) Because, while it appears in the American edition, it is not in any of the British ones of the "Collected Works"—having hitherto been used by myself only in magazine form, and in a volume entitled "The Wider Hope."

I desire now to place the Essay where it may be permanently accessible. The late DR. COX, of *The*

Expositor, in his well-known book entitled "Salvator Mundi," dwells on this thoughtful and suggestive contribution to one of the profoundest inquiries which can engage the pilgrim's mind. Elsewhere the essay has been freely discussed by theologians of different schools.

I cannot close without expressing my warm thanks to MRS. BAIRD SMITH (FLORENCE DE QUINCEY) and MISS EMILY DE QUINCEY for examining these proof sheets, and enabling me to refer to them on various points. I have striven, by patient search and careful consideration, to show, by the impressions of friends and associates of varied character and attainment, what manner of man DE QUINCEY really was.

It has, indeed, been a labour of love. In old Scottish fashion I have sought to place this "stone upon the cairn" of the man who treated me and counselled me with an almost paternal tenderness.

Above and beyond all questions of intellectual power, of scholarship, or beauty of style,—*what human lesson stands out clear and strong throughout these recollections?* That, surely, *of perfect, unswerving kindness in daily life;* an antique, chivalrous courtesy and gracious consideration for people of every class, whatever their temper, whatever their foibles.

If ever man attained unto the full measure of that Scripture which ordains—"having compassion one of another, love as brethren, be pitiful, be courteous"—that man was THOMAS DE QUINCEY.

JAMES HOGG.

11th August, 1895.

THOMAS DE QUINCEY:
HIS FRIENDS AND ASSOCIATES.*

I.

WE should not assert for De Quincey a double personality. There was as little in him of the Dr. Jekyll and Mr. Hyde as in men of the most ordinary turn and type. But he did exhibit very unexpected traits. He revealed some tendencies that seemed almost incompatible. He has been spoken of as a mere dreamer, a solitary, a man apart, a kind of hermit by nature and constitution, whose great aim in life was to escape from everything like sociality and companionship. Greater error there could hardly be. All through his life his hunger for intercourse with others was very keen. Mrs. Baird Smith, in one of her contributions to his Memoir, finely tells how, wherever he went, he surrounded himself with friends, and had so little tact in laying down rules and in keeping to hours that a good deal in his sudden disappearances and settlement in new abodes had to do with this—escapes from the penalties his accessibility had imposed upon him. He himself seriously repeats the confession that, though no man had lived more in solitude than he had, yet that no man could ever have more regretted it. From infancy to old age, we

---

* By Alexander H. Japp, LL.D. (" H. A. Page "), Author of "Thomas de Quincey : His Life and Writings ;" Editor of his " Posthumous Works," " Memorials of the De Quincey Family," &c.

find in him this unique combination—love of meditation, and quick reactions which demanded the stimulus of contact with common human nature. There was in him none of the impatience with the ignorant and rude that is so commonly associated with culture, with the love of meditation and of abstract thought. Wherever he goes he has, in a very marked degree, the art of making himself at home. If others cannot sympathise with him in his lofty thoughts and imaginings, he can sympathise with them, in their thoughts and concerns, and in such a measure that he gains at once their secret and their affection. As we follow him through his long life, we find him a kind of centre of attraction for persons of the most contrasted natures, temperaments and social positions : his rare courtesy, which was born of his quick sympathies and kindly hospitalities, which delighted in making all with whom he had to do completely at home, has been celebrated by all with whom he came into contact; and by servants as decidedly as by their masters. In his "Confessions" he tells us:—

"At no time of my life have I been a person to hold myself polluted by the touch or approach of any creature that wore a human shape. I cannot suppose, I will not believe, that any creatures wearing the form of man or woman are so absolutely rejected and reprobate outcasts, that merely to talk with them inflicts pollution. On the contrary, from my very earliest youth, it has been my pride to converse familiarly, *more Socratico*, with all human beings—man, woman, or child—that chance might fling in my way ; for a philosopher should not see with the eyes of the poor limitary creature calling himself a man of the world, filled with narrow and self-regarding prejudices of birth and education, but should look upon himself as a catholic creature, and as standing in an equal relation to high and low, to educated and uneducated, to the guilty and the innocent."

In endeavouring, then, to present a picture of De Quincey among his friends and associates, within a moderate compass, we shall find ourselves embarrassed by wealth and variety rather than by lack of material; and the very contrasts in those whom we shall summon before our readers in his company will often have even the effect of oddity which now and then only deepens the interest and sometimes adds to the pathos of the circumstances.

II.

De Quincey, as is well known, was born in or near Manchester in 1785. His father was engaged in business, and when De Quincey was quite a child he built a country house in what was then a rural solitude named Greenheys. It was called Greenheys Hall. De Quincey's earliest recollections were connected with this house. He has frequently expressed his thankfulness that his childhood was passed in the country, and in the society of sisters, and not of rough brothers. The first event that made an impression on his mind was the death of his sister Jane when he was about two. He missed her childish society and prattle, but tells us that he knew little more than that Jane had disappeared. She had gone away but perhaps she would come back.

An attack of ague soon thereafter led to his being completely in the hands of nurses; and though he was made much of and petted, and some of his lady friends among them Miss Watson, (one of the two orphan heiresses, whose guardian was Mrs. Schreiber, his mother's bosom-friend,) thought and spoke of him as "a doll that could talk," his mental development was very marked

and precocious. Music, certain sights and sounds of
nature would so affect him that he would almost shed
tears. When he was about six years old, his sister
Elizabeth died, aged nine. Her influence on him had
been great, and he does not fail to celebrate it in his
own style. " Perhaps," he says, "the natural precedency
in authority of years, united to the tender humility with
which she declined to assert it, had been among the
fascinations of her presence;" and his apostrophe to
her, and his description of the effect on himself of
seeing her lying in her coffin, belong to the most
touching and effective of his writings. At all events,
it left a very lasting result on his mind, for many
references are made to it even in his productions of
later days.

The death of his father shortly after confirmed the
impression. An able man, who had so devoted himself
to business that all had prospered with him, yet with a
great deal of culture and marked ability in the literary
way, having himself written accounts of his travels, some
portions of which were published and received the
praise of discerning critics. He had been early
threatened with phthisis, and had been ordered abroad.
He only returned home to die. His famous son, in later
days, was wont to regret that he had known so little of
his father, who, from all he could discover, was a good
and upright man, and fitted perhaps to accord him
the sympathy which he often failed to find.

III.

Changes soon came on the death of his father. The
Rev. Samuel Hall, who had been a very intimate friend
both of his father and mother, and who was the most

active of the guardians appointed under his father's will, was a clergyman in Salford; and it was decided that Thomas and his elder brother William, who had hitherto been at a public school, should now go daily to Mr. Hall's for their lessons. Mr. Hall, it is evident, was a most conscientious, methodic man, with a real interest in the welfare of the family, but with no sort of sentiment or any touch of that tact of sympathy which goes for so much in the management of boys—at all events, such boys as our subject. William was of a very different temperament from Thomas. He was active, spirited, haughty, adventurous, and sought to engage the weaker younger brother in all his diversions and escapades. On their walks from Greenheys to Salford daily he found means to gratify his tastes. He picked a quarrel with some mill-boys, and, though his contempt for Thomas's "physics" was intense, he aimed at bringing him up to his own standard by putting him into positions of the greatest risk. More than once Thomas was taken prisoner by the mothers and sisters of the boys with whom they had fought, to be treated by them in such a manner as made him the less disposed to enter on such contests any more.

Even the pastimes of the two brothers bore the impress of the temperament of the elder. They established themselves as the sovereigns of two imaginary kingdoms—that of William always exercising a kind of suzerainty over that of Thomas; and the suggestion to Thomas that the people of his kingdom had tails grieved the sensitive little boy as much as though it had referred to something real. The passage in the "Autobiographic Sketches" in which he tells of this is at once whimsical, humorous, and pathetic.

William's mind was active too. He alighted on the most extraordinary ideas, and was fain to work them out. He tried to invent a machine that would enable him to walk up perpendicular walls like a fly : he was much exercised by the problem whether all the people on the earth could fight all the ghosts were they but endowed with powers of using arms and inflicting wounds; and he kept everybody about him in a condition of unrest and anxiety.

De Quincey would fain attribute to this rough discipline some beneficial results. But for this he thinks he might have passed into such a condition of helpless dreamy melancholy as would have been fatal. But, happily for him, it was not in the nature of such arrangements to last very long.

IV.

Mrs. de Quincey got tired of Greenheys and went to live in Bath. William, who had shown some turn for painting, was sent as a pupil to the then famous Mr. Loutherbourg, the Royal Academician, and before long died there of fever. Thomas and his younger brother Richard, of whom he writes so delightfully in the "Auto-biographic Sketches" as "Pink," (telling that he was called "Pink" because he was so handsome,) were sent to the Bath Grammar School, then under Mr. Morgan, a distinguished Etonian and fine scholar. De Quincey was captivated by Greek, and made remarkable progress in it to the delight of Mr. Morgan, who was wont to point him out to visitors. While he was at this school he made the acquaintance of Lord Westport—an acquaint-ance which grew to intimacy. It is quite clear from letters and other documents that both by his teachers and his fellow-scholars De Quincey was looked upon as a boy of the greatest promise—in fact, as already a celebrity. He himself tells us that while here, much encouraged by Mr. Morgan's attainments and countenance, he so devoted himself to Greek that he could talk quite familiarly in it; and that, as he read any English ordinary book or newspaper, he was constantly translating the English into Greek as he went along, and so mastered it, that Mr. Morgan would say of him, "that boy could harangue a Greek audience with as much ease as you or I could an English one," and so on.

While here he met with an accident, having been struck in the head with a ruler, which left more serious results than were at first suspected. He was attended by Dr. Mapleton of Bath, whose letters about him, and letters of schoolfellows and others that still exist making inquiries as to his state, set this fact beyond all doubt.

V.

His mother, we are told, withdrew him from the Bath Grammar School because she was shocked at hearing of compliments paid to him in his presence. Mrs. de Quincey was the daughter of an officer who had latterly held some post in the King's household—a post of such importance as entitled him to be ranked as one of the *armigeri*, or esquires—a thing on which De Quincey in his "Autobiographic Sketches" is fain to be a little jocular; but, descended from soldiers, Mrs. de Quincey, though a woman of fine intellect and highly conscientious, deeply concerned for the welfare of her children, was yet in some measure inclined to drill and to be exacting as to points of order and propriety. It is much to be feared, she had too little sympathy with them

and toleration for them in the peculiarities of character
which, it is evident, very early made their appearance in
her boys, and certainly not less in Thomas than in the
others. They were apt to have ideas and ways of their
own, and to stick to their own ideas and ways. The
serious manner in which she dealt with them for little
tricks and pranks, such as any boys might have been
guilty of, is indicative of character. A very staid,
dignified, prudent, well-bred woman, with a gift for
expressing herself in very clear idiomatic English, as her
letters show, and fully justifying what her son said of her
in regard to her ability with the pen.

But she perceived at a very early date a vein of
erratic and, as she regarded it, self-assertive character
in her boys, and was fain to curb it. She took such
ways to do so as did not aid the impression on their
minds of her loveableness. She was always on the
watch, lest anything should be done to encourage them
in this, and was very slow to perceive, or, at any rate, to
show that she perceived, anything uncommon or clever
or promising in them. On their side, they regarded her
as a jealous mistress, rather than as a fond mother. We
have proof of this, alas! in only too many ways. She
removed De Quincey's younger brother "Pink" from a
school where he was happy and comfortable and doing
well to one where the master was a simple tyrant, fond
of physical chastisement, but a religious professor; so
that "Pink" ran away to sea, and did not return for
some years, and, when he did, though he revealed himself
to Thomas, he did not do so to his mother, and such
difficulties arose from this cause as in her mind threw
serious doubts on his identity, and led her to say at first
that Thomas and the rest had been victimized by an
impostor.

Another proof is found in Thomas's many references to her, which are always couched in a tone of admiration for her grace and self-control and prudent management, but as clearly suggest a certain sense of coldness and distance and stately unbendingness on her part. Here is one of Thomas's pictures of her :—

"It may seem odd, according to most people's ideas of mothers, that some part of my redundant love did not overflow upon mine. And the more so, if the reader happened to know that she was one whom her grown-up friends made the object of idolising reverence. But she delighted not in infancy, nor infancy in her. The very greatness of some qualities in her mind made this impossible. Let me make a sketch of her; for she well merits it. Figure to yourself a woman of admirable manners, in fact, as much as any person I have ever known, distinguished by ladylike tranquillity and repose, and even by self-possession, but also freezing in excess. Austere she was in a degree which fitted her for the lady-president of rebellious nunneries. Rigid in her exactions of duty from those around her, but *also from herself;* upright, sternly conscientious, munificent in her charities ; pure-minded in so absolute a degree that you would have been tempted to call her 'holy'—she yet could not win hearts by the graciousness of her manner. That quality, which shone so brightly in my sister, and the expansive love which distinguished both her and myself, we had from our father. And a peculiarity there was about my mother which is not found, or anything like it, in one mother out of five hundred. Usually mothers defend their own cubs, right or wrong ; and they also think favourably of any pretensions to praise which those cubs may put forward. Not so my mother.

Were we taxed by interested persons with some impropriety of conduct? Trial by jury, English laws of evidence, all were forgotten ; and we were found guilty on the bare affidavit of the angry accuser. Did a visitor say a flattering thing of a talent or accomplishment possessed by one or other of us? My mother protested so solemnly against the possibility that we could possess either the one or the other, that we children held it a point of filial duty to believe ourselves to be the very scum and refuse of the universe. Yet, with all this absence of indulgent thoughts toward us or any of us, no mother can ever have lived who was more vigilant to see that we received to the last fraction every attention due to our health, to the decorum of our manners, and to the proprieties of our dress. . . . That I do not exaggerate the austerity of my mother's character, and the awe which it breathed around her, is certain from what I recollect of the deep impression produced upon her servants. Except as regarded the waiting at table, she never communicated with them directly, but only through a housekeeper. Sometimes, however, when a feud arose among them, it was remembered that in the last resort an appeal lay to ' mistress.' But rare were the cases in which this final remedy was tried. And as one out of a hundred similar testimonies to this impression, there occurs to me the lively *mot* of a housemaid who, on being asked why, in case of a supposed wrong, she had not spoken to her mistress, replied—'Speak to mistress! Would I speak to a ghost?'"

Even in the case of the girls—his two sisters, Jane and Mary—they were apt in relation to their brothers to do certain things, and to do them in such ways as their mother had not been consulted about, and perhaps would not have had her approval, if she had been consulted. And this mostly in matters where the girls were anxiously aiming at keeping the boys on good terms with their mother, and to preserve alive in them a sense of home-feeling.

Whether Mrs. de Quincey withdrew Thomas from the Bath Grammar School on the grounds alleged, or merely in consequence of the injury he had received to his head, we need not here inquire further; but it is certain that when he recovered so far as to resume his studies she kept him at home and engaged a tutor for him. This tutor was a Frenchman, who, as Miss de Quincey tells, had escaped from his own country during the Revolution, glad to keep his head where it was originally placed; and who clearly had a sad job in managing his precocious pupil. "Oh, Master Tomma, do be parswaded! do be parswaded!" were the sounds too often to be heard issuing from the tutorial room; and the Frenchman's authority was not likely to be increased when it became known to the pupil that the tutor had fallen in love with his mother and had wished to marry her! Not improbably the complications arising from this situation and the need of a more decisive control for Thomas led to the abandonment of this plan; though we have in it some proof of the truth of what De Quincey wrote when he said that at Bath, as a boy, he saw a good deal of the French refugees, and had many opportunities of talking with them, and learned much from them.

One of the cheering elements at this time for the young sufferer were the visits paid by Lady Carbery (formerly Miss Watson) to Bath. She never ceased to be affectionately interested in her "little doll that could talk."

VI.

The next move made on Thomas's behalf was characteristic. He was sent to Winkfield School, where for
some little time "Pink" had already been. We know
that this school was chosen by the mother more on
account of the religious reputation of the master than
of anything else. De Quincey, at all events, had nothing
to say in favour of the school as regards *the* things that
would have made it most suitable for a boy like him.
It was a small school, only from twenty to thirty boys ;
Mr. Spencer being also rector of the parish. It is
evident that though, on De Quincey's own statement,
Mr. Spencer was no great scholar, he and his family
found a source of much satisfaction and pleasure in the
school-work ; Miss Spencer doing not a little to forward
more "liberal" studies than is often commended to the
boys at public schools, lending books of general literature to the lads and discussing their contents with them.
A literary magazine called *The Observer* was issued, to
which De Quincey contributed. Mrs. de Quincey no
doubt had good reasons for feeling satisfied with the
school, and with "Pink's" life and progress there ; but
what may well have been an excellent and suitable
school for a boy like "Pink," may not have had quite
the same recommendation for the elder brother, who
had made such remarkable progress both at Salford and
at the Bath Grammar School. De Quincey's stay at
Winkfield, however, was not unprofitable, nor was it
wholly uncongenial, though he himself says that he
was entirely without the stimulus he had found so fully
at the Bath Grammar School. He had quite recovered
from the injury he had received, and was more spirited,

lively, and inclined for companionship there than one would have expected him to be. He was held in much regard by the other boys, several of whom became close friends of his, more especially two brothers Tom and Edward Grinfield, with whom, for a time after leaving Winkfield, he kept up a correspondence. Thomas Grinfield became Rector of Clifton, and Edward also had a living in the Church of England, and contributed largely to theological literature and to Greek scholarship. The latter, De Quincey met again at Oxford.

It was while at Winkfield that De Quincey sent in for competition to the proprietors of the "Juvenile Library" a verse translation of Horace's twenty-second Ode. The first prize was awarded to Leigh Hunt, De Quincey's senior by a year, who had just left Christ's Hospital, where he had been "first deputy Grecian." De Quincey stood third, but, as he himself tells, the opportunity was given for anyone interested to judge in the matter as the three versions of the ode were published in the magazine. Dr. R. Garnett, who printed the version of De Quincey in his edition of the "Confessions" in the Parchment Library Series, holds that De Quincey should have had the first prize—an opinion he was not, however, the first to avow, as we shall see by-and-by. Here is De Quincey's translation—surely a very finished performance for a boy not yet fifteen :—

THIRD PRIZE TRANSLATION OF HORACE,
(ODE 22, LIB. I.)
By THOMAS QUINCEY. Aged 15.
Of Mr. Spencer's Academy, Winkfield, Hants.

Fuscus! the man whose heart is pure,
Whose life, unsullied by offence,
Needs not the jav'lines of the Moor
In his defence.

Should he o'er Lybia's burning sands
　　Fainting pursue his breathless way
No bow he'd seek to arm his hands
　　　　　Against dismay.

Quivers of poisoned shafts he'd scorn,
　　Nor, though unarmed, would feel a dread
To pass where Caucasus forlorn
　　　　　Rears his huge head.

In his own conscious worth secure,
　　Fearless he'd roam amidst his foes,
Where fabulous Hydaspes pure
　　　　　Romantic flows.

For late as in the Sabine wood
　　Singing my Lalage I strayed,
Unarmed I was, a wolf there stood ;
　　　　　He fled afraid.

Larger than which one ne'er has seen
　　In warlike Daunia's beechen groves,
Nor yet in Juba's land, where e'en
　　　　　The lion roves.

Send me to dreary barren lands
　　Where never summer zephyrs play,
Where never sun dissolves the bands
　　　　　Of ice away.

Send me again to scorching realms
　　Where not one cot affords a seat,
And where no shady pines or elms
　　　　　Keep off the heat.

In every clime, in every isle,
　　Me Lalage shall still rejoice ;
I'll think of her enchanting smile
　　　　　And of her voice.

ATTESTATION.

The aforegoing is the unassisted translation of Master Thomas
Quincey, a student of this academy, under the age of fifteen years.
　　　　EDWARD SPENCER, Rector of Winkfield, Wilts.
　June 3, 1800.

In one of his mother's letters to him at Winkfield we find the following—interesting on two accounts—further record of Lady Carbery, and light on his mother's way of dealing with a boyish lapse.

"Poor Lord Carbery continues very ill : I am persuaded never likely to recover. They have lodgings in Milsom Street for the present ; but probably will remove to the Hot Wells. Her ladyship was here on Wednesday evening, and is as handsome and amiable as ever ; but I fear terribly surrounded with Irish people of rank who wish to make her racket about like themselves. . . .

" My dear boy, I will never after this mention the affair of Bowes, and perhaps shall never think of it again ; but just to remark that you are wrong to blame Mrs. Pratt about it. You acknowledge that the appearance of being with Bowes was unfavourable, and as long as we are weak creatures unable to form certain or intuitive judgments, we must continue to get the help we can in forming our opinions ; appearances, unfortunately, are all we have to judge actions by, and those on the particular action in question were really against you. If therefore Mr. and Mrs. Pratt put a construction upon your intentions, which excused you with respect to themselves, surely they did a thing as kind as possible, for they could not think it was right for you to be with Bowes, either with respect to me or for your own sake."

The affair of Bowes was nothing but the most innocent schoolboy freak referred to in the Memoir, a matter of which not one parent in ten would ever have taken any notice.

VII.

All this while correspondence had been kept up with young Lord Westport, who was inclined not only to make a friend of De Quincey, but to look up to him as a kind of mentor.   Lord Westport's tutor, the Rev. Thomas Grace, and his father, the Earl of Altamont, had evidently been as favourably impressed by De Quincey as Lord Westport himself had been.   The plan of going on a visit to Ireland with them had been often spoken of; and, on De Quincey leaving Winkfield School, opportunity was found to carry it out.   Many arrangements, of course, had in these days to be made for such a journey, when posting and slow-sailing mail packets were the only means of travel ; and, of course, it was a great event for the young scholar.   Here is part of a letter from Mr. Grace, which shows how the visit was looked forward to by himself and Lord Altamont :—

" Westport is not put down in many of the old maps, but it is situated exactly on the spot marked Newport in them, at the eastern extremity of Clew Bay, and due west of Castlebar; its distance from Dublin is one hundred and thirty-five Irish miles.   It is not certain that I shall go all the way, perhaps only to the Head ; but in this you will find no disadvantage.   Lord Westport is to have a French servant, who, I hope, will speak nothing to either of you but in that language, and if it is not Westport's fault, you will more than supply my place. Lord Altamont expresses great pleasure at the prospect of your society, and I have no doubt but you will be pleased with him and improved by his conversation."

De Quincey has himself told in outline the whole story

of that trip, and letters exist to attest that he was accurate down to the merest details. He tells his mother and sisters a great deal about the journey, that, for one thing, in the packet he met the Countess of Conyngham. "Her ladyship," he says, "who sat the whole time in her coach, seeing me sitting on deck reading, called me to the coach window, where she talked with me for about five minutes, and then made me come into the coach and stay the remainder of the day with her. She conversed with me for above eight hours, and seemed a very pleasant and sensible woman. She is pretty, and something or rather very like a person I have seen, but whose name I cannot recollect. She gave me an invitation to come and see her at Slaine (Lord Conyngham's country-seat), about twenty-four miles from Dublin."

He facetiously describes a drive he had from Dunleary to Dublin in a "jingle," which he defines as "a rotten sociable drawn by one skeleton;" describes the last sitting of the Irish House of Lords, at which he was present, and also an installation of the Knights of the Blue Riband, Lord Altamont being one, and remarks that every one comes to Lord Altamont "with open mouth to tell him they hear that he is soon to be created a marquis." In the Cathedral he again met Lady Conyngham, and was introduced to her husband, who renewed the pressing invitation to Slaine, which De Quincey could not accept as they were leaving for Westport next day.

"Directly behind me," he writes, "stood Lord Grey de Wilton. A Mrs. Sparrow, who was near us, happening to ask some questions of me respecting Lord Altamont's dress, Lord Grey instantly looked at me, and asked if my name was not De Quincey: on my answering 'Yes,' 'Oh, sir,' said he, 'you're a young

C

countryman of mine, and so we must shake hands.'
How his lordship should know me, I can't tell, because
I never recollect having seen him, except once or twice
when I was at the Manchester Grammar School on
speech day."

The account of the journey to Westport is very naïve
and attractive in many ways—certainly not alone for his
description of that meeting with Miss Blake, the sister of
the Dowager Countess of Erroll, and of the impression
she made on him—educing in him for the first time,
according to his own report in the "Autobiographic
Sketches," those feelings of admiration and love which
he had never before felt towards any woman.   But it is
very noticeable that, though he mentions the meeting
with Miss Blake in a letter to his mother, he is silent
there with regard to the element which he elsewhere
celebrates in such characteristic style.   In a letter to his
sister Mary, he thus describes Westport :—

" The house is fine and large and not much injured by
the French and the rebels.   The grounds are very
beautiful, though not kept in the very best order.   There
are two parks, fine groves and lawns, through which runs
a fine river, every now and then rolling with a tremendous
noise over artificial weirs.   We spend all our time in
reading, writing, riding, bathing, hunting, shooting and
boating.   All these, except the two last, the Irish think
it a disgrace not to understand.   Notwithstanding the
dangerous places through which we are continually
riding, I have never yet been thrown."

It is quite evident that De Quincey approved himself
as much the companion of the father as of the son,
entering with interest and zest into all his works and
improvements, and often going round large portions of

his estates with him : as well as in some measure re-awakening in the Earl his taste for the classics, of which they read and talked much together. The ode which De Quincey had translated was often spoken of, and it was read to a party there of whom Lord Morton was one. " Lord Morton," he says, " took particular interest in literature ; and it was, in fact, through *his* kindness that for the first time in my life I found myself somewhat in the situation of a literary lion." Lord Morton had read and compared the trio of translations and " protested loudly that the case admitted of no doubt ; that gross injustice had been done me ; and, as the ladies of the family were much influenced by this opinion, I thus came not only to wear the laurel in their estimation, but also with the advantageous addition of having suffered some injustice. I was not only a victor, but a victor in misfortune."

VIII.

Various letters addressed to De Quincey after his return from Ireland by Lord Altamont have been pre-served, and abundantly prove the friendly and affec-tionate feelings that had been produced towards him. We believe we cannot do better than present some of these letters here, as it is clear enough that Lord Altamont and his family were proud to rank De Quincey among their friends. Here is letter No. 1 :—

" Westport House, *Sept.* 22, 1800.

" MY DEAR DE QUINCEY,—I am to thank you much for your kind letter from Parkgate, which reached me yesterday. The only letter which came here for you since you left us has been carefully forwarded. I shall

receive your ode, or anything else from your pen, with
particular pleasure, whenever your leisure allows you to
bestow any of your valuable time less worthily than your
present pursuit, which is, and ought to be your own
improvement.

"I trust you will continue your recollection of your
Irish friends ; and as you were so good an Englishman
here, so I hope you will argue for us when we are un-
justly censured by those who, from not having claims of
their own, may have been refused those marks of attention and regard which I can answer for your having met
with everywhere—from the wilds of Croagh Phadrig—
vulgariter Crook Patrick—to the drawing-room at St.
James's ; and I really should regret having made your
acquaintance if I did not hope for a continuance of your
friendship and remembrance.

"Lady Altamont is not yet arrived, but I expect her
hourly : she will join me in thanking your mother for
allowing you to come over here. I hope most sincerely
that you got back to her in perfect health and safety. I
am afraid Lord Pickle was a tart companion on your
journey. I don't expect his disposition to riot was
controlled by the sagacity of his mentor Largeaux [his
French valet].

"Our stormy weather has begun here, and a part of
Mr. Campbell's dam, in which you may recollect I was
engaged to keep up water behind my house, has been
carried away, and gone I know not where—perhaps to
add to the soil on the shores of our next Western neighbour, North America. . . .

"The season has been generally not healthful in Ireland ; but we are promised abundance and better times in
future. Adieu, my dear little friend : pray recollect Westport enough to consent to return to it when you cannot

consent to employ yourself better. Believe me, affectionately and sincerely yours,   ."ALTAMONT."

This letter was addressed to De Quincey, "the Rt.
Honble. Lord Carbery's, Laxton Hall, near Stamford,
Leicestershire," proof, if proof were needed, that De
Quincey paid a visit there, as he says in the chapter
headed Laxton in the "Autobiographic Sketches," when
he did something to teach Lady Carbery Greek, in return
for some aid from her in Hebrew.

The Altamont family had been most desirous that De
Quincey should join Lord Westport at Eton—a thing
which we are somewhat surprised to learn that Mrs. de
Quincey was inclined to regard with favour. We have
documentary evidence in the shape of letters from De
Quincey himself to prove that the objection to Eton
came from him : he had visited Lord Westport at Eton,
and had there seen some things which did not attract
him to it. The next thing thought of for him by his
guardians was that he should go to the Manchester
Grammar School, where, after a year or two, he would
secure a certain sum per annum which would do much
to make his circumstances comfortable at college, as all
the interest from his share of the sum left by his father
did not yield more than £150 per annum. His father
died young, and had for some years prior to his death
been in bad health ; so that it speaks much for his
business tact that he should have left so much as, divided
among the children, would yield per annum £150 to four
boys and £100 per annum to two sisters, besides an
income to his widow. We shall devote another section
to the Manchester Grammar School ; we have said this
much here to preface the remark, that the second letter
from Westport was addressed to "the care of G. Lawson,

Esq., Long Millgate, Manchester,"—the Manchester
Grammar School, and that by this time Lord Altamont
had become Marquis of Sligo, and Lord Westport
advanced to the courtesy-title of Earl of Altamont.
Here it is :—

"Westport, *Jan.* 12, 1801.

"MY DEAR LITTLE FRIEND,—I have just had the
pleasure of a line from you, after having for some months
expected it. Your remembrance of me is highly
gratifying.

"I am just now recovering from a severe and dangerous illness—two fevers, the one following the other,
which brought me to death's door, and from which I have
escaped most miraculously. I am not yet sufficiently
recovered to think of setting out upon a journey, which
keeps me in Ireland, though I purposed to have passed
the last two months in London.

"In course of the Spring I still purpose being in
England, and I trust I shall not leave it without seeing
you somewhere or another. I have very flattering
accounts of my boy : he has profited by your good
example. As to the long-promised ode, I shall receive
it with much pleasure whenever you are so good as to
send it. I am sorry, however, that I cannot undertake
the polishing part of it, though I imagine it will not
require any, from the specimen of a similar kind which
I saw from the same hand.

"Direct always to me in Dublin. We are perfectly
tranquil here, and better off in point of food than you
are in England. My great water-works which you saw
me engaged in have succeeded to my utmost satisfaction. Whenever you pay me another visit you will
find great alterations and improvements made here.
You are in the midst of industry in Manchester, and I

make no doubt profiting by it. It is the real source of wealth, prosperity and happiness, both national and individual. Were I where you are I would soon understand the process of cotton-making. When in Lusatia and Silesia I learnt check-making, and brought it home here in tolerable perfection. I never indeed went anywhere without trying to pick up something for the improvement of my neighbourhood. You tasted the ale which I learnt to make by a visit to Lord Bath's, and you saw also, I believe, the industry of every kind round Westport exceeds that of all the rest of Ireland through which you passed. Believe me,

"Ever affectionately yours,

"SLIGO."

Clearly, a man of real productive and organising character—always learning something, anxious to improve his neighbourhood. *O si sic omnes !*

The next letter is dated from Grafton Street, London, May 5th, 1801, and is as follows:—

"MY DEAR DE QUINCEY,—Your letter directed to Dublin came to me from thence to-day. I shall be very glad to get the long-promised ode when it is completed.

"The disorder you complain of is certainly of recent acquirement, and therefore may the more easily be got the better of, as I sincerely hope it will and speedily. When we were more acquainted you had no disposition to idleness at all. I have been here some weeks, and have just sent my boy back to school, having had him here for the holidays. If he had as little of the disease of idleness as you have, I should do more with him than I expect to do; but he has a great deal of good in him, and what is not right I hope is corrigible. I wish you may be at leisure to pay us another visit at Westport soon. Our good news recently will, I hope, ensure our tranquillity; but I am sorry to assure you, from the extravagant demands of the First Consul, peace is out of the question for the present. Believe me, with sincere regards,. "Yours affectionately,

"SLIGO."

IX.

Very touching it is to read his protests against going to the Manchester Grammar School. He was eager to proceed to the University, for which he held he was perfectly prepared. His mother and guardians argued that his income was not enough to enable him to do this with any measure of comfort. He must either go to Manchester or enter a lawyer's office. Of the two evils he chose what he thought the least. He went to Manchester. But the discipline of the school—the whole of the arrangements which he held made no due allowance for exercise and fresh air—combined with what he found the utter incompetence, pretence and pedantry of the headmaster, Mr. Lawson, put him sadly at odds with the life of the place and all that went on there. From one who knew well about the Manchester Grammar School and Mr. Lawson, we learn that the formula with which Mr. Lawson was too much in the habit of addressing his pupils was—"Psha, blockhead!" That formula would hardly fit De Quincey. He fell into low spirits, which by-and-by brought on ill-health. Notwithstanding all this there arose some relief on the monotony and shadow of his life. First of all, he found that some of the boys there were remarkable boys—in some things, at all events, his equals; in other things, it may be, one or two were even his superiors. One there was who, for knowledge and power of philosophic thought, extorted his admiration on their first meeting—one who, on the evidences of Christianity, could present wholly new ideas, and, in De Quincey's opinion, picked a lock which neither Grotius nor Paley had quite succeeded in opening ;. and had thus indicated the outline of a better work than either had accomplished. De Quincey's admiration was awakened and also his desire to attain closer friendship with this youthful seer in the guise of a Manchester Grammar School-boy. In his "Confessions" he does full justice to the boy G——, and the stimulating and suggestive character of his talk. The boy G—— was none other than Ashurst Gilbert, later Bishop of Chichester. But he found out as time went on that Gilbert did not altogether stand alone, and he sets down his deliberate estimate of the boys then at the Manchester Grammar School in these terms :—

"I learned," he says, "to feel a deep respect for my new schoolfellows ; deep it was then, and a larger experience made it deeper. I have since known many literary men—men whose profession was literature, and who sometimes had with one special section or nook of literature an acquaintance critically minute. But amongst such men I have found but three or four who had a knowledge which came as near to what I should consider a comprehensive knowledge as really existed among these boys collectively. What one boy had not, another had ; and thus, by continual intercourse, the fragmentary contributions of one being integrated by the fragmentary contributions of others, gradually the attain-. ments of each separate individual became, in some degree, the collective attainments of the whole senior common room."

Mrs. Baird Smith has thus furnished evidence that, if

De Quincey, to his surprise, found the attainments of his schoolfellows noticeable, they did not fail to carry away similar impressions regarding him, and that he never passed out of the remembrance of some at least among them. She writes :—

"I have been trying to find, but as yet without success, the place where he mentions in his works that, of his two schoolmates in the first form of the Manchester Grammar School, the one became a bishop, and the other was hanged for sheep-stealing ; so at least he had heard in later years. So far as our poor friend the sheep-stealer is concerned, I cannot be sorry we have had no confirmation of the report of that catastrophe. But some few years after my father's death we had a most pleasing confirmation of the other part of the account, in making the greatly-prized friendship of the daughter of this very schoolfellow, the bishop. At her house we met the delightful and gracious old man himself, who had remembered my father with life-long regard and interest. My father's enduring regard for his schoolfellow, the young G—— of the 'Confessions,' is 'writ large' in his remembrances of the Manchester Grammar School."

Another circumstance that arose to reconcile him for a while longer to Long Millgate was the appearance there of Lady Carbery on a long visit. She not only found means of entertaining him, but brought to the school at special times followings of distinguished people such as rejoiced Mr. Lawson's heart. "She did not forego," De Quincey says, "her purpose of causing me to shine under every angle ;" and we may be sure that, if any means had suggested themselves to Mr. Lawson of binding his clever pupil to Manchester, he would not have been slow to make use of them.

Another attraction there was of a very different kind. A family of the name of Clowes had been from earliest days great friends of his father. One of this family was the Rev. John Clowes, M.A., Rector of St. John's, Manchester. He was a Swedenborgian, and by his writings and otherwise had done not a little to recommend Swedenborgian doctrines to members and clergymen of the Church of England. De Quincey, whose thoughtful meditative ways made him a fit companion for scholarly people advanced in years, became a privileged friend of old Mr. Clowes, and, as he says, found free admittance at any time and at such times as most others would not have been admitted at all. He speaks of the reverential apostolic look of Mr. Clowes, and says he always reminded him of the Apostle John. De Quincey gives some taste of the conversation that passed between them on poetry, the classics, literature and so on, but always the conversation at last turned to sacred things. The house for its quietude and air of complete half-dimmed repose was like the Castle of Indolence, and De Quincey tells us that the old butler always put him in mind, by his noiseless step, of the porter or usher of that castle, who was shod in felt. Here, surely, is a very fine picture of this old and reverent friend of our subject :—

" Daily and consciously he was loosing all ties which bound him to earlier recollections ; and in particular I remember—because the instance was connected with my last visit as it proved—that some time he was engaged daily in renouncing with solemnity—though often enough in cheerful words—book after book of classical literature, in which he had once taken particular delight. Several of these, after taking his final glance at a few passages to which a pencil-mark on the margin directed

his eye, he delivered to me as memorials in time
to come of himself. The last of the books given to
me, under these circumstances, was a Greek 'Odyssey'
in Clarke's edition. 'This,' said he, 'is nearly the
sole book remaining to me of my classical library,
which for some years I have been dispersing among
my friends. Homer I retained to the last, and the
'Odyssey' by preference to the 'Iliad,' both in com-
pliance with my own taste, and because this very copy
was my chosen companion for evening amusement
during my freshman's term at Trinity College, Cambridge, whither I went in the spring of 1743.* Your
own favourite Grecian is Euripides, but still you must
value—we all must value—Homer. I even, old as I
am, could still read him with delight ; and as long as
any merely human composition ought to occupy my
time, I should have made an exception on behalf of
this solitary author. But I am a soldier of Christ: the
enemy, the last enemy, cannot be far off ; *sarcinas
colligere* is, at my age, the watchword for every faithful
sentinel, hourly to keep watch and ward, to wait and to
be vigilant. This very day I have taken my farewell
glance at Homer, for I must be no more found seeking
my pleasure among the works of man ; and, that I may
not be tempted to break my resolution, I make over this
my last book to you.' The act was in itself a solemn
one : something like taking the veil for a nun, a final
abjuration of the world's giddy agitations. Me it
impressed powerfully in after years. Farewell, my early
friend ! holiest of men whom it has been been my lot to

---

* De Quincey is hardly accurate here : 1763 was Mr. Clowes's
freshman's year. Mr. Clowes's very venerable aspect led De
Quincey to exaggerate his age. He lived many years after De
Quincey's intercourse with him, and wrote a good deal.

meet. Yes, thirty years are past since then [*i.e.*, since 1802, when he parted from Mr. Clowes], and I have yet seen few men approaching to this venerable clergyman in paternal benignity—none certainly in childlike purity, apostolic holiness, or in perfect alienation of heart from the spirit of this fleshly world."

X.

By this time De Quincey's mother, in gratification of a fancy she had for new houses and for altering and improving them, had removed from Bath, and taken up her abode at the Priory, Chester—a quaint and pretty little house, as De Quincey has described it—"a gem in the field of the picturesque." On his mother's visits to Manchester, he poured many a tale of his woes into her ears, and wrote long letters urging his reasons why he should be removed from Manchester—his health at last being the main point dwelt on. Neither his mother nor his guardians would listen to his requests; his mother arguing with him in this style—very good, it may be, from the prudential common-sense point of view, but not likely to weigh, as it was meant to do, with a lad like De Quincey in ill-health, and wholly out of sympathy with his surroundings :—

" I must here repeat what I believe is true, that you cannot be admitted to the University till you are eighteen (that, however, may easily be ascertained) ; you may enter your name on the books when you are sixteen, and there is some advantage in doing so. This I am pretty sure Charles Cowper did ; and though, like you, he wished to have gone at an earlier age, he did not, because, as I believe, he could not. Supposing this to be the case, is it possible you can wish to loiter away

two years at home?   Surely Mr. Lawson's school may
afford you a better opportunity for study than you could
have in any other family !   I would urge you to consider
that the language you use when you say 'I must' or 'I
will' is absolute disobedience to your father's last and
most solemn act, which appoints you to submit to the
direction of your guardians, to Mr. Hall and myself in
particular, in what regards your education.   I cannot
think you believe a total revolt from our rule will make
you in any sense great if you have not the constituents
of greatness in you, or that waiting the common course
of time and expediency will at all hinder the maturity
of your powers if you have them.   What to say to you
on the subject of pecuniary advantages I scarcely know,
since you are so unhappy as to think £100 a year added
to your own fortune despicable, and that the honourable
competition with your equals for the reward of literary
superiority is a degradation.   Were I to fix upon the
most independent mode of obtaining such a sum, I am
sure I should be very apt to name those very academic
prizes ; so much do you and I differ."

It is evident enough, however, that De Quincey's
determination to leave the Manchester Grammar School
was not due to any lack of appeals to his vanity.   Even
Mr. Lawson, who seldom gave praise, paid him compliments.   On that memorable celebration of the Christmas
breaking-up, much honour was done to him for his part
in the proceedings—the recitation of a Latin poem on the
recent conquest of Malta—*Melite Britannia subacta.*
Lady Carbery smiled upon him, and brought in her
train every person of rank and influence she could prevail upon to go.   Here is a rather more detailed account
than he gave in the "Autobiographic Sketches":—

"Lady Carbery, ever intent upon doing me honour, had come down with all the splendour of equipage that she could muster, and surrounded by all the friends— old friends or new friends—that she could influence. Whoever it was on that day that failed to be happy, the headmaster—the *Archididascalus*—was not the man. To the seventh of the heavens he was elevated by the pomps and vanities of this wicked world which invested and took by storm the ancient school. Three lords at the very least there were, viz., Lord Massey, with his brother and his lovely wife, on *my* account ; Lord Grey de Wilton as an old *alumnus* of the school, and Lord Belgrave, his son-in-law. Many others of distinction glorified the hour for *him ;* and all Millgate came forth to witness his glory."

Nothing, however, would avail with him. His contempt for Mr. Lawson grew as time went on, and he resolved to run away. He wrote to Lady Carbery for a loan of £5. She sent him £10, saying that even if it were never repaid, she should not be ruined by it. He himself thus wrote of his feelings then :—

" I had but some eighteen months more to serve. Oh, wherefore could I not have been wiser ? Wherefore did I not hear that secret whisper of monitorial wisdom, that even then went sighing over the evil choice which I made ? Wherefore was it that to thee I should so obstinately have been deaf ? For my powers of long-suffering were great ; and the burden that oppressed me I *could* have borne—had I not suffered at that time under the falsest medical advice. There is no misery which cannot be simulated by a deranged liver ; and] for me at that time this curse existed under a double agency, viz., want of exercise in the first place ; and, secondly, medical

counsel the most extravagantly erring that in this erring
world I have ever known."

He did carry out his resolution in a very characteristic manner ; and, as he himself has told in the most
piquant style, he went first to Chester, as he had learned
that his uncle, Colonel Penson, home from India, was
there, and he wished to see him.   His mother was horri-
fied ; but his uncle seemed to regard it as not unnatural
that a lad should prefer to go wandering about the
country to being kept stuffed up in a Manchester school ;
and, by the Colonel's influence with his sister, Thomas
was allowed to go off for a tour in Wales till some
definite arrangements could be made.   He did go off,
and so long as he kept up any correspondence with his
friends, he received a pound per week ; but by-and-by
he got too afraid of being pounced on and sent back to
Manchester, and chose to be without any communications.

That he was wandering about Bangor at the time he
says he was is proved by the fact that the fourth and
only further letter from the Marquis of Sligo that has
been preserved, was addressed to him there, though it is
clear De Quincey had not told Lord Sligo the whole
story about his running away, and the reason he was
then there.   It is as follows :—

                    "Westport House, *Nov.* 8, 1802.

"MY DEAR LITTLE FRIEND,—I derived great
pleasure from the note you so kindly addressed to me
from Bangor, which came to my hands yesterday.

"Altamont left us about fourteen days ago. I am
almost surprised that you did not meet him, as he went
to Holyhead and through North Wales. Whenever
your business or your idleness allows of it, I shall be

happy to have a line from you, and shall always feel 'a sincere interest in all which concerns you. When you come to Bangor next, I hope you will recollect how short a distance it is from hence. I should much like you to see all the great works of improvement in which I have been engaged and generally got through successfully. Our great misfortune in these parts for some years to come will be our entire dependence on peace for the comfortable possession of what we have. I never hear of anything like another revolution in France, without trembling for the effect it may have upon us here ; for our rebellions and the French invasion have left bad effects, which it will take many years wholly to wipe out. Adieu, my dear little friend,

" Believe me, very truly and affectionately, yours,

"SLIGO."

When De Quincey cut himself off wholly from his family, he wandered about on the Welsh hills, sleeping in the open air, and finding at the last, when his money was low, a very precarious diet in the wild-berries ; he even resorted to the expedient of trying to sleep under a kind of umbrella tent, but in wind he found it unmanageable and abandoned it, and sometimes for days he had a home with the simple peasants in return for little services he could render. In one family he remained for some days—wrote letters on business for the men and wrote love-letters for the girls ; and he declares they would have kept him there as long as he chose to stay, but when the father, who had been absent, came home, he looked at the matter in another light, and De Quincey left.

Like to like. In the course of his wanderings, he met with one or two who could aid him towards what he sought. One of these was a Mr. de Haren, who told him

D

about the wealth of German literature and lent him one of Haman's books, so that it was in the most unlikely of places that he got his first impulse to the study of German literature.

But at length matters got so bad with him that he felt he must make a change, and rather than deliver himself up to his guardians, he found a chance of going to London, of which he duly took advantage.

XI.

His sufferings during what he calls his " London novitiate," form the subject of one of the most startling chapters in the "Opium Confessions." He found sleeping accommodation in the office of one Brown or Brunell, a shady attorney, in one of the houses at the top of Greek Street, Soho. He had applied to a man named Dell, a Jew, for a loan of money on his expectations, producing to him, among other things, in proof of his identity, the bundle of letters from Lord Sligo and Lord Altamont, some of which very letters we have already presented to the reader. Brunell was the legal agent through whom this Dell did his business, or a part of his business. De Quincey gives a very powerful picture of the kind of life lived by such professional men (who, as he says, have laid down their consciences as rich folk sometimes do their carriages, finding them too expensive or inconvenient). Brunell, however, was fond of literature and liked to converse with the young student who had thus strangely come in his way, and he was willing that De Quincey should have house-room, that is, live and sleep in the large half-empty house where he could (Brunell sleeping somewhere else), and he would often give the lad a share of his breakfast for the luxury of a talk about authors and books.

De Quincey at a time when his statements could easily have been checked by references to persons still living, made no secret about the house or the man, as is proved by his remark to Mr. Woodhouse, who writes:

"The house in which the opium eater lived, as mentioned in his 'Confessions,' rent free, and which is in a street leading out of Oxford Street, is in Greek Street, partly in the Square on the right hand as you go down from Oxford Street. The master had other offices elsewhere, at which he carried on his game. He went by several names." [Garnett, p. 208.]

Strangely mingled are the threads of good and bad in human nature. Brunell in his own way meant to be kind, and was kind to the runaway schoolboy. He did what he could for him in various ways, though the loan of money was long in coming.

De Quincey, however, had a companion in the large half-empty house. A little girl, of whom he says that he never knew whether she were an illegitimate child of Brunell's or what.

" The only other nightly inhabitant of the large house," he writes, "was a little girl, a poor, forlorn child, apparently ten years old, hunger-bitten and wretched. Great was the joy the poor creature expressed when she found that I was to be her companion through the hours of darkness. From the want of furniture in the large house, the noise of the rats made a prodigious echoing on the spacious staircase and hall, and amid many real bodily ills, the forsaken child had suffered much from the self-created one of ghosts."

Some critics think that Dickens must have had in his
eye this picture when he drew the Little Marchioness.

They did the best they could to be comfortable ; but
the exposure here and the effects of the exposures in
Wales had their own effect ; so that De Quincey tells us
he now suffered much from a gnawing pain at the bottom
of the stomach which made sound sleep impossible—
all that he got being, so he says, a kind of dog-sleep.

Naturally, he was often about the streets, and on his
own principle of holding it no contamination to talk with
any creature in human form, he came to be on speaking
terms with some of the women who "walk the streets."
With ·one in particular he formed, as he says, a friendship, and often talked with her—they were companions
in misery, that was all. She had suffered great wrongs,
and he was fain to try and aid her, in as far as he could,
to get some justice from those who had wronged her.
One night the two were sitting on a door-step when,
owing to his lack of proper food and attention, he fell
forward suddenly in a faint. She quickly caught and
supported him, and having put him in as comfortable a
position as she could, ran off and spent her last sixpence
in procuring wine and spices which revived him—but for
that, his own idea was that he must have died.

Just after this, he found an opportunity to go down to
Eton to try to get from friends there some aid to raise
money, and he had arranged to meet this benefactress
again on his return on a certain evening, at a certain
place. He never did meet her again, though he tells that
for a long time he never ceased to hope and anxiously
to search for her ; and his account of these things and
his apostrophes to Ann of Oxford Street, form some of
the most touching passages in the "Confessions."

XII.

Gradually, the way opened, through the offices of a gentleman—a friend of the family—whom he had accidentally met in London, to a reconciliation with, and a restoration to, his friends. But for a time it was deemed advisable that he should reside with a family known to his mother—that of Mrs. Best, at Everton, Liverpool, till at all events his guardians had come to some agreement with him respecting his future. While there he received the following letter from the Rev. Samuel Hall, his guardian, which will further throw light on Mr. Hall's character, and suggest the incompatibility that was certain to arise between him and a young man like De Quincey.

"*Manchester, June* 7, 1803.

"SIR,—As you have thought proper to revolt from your duty on a point of the utmost importance to your present interest and future welfare—as you have hitherto persisted in rejecting the wishes of your guardians, who could be governed by no motives but those of promoting your real benefit, you cannot be surprised to hear that they have no new proposition to make. But, notwithstanding all that has passed, if you have any plans in agitation that seem entitled to notice, they are willing to pay them every degree of consideration.

" They trust that by this time you are convinced that it was (to speak the least of it) a rash step for a young man of seventeen to throw himself out of the protection of his friends and relations into the wide world, and to have nothing to trust to but the charity or compassion of strangers ; and they still cherish the hope that you will

renounce your errors, and endeavour to remove the
impression of former misconduct by correct and proper
behaviour for the future.

> "I am, sir,
>> "Your very humble servant,
>>> "SAMUEL HALL."

A very good letter for a commonplace man to write
to an ordinary commonplace boy, caught in a fault for
which dicipline was the proper punishment, but hardly,
it will surely be admitted, the kind of missive to have the
effect of conciliation on the mind of a youth like
De Quincey.

By-and-by, however, mainly through the influence of
his friend Mr. Kelsall, and of his uncle, Colonel Penson,
De Quincey wrote a letter, agreeing to certain points—a
letter so characteristic that we must quote the following
passages.

> "Everton, *June* 23, 1803.

"SIR,—I learned from Mr. Kelsall, when he was last
in Liverpool, that, on my pledging myself to enter into
a profession, my mother's scheme of sending me to
college would receive your sanction ; I mentioned this, a
few days ago, in a letter to my mother, and yesterday I
received an answer in which she expresses hopes of the
same sort. I write, therefore, sir, to say that, if any
assurance on this point—short of an absolute promise—
can have weight with you, I am ready to give it. I
object to an absolute promise, not out of any desire to
secure a decent method of evading my engagements, but
because there appears something more than rashness
in binding ourselves, by a solemn obligation, to perform
what the uncertainty of human events hourly tells us we
may never have the power of performing ; and, assuredly,

under whatever circumstances it could be required of me, I shall consider an assurance as binding as a promise. . .

"Sorry as I am, however, to lie under the imputation of having expressed sentiments towards Mr. Hall so contrary to those which I really feel, I should be still more sorry if I thought it possible that, in thus disavowing such sentiments, I could be suspected of acting a part for the purpose of compassing a favourite point. I may, therefore, observe that, with me, going to college is not a favourite point; at least, I mean, it is not an object which I have looked to with any ardour of desire. In whatever I feel of inclination for academic pursuits, I am influenced entirely by my mother's wish that I should quit a mode of life which she considers useless and inactive ; and in thus attempting to obtain your approbation and furtherance of such a plan, I am actuated by the joint wishes of my mother and myself, that, on entering into a new scene of life (at the best, perilous and expensive), I should do it not with a mere negative forbearance of opposition on the part of my guardians, but with that positive consent and union of all parties which give stability to any scheme—spirit and animation to any hopes.

"I am, sir, with high respect,

"Your humble servant,

"THOMAS DE QUINCEY.

"The Revd. Samuel Hall,
   "near St. Peter's Church,
     "Oxford Street,
       "Manchester."

Very soon after this he proceeded to the Priory, and of his stay there, and of the conversations and discussions he had with his uncle, he has given a very lively and humorous account. Before long, arrangements were made, whereby he should enter Worcester College, Oxford.

During his stay at the Priory, he wrote to Wordsworth a letter in which he tells of the deep impression produced on his mind by the "Lyrical Ballads," and the poems that had followed, a letter to which Wordsworth replied at great length, and in the course of his reply he said—

"It would be out of nature were I not to have kind feelings towards one who expresses sentiments of such profound esteem and admiration for my writings as you have done. You can have no doubt but that these sentiments, however conveyed to me, must have been acceptable ; and I assure you that they are still more welcome coming from yourself, and in the terms they do. A sound and healthy friendship is the growth of time and circumstance ; it will spring up and thrive like a wild flower when these favour ; and, if they do not, it is in vain to look for it. . . . . I am going with my friend Coleridge and my sister upon a tour in Scotland for six weeks or two months. This will prevent my hearing from you as soon as I could wish, as most likely we shall set off in a few days. If, however, you write immediately, I may have the pleasure of receiving your letter before our departure ; if we are gone, I shall order it to be sent after me. I need not add that it will give me great pleasure to see you at Grasmere if you should ever come this way. . . You speak of yourself as being very young, and therefore may have many engagements of great importance with respect to your worldly concerns and future happiness in life. Do not neglect these on my account ; but, if consistent with these and your other duties, you could find time to visit this country, which is no very great distance from your present residence, I should, I repeat be very happy to see you."

XIII.

His life at Oxford was very solitary and unlike that pursued by most students. Professor Wilson was then one of the most brilliant personages there, carrying all before him in certain ways; and it is significant of De Quincey's hermit-like mode of life that he never so much as heard of Wilson and his achievements, not to speak of knowing him. Edward Grinfield was at Lincoln College, and sometimes saw his old schoolfellow; but failed to improve the friendship, anxious as he was to do so. De Quincey was intent on his own peculiar· interests, read much in out-of-the-way books; took up the study of German and Hebrew, in which he found aid from a Jew named Schwartzburg; and suffered so much from neu-ralgia and pain in his stomach, that he was frequently prostrated. In spite of all this, he found pleasure, relief, the greatest delight even in the study of the works that had by this time proceeded from Wordsworth and Coleridge. He regarded them, while yet in many quarters they were looked on with contempt, as the greatest poets of recent times, and was never tired of commending them to those whom he knew or corre-sponded with, as letters to his sisters still existing would suffice to prove. If he attained any notice for a while, it was more for oddity than for anything else, and a story is told of his coming into the dining-hall without a waistcoat—by a thoughtless movement, discovering the nakedness of the land, and suffering a mild reprimand from the master for his neglect in this important matter·

One of the chief pleasures of his life then was the

receipt of letters from Wordsworth. The next is dated
" Grasmere, March 6, 1804," and had been addressed to
St. John's Priory, Chester, forwarded to Mrs. de Quincey,
who had by this time gone to Bath, and by her sent on to
Worcester College, Oxford. In it Wordsworth says :—

" Your last letter gave me great pleasure: it was indeed
a very amiable one, and I was highly gratified in the
thought of being so endeared to you by the moral effect
of my writings. I am afraid you may have been hurt at
not hearing from me, and may have construed my silence
into neglect or inattention. I assure you this has by no
means been the case. I have thought of you very
often, and with great interest, and wished to hear from
you again. . . .

" We had a most delightful tour of six weeks in Scotland : our pleasure, however, was not a little dashed by
the necessity under which Mr. Coleridge found himself of
leaving us, at the end of something more than a fortnight,
from ill-health and a dread of the rains (his complaint
being rheumatic), when, after a long drought rain
appeared to be setting in. The weather, however, on the
whole was excellent, and we were amply repaid for our
pains. As, most likely, you will make the tour of the
Highlands some time or other, do not fail to let me
know beforehand, and I will tell you what we thought
most worth seeing, as far as we went. Our tour, though
most delightful, was very imperfect, being nothing more
than what is called the short tour, with considerable
deviations. . . .

" By this time I conclude you have taken up your
abode at Oxford. I am anxious to hear how far you
are satisfied, and, above all, that you have not been
seduced into unworthy pleasures and pursuits. The

state of both the universities is, I believe, much better than formerly, in respect to the morals and manners of the students. I know that Cambridge is greatly improved since I was there, which is about thirteen years ago. I need not say to you that there is no true dignity but in virtue and temperance, and, let me add, chastity; and that the best safeguard of all these is the cultivation of pure pleasures, namely, those of the intellect and affections. I have much anxiety on this head, from a sincere concern for your welfare and the melancholy retrospect which forces itself upon one, of the number of men of genius who have fallen beneath the evils that lurk there. . . . Love nature and books : seek these, and you will be happy ; for virtuous friendship and love and knowledge of mankind must inevitably accompany these, all things ripening in their due season.

"I am now writing a poem on my own earlier life : I have just finished that part of it in which I speak of my residence at the University ; it would give me great pleasure to send this work to you at this time, as I am sure, from the interest you have taken in the L. B., that it would please you, and might also be of service to you. This poem will not be published these many years, and never during my lifetime, till I have finished a larger and more important work to which it is tributary [' The Excursion']. Of this larger work I have written one book and several scattered fragments : it is a moral and philosophical poem : the subject whatever I find most interesting in Nature, Man and Society, and most adapted to poetic illustration. To this work I mean to devote the prime of my life, and the chief force of my mind. I have also arranged the plan of a narrative poem ; and if I live to finish these three principal works, I shall be content. They are all to be in blank verse.

I have taken the liberty of saying this much of my concerns to you, not doubting that it would interest you."

It was during his second year at Oxford that De Quincey first tasted opium when on a visit to London ; and his celebration of that incident and "the beatific chemist," who supplied to him the mystic nepenthe near the Pantheon, readers of the "Confessions" are not likely to forget. This introduction to opium is of the greatest importance, as the habit grew upon him and came so entirely to colour the strain of his life and genius. According to his own account it wonderfully quickened mental activity during its first stages, allaying pain, and imparting a clearness and calm penetration to the intellect. At all events, it did not operate in any way against his success at Oxford, for when he went up to examination for his degree, he astonished the examiners, who declared that in him they had the cleverest man they had ever come in contact with ; and the verdict of Dr. Goodenough, the Master of Worcester, is quite in accord with theirs. But his shyness was too great to permit him to undergo the viva voce, (at which, they had said, if he only did as well as he had done at the written, he would carry everything before him) ; and he disappeared from Oxford to the regret of all, without having taken his degree.

XIV.

We next find him in London, making some attempt to study law, and keep his terms with a view of being called to the bar; but his real concern was in such associations as those he now formed with Charles Lamb

and Coleridge. He describes visits to both of these
distinguished writers: with Lamb, at the India House,
and at his home, and with Coleridge, who was then
located with Mr. Stewart, at the "Courier" office in the
Strand. It was at this time, too, that his brother Richard
("Pink"), returned from his first odyssey of wanderings
and adventures, spent some time in London; and the
younger brother was as much taken with Lamb as was
the elder; for in his after letters, "Pink" often referred
to Lamb, and how he refused to be humbugged by a
certain picture-dealer. Coleridge he had first met when
at Mr. Poole's in Nether-Stowey, and the acquaintance
was now renewed and passed into close friendship. De
Quincey by-and-by, through Mr. Joseph Cottle in Bristol,
presenting Coleridge with £300, to enable him, with
an undisturbed mind, to pursue his literary and philosophical work. Coleridge was now busy preparing
lectures; and Mrs. Coleridge was about to go on a
visit to Southey and the Wordsworths. As Coleridge,
because of his engagements, could not accompany her,
De Quincey agreed to do so. This was his first introduction to the Wordsworths personally. He was so
attracted by their society and by the district, that he
resolved to settle there. By-and-by he took a lease of
Dove Cottage, in which Wordsworth had for some time
lived, before entering Rydal Mount; Miss Wordsworth
(Dorothy) taking the greatest interest in the furnishing
and fitting up of his cottage, while De Quincey was in
London or elsewhere. Between her and De Quincey
there sprang up the closest friendship, which has record
in the most delightful letters, many of which are to be
found in the first volume of the "De Quincey Memorials." De Quincey, too, became the great friend of
the Wordsworth children, who used to long for him,

and speak of him as "their greatest friend,"—with Tom
and with little Johnny, who "never forgets him in his
prayers," and with little Catherine, whose beauty and
sweetness caused him to regard her as "the impersona-
tion of the dawn and of infancy," and whose sudden
death worked something like a revolution in his mind
and fancy, so affected was he by it. Here are some
snatches from Dorothy's letters, which will justify these
statements :—

"Johnny improves daily; he is certainly the sweetest
creature in the world ; he is so very tender-hearted and
affectionate. He longs for your return, and I think he
will profit more than ever by your conversation, though
great was the improvement that you wrought in him ;
indeed, he owes more to you than to any one else for the
softening of his manners. He is not famous for making
extraordinary speeches, but I must tell you one pretty
thing he said the other day. His mother and he were
walking in the lane, and, looking at the daisies on the
turf, when he said, ' Mother, the poor little daisies are
forsaken now.' ' Forsaken, Johnny, what for ? ' ' Well,
because there are so many other pretty flowers ! ' . . .
Little Tom has been poorly and looks ill ; he often lisps
out your name, and will rejoice with the happiest at your
return. I must remind you of your promise you made
to Johnny to bring him a new hat. I bought one for
Tom at Kendal, but, remembering that you would bring
Johnny one, I did not buy one for him. Let it be a
black one if you have not already bought one of another
colour." . . .

When De Quincey at length returned to Grasmere,
one of the most important incidents that occurred to him
there was his introduction to Wilson, which he owed to

Wordsworth, and later his making the friendship of Charles Lloyd. In Wilson he found much of an answering spirit on some sides—in love of poetry and delight in nature, and fondness for long tramps on the mountains, while even in some forms of sport they were congenial; for De Quincey had, after all, a bit of the John Bull in him. Very eloquent are his descriptions of many points in their association, and the complete freedom of friendship that before long grew up between them with talk of many plans of excursions and travels, and something almost like a common purse by-and-by. We can see them with the mind's eye as they go on their rambles in that lovely region—Wilson tall, splendidly formed, almost leonine of look, with long fair locks waving in the breeze; De Quincey very short of stature and slight, yet able to undergo a great deal of fatigue, and not at all put to disadvantage in the walking way by Wilson's great strides. There they go, an odd-looking pair, as a stranger would have said, discussing the last poem of Wordsworth which he had just read to them before they left his house, or deep in some knotty problem of Platonic metaphysics, or keen to disentangle some doubtful collocation in their last talk with Coleridge, who, by this time, was at the lakes with Southey, busy on 'The Friend.' It is funny, but one of Wilson's playful names for De Quincey was Plato.

The plans for excursions they had so liberally formed were knocked on the head by the sudden loss of a great part of Wilson's fortune through the mismanagement, or worse, of a relative who was also his agent, making it necessary for Wilson to leave Elleray and betake himself seriously to the study of law in Edinburgh, where before long De Quincey on a visit will rejoin him.

But in poor Charles Lloyd, De Quincey found the

most of an answering spirit on the higher ground of
sentiment, imagination, phantasy. Very fine is his account of his contact and conversation with Charles Lloyd
—sympathetic, rarely comprehensive—and touching in
the highest degree is his story of poor Lloyd in his
alienation of mind ; how once, when he escaped from
those in charge of him, he made his way direct to
De Quincey's cottage, much to his friends' concern and
perplexity. There is much of the idyllic in De Quincey's
life among his friends and daily companions at this time.
Wordsworth, with his profound meditation, Dorothy,
with her suggestive words, in which quaint originality
and fine sentiment and love of nature went hand in hand ;
and the children, whose attractions for De Quincey were
even more strong and enduring than those of their
father's philosophy.

When he was alone, has he not told of the delight he
found in his nocturnal rambles through the silent valleys
of Cumberland and Westmoreland ; and how, in the lights
in the distant windows, he could read as by mystic
hieroglyphics, the passage of the hours. But no man
need trust to the continuance of such idyllic days, or, if
he does trust, he is sure to be disappointed.

XV.

A visit paid to Wilson in Edinburgh brought him
among a brilliant band of new friends and associates.
Now, he met Lockhart, Sir William Hamilton, and his
brother, Captain Thomas Hamilton (" Cyril Thornton ") ;
Sir William Allan, President of the Royal Scottish
Academy ; R. P. Gillies, Advocate, the clever *raconteur*,
whose position in Edinburgh was so unique, and whose

talents were so varied, and whose later life, alas! was so shadowed and forlorn. De Quincey has suggestively described it.

Here he found himself in his element, and has made due record of the fact in many of his essays and in the "Autobiographic Sketches." But, by this time, the opium had begun to dash its delights with penalties ; and in this circle it is clear that to keep himself up to the mark he was tempted to indulge too far. All tell of his brilliant talk, of his finely turned sentences as perfectly framed as though they had been written and revised, of his wealth of out-of-the-way learning, and his aptness at capping an anecdote or a quotation. "The talk might be of beeves," wrote Gillies, "but De Quincey could take his share in it, and from that could cunningly lead the conversation round to Chaucer or Homer, or, it might be, to Plato or Ptolemy, or to the Greek Dramatists, or even to the Talmud or some Hebrew Rabbi." After a lengthened stay, that was much enjoyed, De Quincey returned to Grasmere with memories that often made him revert to Edinburgh.

XVI.

De Quincey's ready sympathies led him always to find friends outside literary and philosophic circles. He was, in this respect, no recluse, nor was he one to stand aloof any way or to pique himself on his education or his birth. Among many of the farmers and yeomen of the Grasmere region, he found friends and associates too. He was interested in these strong characters, their fine natural intelligence and their shrewd ways. He appreciated the "salt" in their speech—was fond to hear

E

them use words almost peculiar to them—words that
told of the Danish element that had made its own mark
there. With one of these, a Mr. Simpson, he became
very intimate and often visited at his house, where he
was warmly welcomed because of his good manners
and unaffected ways; the light he could throw on many
things to a man, in whom the hard, rough work of
yeoman life in Westmoreland had not quenched the
more liberal curiosities. And, by-and-by, the daughter,
Margaret, a young girl (of whom one who saw much
of her declares that she was both beautiful and handsome), was much attracted by the visitor, as before long
he by her, and gradually affection sprang up between
them. One new inducement to overcome the opium
enemy which had gained too great a hold arose from
De Quincey having become engaged to Margaret
Simpson, and in this by dint of resolution he so
far succeeded as to justify their being united in
marriage.

Then he had to try what he could do in a practical way
to improve his fortune, which, never large, had been much
eaten into by gifts to friends, by loans, and in many
other ways. He began to write in many places—he had
already contributed to *Blackwood's Magazine;* he wrote
for, the *Westmoreland Gazette*, and, by-and-by for the
space of a year was its editor—a post which we can
scarcely conceive as congenial to him, though he was
certainly very energetic and active in it. Children had
been born to the pair, and we can realise how a man
like De Quincey would realise painfully his incapacity
to cope with the demands thus made upon him. The
sense of this incapacity led him to try to draw strength
from the opium, and of course the opium painfully
avenged itself on him in the end, with such complete

paralysis of productive function as made him wretched. He has described all this in his " Confessions,"—the depth of despair and helplessness to which he sank, "as though twenty Atlantics were heaped upon him," till at last he grew afraid to sleep and shrunk from it as from the most dreadful of tortures. Awful wretched dreams it brought—dreams that transformed all about him into crawling horrors and monstrosities unspeakable.

Amid all this his wife was a ministering angel—never complaining ; but with the utmost tact and tenderness, applying herself unweariedly to his relief and comfort. He has celebrated her devotion in the " Confessions." "Thou wast my Electra !" he exclaims, "and neither in nobility of mind, nor in long-suffering affection, wouldst permit that a Grecian sister should excel an English wife." And not improbably he had her in his thoughts too when he penned the beautiful concluding passage in that essay—"The Loveliest Sight for Woman's Eyes," which is given in the first volume of the " Posthumous Writings " :—

" And pertaining also to this part of the subject, I will tell you a result of my own observations of no light importance to women. It is this : Nineteen times out of twenty I have remarked that the true paradise of a female life in all ranks, not too elevated for constant intercourse with the children, is by no means the years of courtship, nor the earliest period of marriage, but that sequestered chamber of her experience, in which a mother is left alone through the day, with servants perhaps in a distant part of the house, and (God be thanked !) chiefly where there are no servants at all, she is attended by one sole companion, her little first-born angel, as yet clinging to her robe, imperfectly able to walk, still more imperfectly in its prattling and innocent

E 2

thoughts, clinging to her, haunting her wherever she
goes as her shadow; catching from her eye the total
inspiration of its little palpitating heart, and sending to
hers a thrill of secret pleasure so often as its little
fingers fasten on her own. Left alone from morning
to night with this one companion, or even with three,
still wearing the graces of infancy; buds of various
stages upon the self-same tree, a woman, if she has the
great blessing of approaching such a luxury of paradise,
is moving—too often not aware that she is moving—
through the divinest section of her life. As evening
sets in, the husband through all walks of life, from the
highest professional down to that of common labour,
returns home to vary her mode of conversation by such
thoughts and interests, as are more consonant with his
more extensive capacities of intellect. But by that
time her child—or her children—will be reposing on the
little couch, and in the morning duly as the sun ascends
in power, she sees before her a long, long day of perfect
pleasure in his society which evening will bring to her,
but which is interwoven with every fibre of her sensibilities. This condition of noiseless, quiet love is that,
above all, which God blesses and smiles upon."

Gradually, after many an effort, many a trial, he
emerged from the worst form of the tyranny, and by-
and-by was able to go to London to try what fortune
might be in store for him there.

XVII.

Through Lamb and Sir T. Noon Talfourd, he was
introduced to Messrs. Taylor and Hessey, the publishers
of the *London Magazine*, to which he began to con-

tribute. It was the custom of this firm to have periodical meetings of their contributors, when they dined together and interchanged views. At these meetings, as was natural, De Quincey's experiences due to opium were often spoken of. This at length led to his being asked to write an account of these. The result was the famous " Confessions " which produced an immediate effect, and placed De Quincey in the front rank of literary men then living. He had found it inadvisable and impossible to take his wife and children to London with him ; and in his notes of life at that period he tells how often as he walked about, he looked to the north and wished for the wings of a dove that he might fly there and be at rest. He occupied lodgings at one place or another throughout the entire period of this visit, with a short exception. For some time he lodged in rooms above the shop of Mr. H. G. Bohn, in York Street, Covent Garden, and there, most probably, the " Confessions " were written. Thomas Hood was then a young man, just beginning his literary career, and was a sort of subeditor, under Mr. Taylor, of the *London Magazine.* He frequently had occasion to call on De Quincey, for whom he came to entertain feelings of real affection, as De Quincey did for him ; and he thus, in his own quaint playful way, at one place makes record of his visits.

" I have found him at home, quite at home in the midst of a German Ocean of literature, in a storm, flooding all the floor, the table and the chairs—billows of books, tossing, tumbling, surging open—on such occasions I have willingly listened by the hour, whilst the philosopher, standing with his eyes fixed on one side of the room, seemed to be less speaking than reading from 'a handwriting on the wall.' Now and then he

would diverge for a Scotch mile or two, to the right or
left, till I was tempted to inquire with Peregrine, in
' John Bull' (Coleman's not Hook's), 'Do you never
deviate ? '—but he always came safely back to the point
where he had left, not lost the scent, and thence hunted
his topic to the end . . . Marry, I have one of his
"Confessions" with his own name and mark to it : an
apology for a certain stain on the MS., the said stain
being a large purplish ring. 'Within that circle none
durst walk but he '—in fact, the impression, coloured, of
a tumbler of laudanum negus, warm, without sugar."

·It was at these meetings at Taylor and Hessey's that
he met Mr. Woodhouse, whose valuable reminiscences of
those days Dr. R. Garnett was fortunate enough to
publish in his edition on his "Confessions" in the
Parchment Library Series—a work which is essential to
all students of De Quincey.

With Charles Knight, too, De Quincey made
acquaintance at this time, and between the two sprang
up a genuine friendship which was never interrupted.
For a short period towards the end of this stay in
London, De Quincey lived at Knight's house, and, as
Knight says, drew to himself the affection of his wife as
well as his own, by his learning, his eloquent conversation,
his affability, his eccentricity and his utter simplicity of
character.   Knight tells of many odd ways and habits—
which only drew them the more affectionately to the
strange little man.   De Quincey contributed several
articles to the *New Quarterly Magazine* and afterwards
many letters passed between these two—one most quaint
and original letter from De Quincey, inviting Charles
Knight to visit him at Grasmere, where, if he chose, " he
should bathe in oceans of milk ! "

Much as De Quincey loved music and delighted in the opera, he tells us how at this time in London, after taking his ordinary dose of opium in the evening, he would forego the temptations opera-ward, and instead would go into the streets and walk among the working folks engaged in their marketings, and would enter into conversation with them. This, indeed, was a favourite resource, he tells us, on the Saturday nights, and from what he saw there, as later on Glasgow Green and elsewhere, he learned so much of the struggles of the poor, and of their kindness to each other that he never ceased to think of them with affectionate regard and sympathy.

XVIII.

After some time spent in Grasmere, while he made many efforts, more or less successful, to keep open his connections with the literary world, in the year 1828 he went to Edinburgh, with the idea that, if he could find engagements, he would settle there. He did find engagements, as the volumes of *Blackwood* for the years that followed will bear witness. He rejoined the circle to which he had been welcomed when in Edinburgh before : found Professor Wilson still as full of life, as friendly and hospitable, spent many an evening discussing knotty points of philosophy with Hamilton, and made many new friends, among them Mrs. Crowe, the author of "the Night side of Nature," in whose house in Darnaway Street, he spent many a pleasant evening. By and by, he began to write in *Tait's Magazine*, contributing to it many chapters of autobiography, and on "Greek literature" among other subjects, and he found in Mr. Tait a liberal editor and a warm friend.

At this time De Quincey saw a good deal of Carlyle, who, with Mrs. Carlyle, was then living at Comely Bank. It is evident, despite some disparaging and cynical remarks in the diaries published by Mr. Froude, that both Carlyle and Mrs. Carlyle then warmly wished to be ranked among De Quincey's friends, and we know that De Quincey came to entertain the warmest feelings of friendship toward them—more especially towards Mrs. Carlyle, who had shown him much kindness, which he never forgot. When shortly afterwards, the Carlyles had gone to Craigenputtock, De Quincey received from them the most affectionate letters—one of which, anxiously urging De Quincey to visit them in their bleak, bare, Dumfriesshire home, is given at length in the Memoir.

By and by, Mrs. De Quincey came to Edinburgh with the children, and they were established first in a cottage at Duddingstone, and then in other parts. But De Quincey was never the man to lay the proper value upon money, and owing to one circumstance and another—his utter powerlessness to take his affairs firmly in hand and deal with them, and his incompetency in keeping proper business records, together with a generosity that was utterly uncalculating—he found himself at length under the necessity of finding sanctuary from his creditors in Holyrood, so to escape imprisonment for debt. There his wife and family went with him. He found many friends in Holyrood as he did everywhere else—his relations with some of them being celebrated by letters directed to them after he had left Holyrood—to one of them, Miss Jessie Miller, he wrote often, and one or two of his letters to her will be found in the Memoir, a cheap edition of which is published by Mr. John Hogg.

Escape from Holyrood was impossible during all days except Sundays ; so that in Edinburgh, as Defoe was in

Bristol, De Quincey was "the Sunday gentleman" for a while. There was naturally much sending out of MSS. and much sending in of proofs from printing offices. To this circumstance we owe one of the most delightful descriptions of De Quincey at this time that we have— from the pen of the late Mr. James Bertram, who was in these days a boy in the shop of Mr. Tait. He tells how courteous and sympathetic De Quincey was ; how even towards a mere errand boy, he never failed in the most perfect consideration, and also how the boy came to like to go there and to treasure up his sayings. Mr. Bertram tells also how inefficient he was in all money-matters, how cheques were rather a trouble to him, and how he would beg the boy when he took them to go to a friend and get them cashed. From others, as well as from Mr. Bertram, we learn that generally he had no notion how matters stood as between himself and Mr. Tait, and, no doubt, it was quite the same in the other cases of those with whom he had relations.

On one occasion he had gone out on a Sunday to consult his lawyer, who lived in Princes Street, on some point, and, forgetful of the lapse of time, found, on rising to go, that it was too late for him "to leap the boundary" as it was called, that is, to escape the observation of sheriff-officers, who, after a certain hour on Sunday, could or might arrest any debtor found out-side. On this occasion his only chance was to stay *perdu* where he was, and this visit was prolonged for several weeks—the utmost care being taken to keep him from observation of any but his tried friends. In the house of that solicitor, a young student, a near relative of his, was lodging, and, on his getting at the secret that the famous opium-eater was there, nothing would satisfy him but that he must be introduced ; pledge of secrecy

on his part having been given. That student enjoyed
many fruitful conversations with De Quincey during these
weeks, and was able to do many services for him, to
relieve the tedium of this queer confinement ; and this
student declared, and indeed deliberately wrote, that he
then learned more from De Quincey than from all his
teachers and books put together. He never spoke of
De Quincey but with gratitude and reverence, notwithstanding the peculiar circumstances under which he had
made his acquaintance. This was the Rev. Dr. Robertson,
of Irvine, whom De Quincey visited, and in whose
biography, by the late Rev. Dr. James Brown, of Paisley,
will be found the full details of what we here have merely
the space to hint at.

One of the friends, whom he made about this time,
was Mr. Hill Burton, the historian. Mr. Hill Burton, in
his volume " The Book-hunter," has given a sketch of
De Quincey under the thinnest of disguises—" Thomas
Papaverius,"—and there he tells how utterly without
business calculation he was—how once he came to him
after dark in great trouble wanting to borrow a trifle of
half-a-crown for some immediate need, and, much to
Mr. Burton's surprise, wished to leave a £5 note as
security for the loan ; Mr. Burton remarking that he
believed if he had taken it he would never have heard
any more of the matter from De Quincey, or that any
claim would ever have been made upon him for it. One
can easily imagine that it was possible for De Quincey
in such circumstances to fall into less scrupulous hands,
as no doubt he did, particularly in two or three cases of
lodging-house keepers. Mr. Charles Knight has told
of an almost similar simplicity in dealing with money
when De Quincey had left his house, quite unnecessarily
for fear, as he said, of giving Mrs. Knight too much

trouble. Mr. Knight found him in a lodging-house, on the South-side of London, waiting until the day should arrive for a draft to become payable to enable him to go home to Grasmere. Needless to say, Mr. Knight cashed the draft, relieved him, and, after hospitalities at his house, sent him off to Grasmere without more delay.

Mr. Hill Burton also speaks of it as a peculiar fact that, though De Quincey had a great love of books, he was in no sense a collector of rare and fine books, and would be just as content with a lot of half-loose leaves as with the most sumptuous edition. What he cared for was the matter, which he quickly mastered by his wonderful memory, rather than for the binding and tooling.

Mrs. De Quincey died in 1837, and was buried in Edinburgh, and he found himself left with a family of young children—one of the most incapable of men to look after them. Many friends they had in Edinburgh, who endeavoured as far as possible to aid him and them ; but things were in the most unsatisfactory condition, when Margaret, his eldest daughter, still a mere girl, took the reins into her own hands ; and with some assistance of friends, rented and furnished the little cottage at Lasswade, which up to the end really remained his headquarters, though, owing to his engagements, he would now and then be called to Glasgow or Edinburgh, and in lodgings in either of these places for a time.

As one instance of the loose, unjustified, statements made in Handbooks or Histories of English Literature, we may cite one (from a larger number recently noted) in a volume published by a writer from whom we should expect better things—published too in Edinburgh where verification would have been so easy for the writer. He says De Quincey "established his *wife and* family

in a cottage at Duddingstone or Lasswade, he himself
preferring for the most part to live in lodgings in Edinburgh. Now this is not only inaccurate and misleading,
but is calculated to give quite a wrong impression of
De Quincey and his habits, erratic though they were.
While De Quincey's *wife* lived, they were mostly together—even as we have seen in sanctuary together. As
she died after a few years in Edinburgh, she certainly
never was established at Lasswade at all. The establishment at Lasswade, as we have said, was due entirely
to the wonderful tact and management of De Quincey's
eldest daughter, Margaret, who, on her mother's death,
or soon after it, seemed to spring at one step from the
girl to the woman. This writer too speaks of 42, Lothian
Street, as "obscure lodgings in Edinburgh"; and, even
though Mr. J. R. Findlay's plate had not been attached
to the house, notifying it as the place where De Quincey
lived during the last years of his life and where he died,
it should have been well known, if not familiar, to a
resident in the Modern Athens.

XIX.

When the proprietors of *The Daily Mail*, in Glasgow,
purchased *Tait's Magazine*, and transferred it to that
city, Mr. Troup became editor, and one of De Quincey's
lengthened visits to Glasgow was connected with
assistance desired from him in relation to that enterprise. When frequently in Glasgow in former days he
had lived at 74, Renfield Street, his main object in
these visits having been to enjoy the society of Professor
J. P. Nichol, the distinguished astronomer, and of Professor Lushington, with one or other of whom he would

sometimes stay for weeks. Among the most cherished recollections of the late lamented Professor John Nichol, as he himself told me, were the walks, when he was a boy, from his father's house to the Observatory with De Quincey whose talk was such then as to cause the lad to regard him as one of the wisest of sages and the most eloquent of talkers. Now, happily, these attractions still remained, so that De Quincey when he accepted the invitation of *The Daily Mail* people and of Mr. Troup, (as told so well by Mr. Colin Rae-Brown) knew that he had the chance of renewing these pleasant associations. Mr. Rae-Brown has told how he found lodgings for De Quincey in a suitable spot; and how assiduously the opium-eater worked to realise all that the new proprietors of the magazine aimed at so far as related to his part of the enterprise. Mr. Troup and he were great friends—the inexhaustible energy of the one was a fit complement for the dreaminess and abstraction of the other—their friendship was certainly based on the admiration of opposite qualities from those that each himself possessed. Troup and De Quincey and a versatile Irishman, I have been told, themselves wrote the whole of *Tait's Magazine* for months running.

When De Quincey returned from this visit, he settled down for a long period uninterruptedly at Lasswade. He had now overcome the excessive craving for opium by the utmost self-denial, systematic persistence in exercise and strict attention to diet; and, though he never claimed to have become a total abstainer from opium, he was now able to content himself with a merely ordinary medical dose or not very much beyond it. Certainly, he never again fell into such excesses as he had done several times in earlier life. The chronic irritation of the stomach had in great degree been sub-

dued ; and, though he had still to subsist on the softest
and most easily digested of food, he enjoyed, in a sense,
more of life than he had done since boyhood. It was the
delight of his daughters to minister to him. When Margaret married Mr. Robert Craig and went to Ireland,
then the chief duty fell to Florence, and when she married
Colonel Baird Smith and went to India, this fell upon
Emily, who, like the other two, faithfully discharged it.

At this time De Quincey was visited at Lasswade by
many celebrities—Americans and Englishmen ; by Mr.
James T. Fields, by Mr. James Payn, and many others,
who all went away impressed by his fecundity of thought,
his eloquence in conversation, and his courtesy and
consideration for others. On one occasion some English
people were present, who, knowing that he was an Epis-
copalian, were making remarks about Presbyterianism
of a qualified kind. He begged them to reserve that
part of the conversation, till the time had come when
it would not be necessary for the maid to go out and
in to the room, as she was a Presbyterian, and he would
not wish her to hear things said about her church, that
would in any way hurt her feelings. Mr. James Payn,
and Mr. Fields, and the Reverend Francis Jacox, have
given their impressions of him at this time. All alike
remark upon his wonderful talk—his power of bringing,
with the utmost ease illustrative references from the
most obscure, or unexpected points ; while yet he was
in no sense like Coleridge, inclined to indulge in monologue ; but had the gracious art in high degree of
bringing out the views of others—a good listener as well
as a good talker. All alike bear testimony, too, to his
utter courtesy. Mr. Fields indeed says happily, "so
perfect was he in this respect, that, if good manners had
not been invented, he would have invented them."

From the outside world came missives from many distinguished persons—from Mary Russell Mitford among others; the edition of his works collected and published by Mr. J. T. Fields, in Boston, had done much for his reputation in America, and strongly recalled attention to him in this country, while he, in the dignified simplicity of the home at Lasswade, enjoyed the respect and affection of his neighbours, simply because of his kindly and neighbourly ways, and not on account of his literary work or fame which most of them could hardly have appreciated. Here is a very characteristic trait felicitously revealed by Mrs. Baird Smith, in a way, too, which fully illustrates what has just been said.

"Nearly the last time we were together, his almost constant companion for some time every day, was the nephew of one of our maids, a child of about four, who solely for the pleasure of conversation, walked round and round a dull little garden with him. Of this boy I remember one story which amused us. He had asked my father, 'What d'ye call thon tree?' To which my father, with the careful consideration he gave to any question, began, 'I am not sure, my dear, but I think it may be a Laurustinus:' when the child interrupted him with some scorn, 'A Laurustinus! Lad, d'ye no ken a rhododendron?' The 'lad' must have been about seventy at the time."

And, in illustration of the same trait, we may here quote the following from the pen of Miss De Quincey:—

"To upper class funerals he never went, but a sad case in the village aroused his sympathy. John Campbell, the shoemaker in the village, had a little boy

drowned. A notification arrived, and an invitation to
the funeral. To our dismay, my father determined to
go, though he had only a dark-blue coat and a brown
one. We thought the wearing of such coloured garments
at a funeral, the people would take as an insult. However, he came up to show himself after he was dressed—
so very like a child, who did not quite like to do a thing
he was warned against, and yet was determined to do it ;
and at length we were coaxed into agreeing that 'the
coat was not so very blue.' But when he got out into
the open, the bridegroom-like blueness of the coat made
us look at each other and sadly smile. Strange to say,
the very people that one would have expected to stand
most on attention to such matters took no notice ; but
the little blue figure among the trappings of woe, was
taken as much loving care of as the silent little corpse
in the coffin. . . The father of an old servant of ours—a
carter at Mr. Annandale's mills—lost a little child by
scarlet fever. An invitation to the funeral was sent in
my father's absence in Glasgow ; and he never heard of
it till afterwards when he returned. He, however, to
make up, wrote such a really touching letter, that we
were told, 'the poor man had it framed, and hung up
over his mantel-piece.' "

XX.

During De Quincey's stay at Lasswade in these circumstances, he was led one day early in 1850 to think
that he might do something that would benefit both
parties if he opened communications with *Hogg's Instructor*, which then had an extensive circulation throughout Scotland and elsewhere. The late Mr. James Hogg
tells how he was surprised one day, when busy in

his office, at being told that Mr. Thomas de Quincey, whose writings he well knew, but had never seen, wished to speak to him ; and, on going down, he was confronted with a very striking little figure, dressed in the most unusual style, and wearing an upper coat which also served for an under one. De Quincey said he had read *Hogg's Instructor* and wished to contribute to it, and here he drew from his pocket a manuscript which he was very careful to brush over with a little brush, which he had with him, before handing the packet to Mr. Hogg. In answer to Mr. Hogg's inquiries, he said that he had walked from Lasswade, and meant to walk back again, as he preferred this to being stuffed into close conveyances.

The article was, of course, accepted,* and led the way not only to many further contributions to *Hogg's Instructor*, and later to *Titan*, but to what was to him, at that age, and with his natural impatience of certain kinds of systematic work, the gigantic under-taking of the " Collected Works." America, through Mr. Field's enterprise, had shown the way ; but Mr. Hogg urged on him the importance of a collection of his writings from his own hand, revised and arranged according to his own ideas.   Finally, he consented to do this, and an agreement was signed ; but lest he should not be able to carry it to a proper conclusion, the volumes were at first titled " Selections Grave and Gay, from the Writings of Thomas de Quincey."

Mr. Hogg had the art of managing and humouring the strange little man, and, in opposition to all manner of head-shaking and hints that he was doomed to failure in this enterprise, by patience and tact he carried the thing to a satisfactory termination. Mr. Hogg, in the Reminiscences which he contributed to the Memoir of

* See page 169.

De Quincey, recalls no end of characteristic points—
how, for example, the poor Opium-Eater, wherever he
went, carried boxes and bundles of books and papers
with him, and how he was apt to lose or to leave them
on the way, giving, as one instance, that of a big box
which he had packed full of valuable things as he
thought with which to occupy himself when on a visit
to Professor Lushington in Glasgow, and how it came
somehow to be left in an obscure bookseller's shop, how
De Quincey forgot the address, and it was not unearthed
until years afterwards through Mr. Hogg's own exertions.
Then, wherever he had had lodgings, he had left
memorials of himself in the shape of such gatherings,
and then sometimes, when circumstances arose to make
him desire to refer to those papers and books, or to get
possession of them, there were difficulties, and claims
made which very often had no real foundation, as Mr.
Hogg from careful investigations in some cases fully
satisfied himself of.

Mr. Hogg also tells with what a keen and unceasing
curiosity he read the newspapers, showing the greatest
interest in all that was going on, and how he followed
up every detail in famous murder cases and criminal
trials, and was ever ready to discuss these with him :
very often throwing the most unexpected and fresh
lights upon them.   Indeed, he industriously made notes,
just as an active newspaper editor would do, of peculiar
facts and touches of character revealed in newspaper
reports, more especially in police-courts; and had
accumulated such masses of material in this kind that
he was never able to recover them, not being equal to
the task of systematic commonplace book-keeping ; but
some of these drawn from the mass have been given, by
way of specimens, and as throwing light on his character

and methods, in the volumes of the "Posthumous Writings," as well as various versions of some famous passages which show how he re-wrote and laboriously corrected in the getting of his finest effects which critics and readers admire.

For a while De Quincey tried to carry on the work at Lasswade, but no end of difficulties, fancied and real, arose : and the upshot of it was that, to be near the press, he took lodgings at 42, Lothian Street, Edinburgh. There both Mr. Hogg and his son James * became constant visitors. The connection developed into a genuine friendship—had it not done so, it is hardly possible we should have had an English collected edition of De Quincey's works. Mr. Hogg, senior, tells with a fine humour about the odd ways of his distinguished author—how his rooms got piled up with books and papers, till he had hardly more free space than just to allow him to write on ; how he would himself attend to making up his fire and cleaning his hearth, rather than be interrupted by any intruding attendant at times when he was absorbed in his work ; how Mrs. Wilson, his landlady, and Miss Stark her sister, came to understand their eccentric lodger, and carefully to watch over him— a thing that was sometimes necessary, as he would frequently set papers alight (a tendency from which his daughters suffered also at Lasswade as well as from what they humorously called the "snowing-up ") ; and how he would sit and sip his little glass of much-diluted laudanum, and talk of no end of big projects—a great History of England in six octavo volumes, and so on !

He made his periodical visits to Lasswade, which remained his head-quarters to the end, and if he failed to go out there for a longer time than usual, he would

* The Editor of this volume.

F 2

write to his daughters the most lightsome, humorous
letters, of which many samples are given in the Memoir.
Sometimes he would arrange for a friend to come for
him at Lothian Street, and then they would walk out to
Lasswade together : Professor Lushington for one often
arranging thus ; and we can easily imagine the kind of
talk that took place between them on the way.   Mr.
Hogg frequently walked out with him to Lasswade, and
he tells how agile the little man was even then, how "at
seventy he had the nimbleness of a squirrel," and easily
outwalked him (though a much younger and taller man)
when once they were fairly in the open, and more
especially when they had heights to climb.

By the nicest management and the art of patience and
good humour on Messrs. Hogg's part, the great work
moved on, slowly yet surely, with many hitches that would
have been almost ludicrous but for the seriousness with
which the Opium-Eater was apt to view them, and for
their effects upon him ; for not seldom, with the task of
searching for missing pages, proofs and notes constantly
going astray among his vast accumulations of miscellaneous matter, he was completely prostrated.   He found
that "stooping killed him," that his memory was not
what it had been, and much else ; and yet the work, in
face of all these things, was done.

Cheering influences amid all this labour and trial were
the visits of Mr. J. R. Findlay, who, in his "Recollections
of De Quincey," has given most attractive and vivid
pictures of him at this time.   Mr. Findlay and his uncle,
Mr. Ritchie, proprietor of *The Scotsman*, were very
fond to tempt the old man eloquent to share their
society in George Square as often as they could ; and
many a delightful evening did De Quincey spend there.
They were fain on one occasion to arrange for a meeting

between Thackeray and the Opium-Eater ; but, owing to the circumstances detailed on page 192, he did not go, and thus these two distinguished writers never met. Indeed, a good deal of *finesse* and management was needed then, as it had been in former times, as Mr. Robert Chambers and his friends well knew, to beguile the recluse of Lothian Street to anything like a formal party—where, as he said, the most distressing thing to him was to hear his own name shouted out before him, as through a long inverted trumpet of fame.

XXI.

He was actually at work on the closing volumes of the " Collected Writings " when the last illness came. He was averse to doctors' treatment ; but he sank so low that his friends were summoned and Dr. Warburton Begbie was called in. It is very characteristic of De Quincey that he soon transformed this distinguished physician into a friend, and Dr. Begbie's account of the last moments along with those of Miss de Quincey, who faithfully attended to and nursed him, furnish a complete record of the last scenes. Dr. Warburton Begbie's account was published in *The Scotsman*, and a large portion of it was reproduced in the Memoir, and there he does full justice to the fine courtesy, frankness, and beautiful humility of the old man. He died on the 7th December, 1859, and lies buried in St. Cuthbert's Churchyard, a stone memorial, erected by his friends, marking the spot.

A very peculiar coincidence was that just as he breathed his last, a letter was received for him from his old schoolfellow, Edward Grinfield, wishing to exchange good wishes before they should be called from earth.

THOMAS DE QUINCEY MARRIED ELIZABETH PENSON.

Issue :—

1. Jane (died about two years old).
2. Elizabeth (died about nine years old).
3. William (died in his eighteenth year).
4. Mary (in 1819 married the Rev. Philip Serle, and died in childbed about eighteen months afterwards).
5. Thomas (born 1785, died 1859).
6. Richard (written of by De Quincey as "My Brother Pink" —supposed to have been killed in the Blue Mountains, Jamaica, after many adventures, when about 25 years of age).
7. Jane (lived to a good old age).
8. Henry (the H. of the "Autobiographic Sketches;" a posthumous child. He belonged to Brasenose College, Oxford, and died in his 26th year).

THOMAS DE QUINCEY MARRIED MARGARET SIMPSON.

Issue :—

1. William (who died about 1835, in his eighteenth year ; referred to by his father as a student of great promise).
2. Margaret (who died in 1871, in Ireland, at the residence of her husband, Mr. Robert Craig. He died in 1886).
3. Horace (an officer in the 26th Cameronians ; was engaged in the China Campaign under Sir Hugh Gough, and died there in 1842).
4. Francis (a medical man, who settled in Brazil and died in Rio Janeiro in 1861 of yellow fever).
5. Paul Frederick (an officer in the 70th Regiment ; fought at Sobraon, and served all through the Indian Mutiny. He was military secretary to General Galloway in the Maori War, and as a reward for services received a grant of land. He settled there and died in 1894).
6. Florence (who married Colonel Baird Smith, the Chief Engineer at the siege of Delhi, where he received wounds from which he never recovered).
7. Julius (who died in 1833, about 4 years of age).
8. Emily.

NOTES OF CONVERSATIONS WITH THOMAS DE QUINCEY.

By RICHARD WOODHOUSE.*

September 28, 1821.—The Opium-Eater was formerly (indeed he is still) a great admirer of Wordsworth. So much was he so, that he could not even bring himself to mention his name in Oxford, for fear of having to encounter ridiculous observations or jeering abuse of his favourite, who was laughed at by most of the Oxonians. Of this he felt himself so impatient that he forbore even to speak upon the subject.

Meeting one time with Charles Lamb, who he understood had praised Wordsworth's poetry, he was induced to mention that poet's name, and to speak of him in high terms. Lamb gave him praise, but rather more qualified than the Opium-Eater expected, who spoke with much warmth on the subject, and complained that Lamb did not do Wordsworth justice; upon which Lamb, in his dry, facetious way, observed, "If we are to talk in this strain, we ought to have said grace before we began our conversation." This observation so annoyed the Opium-Eater that he instantly left the room, and has never seen Lamb since.

"This anecdote the Opium-Eater told me," said Hessey, "himself, along with some others of a similar tenor, in exemplification of points in his own character. He told it with much humour, and was quite sensible

* See Preface, page ix., and page 103.

how ridiculous his conduct was ; and he will be glad to
see Lamb again, who he supposes must have long since
forgotten or forgiven the circumstance."

On Wednesday the 28th, and Thursday, 29th October,
1821, I passed the evenings at Taylor and Hessey's, in
company with the author of " Confessions of an English
Opium-Eater," published in Nos. 21 and 22 of the
London Magazine. I had formed to myself the idea
of a tall, thin, pale, gentlemanly-looking, courtier-like
man ; but I met a short, sallow-looking person, of a very
peculiar cast of countenance, and apparently much an
invalid. His demeanour was very gentle, modest, and
unassuming ; and his conversation fully came up to the
idea I had formed of what would be that of the writer of
those articles. He seems well acquainted with many of
the literary men of the present day. He has for some
time past lived near Wordsworth in Westmoreland, near
Grasmere, where he had met Southey, Wilson, and the
Edinburgh men. He knew Sir Walter Scott, Lockhart,
and the majority of the *Blackwood* writers. I learned
from him that he was for some time at Morgan's school
in Bath, where I had been about two years after he left
it, and that Morgan was the "ripe" scholar he alluded to
in his " Confessions." He was a day-boarder there ; he
was at first under Wilkins, the under-master (who now
has the school), but he used always to show his Latin
verse exercises up to Morgan with the two upper classes.
He says he has often observed Morgan pointing him out
with his cane to the boys in his upper classes, particularly when they brought up their verses to him, and the
larger boys would threaten him and compel him to do
their exercises for them.

From Morgan's he was removed to the Rev. Mr.
Spencer's, at Winkfield, near Bath, where two of my

brothers went. He found a great difference between
the two masters. Being one of the head boys in this
latter school, he found he could do pretty much as he
pleased. He with some of the others at that school
set up a periodical work, as it may be termed, in conjunction with one of Mr. Spencer's daughters. They
each furnished in turn written essays or disquisitions.
Of these they collected about eighty, "some of which,"
said the Opium-Eater, "I met with among my papers
within the last three months." It was from this school
that he took his departure so unceremoniously.* He is
now thirty-six years of age. His constitution is much
shattered. He has reduced his daily potion of laudanum
from 8,000 to about 80 drops, but he occasionally takes
more, and whenever he is obliged to do this for any
length of time the consequence is a great irritation in his
stomach—he feels there an itching which he is obliged
to bear, and unable by any means to allay. This is
accompanied by a tendency in his stomach to turn
everything to acid, and no alkaline medicine has any
effect upon this. The only medicine that reaches this
disorder is that prescribed by the surgeon he alluded to
in his "Confessions." He says this sensation of itching is
so dreadful that if it were to last much longer than it
usually does (about eight or ten hours), it would drive
him out of his mind.

The Opium-Eater appears to have read a great deal,
and to have thought much more. I was astonished at
the depth and *reality*, if I may so call it, of his knowledge. He seems to have passed nothing that occurred
in the course of his study unreflected on or unremem-

* Woodhouse must of course have misunderstood De Quincey,
as the school from which he absconded was the Manchester
Grammar School.

bered. His conversation appeared like the elaboration of a mine of results: and if at any time a general observation of his became matter of question or ulterior disquisition it was found that he had ready his reasons at a moment's notice; so that it was clear that his opinions were the fruits of his own reflections on what had come before him, and had not been taken up from others. Indeed, this last clearly appeared, since upon most of the topics that arose he was able to give a very satisfactory account, not merely of *what books* had been written upon those subjects, but of *what opinions* had been entertained upon them, together with his own judgments of those opinions, his acquiescence in them, or qualifications in them. Upon almost every subject that was introduced he had not only that general information which is easily picked up in literary society or from books, but that minute and accurate acquaintance with the details that can be acquired only from personal investigation of a subject and reflection upon it at the same time. Taylor led him into political economy, into the Greek and Latin accents, into antiquities, Roman roads, old castles, the origin and analogy of languages; upon all these he was informed to considerable minuteness. The same with regard to Shakespeare's sonnets, Spenser's minor poems, and the great writers and characters of Elizabeth's age and those of Cromwell's time. His judgments of books, of writers, of politics, were particularly satisfactory and sound. He is a slight Danish scholar, a moderate Italian, a good Frenchman, except as to pronunciation, and it seemed to me an excellent German scholar. He spoke of writing German articles and translations for the *London Magazine.* He had an immense fund of literary anecdotes respecting the living writers. He had, he said, conducted a journal in the north (*The Westmoreland Gazette*). It was set up with a view of supporting the Lowther interest. "But," said he, "I so managed it as to preserve my independence, and it happened that during the year and a half that I was the conductor of the paper, the name of Lowther was scarcely ever mentioned in the leading articles."

November 3rd, 1821.—This evening also I passed in his company, and had fresh reason to admire the variety and extent of his acquisitions in the different branches of knowledge, and the soundness of his judgments. I was also pleased with the candour with which he confessed his unacquaintance with different subjects, at the same time showing by his remarks that he had very good general knowledge of the outlines of them, and of the groundworks on which they were erected. He has gone very deep in the German metaphysics, and particularly studied Kant's works. He is well acquainted with Coleridge, and they have in a great measure pursued the same studies. But he observed that Coleridge had mixed up his own fancies and mysticalities so much with the Kantian philosophy, that it was difficult for him (the Opium-Eater) to judge of the exact extent of Coleridge's acquaintance with Kant's system. He thinks very meanly of Dugald Stewart, who has no originality or grasp of mind in him, who constantly misunderstands and misquotes writers from taking their opinions at second-hand from others, and then falling foul of them. He has taken the account of Kant, as well as some passages of rank nonsense cited as Kant's, from a French writer whom he quotes and praises much in his introductory dissertation prefixed to one part of the *Encyclopædia Britannica* Supplement (Degerando). All Dugald Stewart's disquisitions are little, and the subject of them of no moment, even if true. He is thought little of at Edinburgh, or on the Continent. In the latter the only consideration he meets with is from his talent as a writer on polite literature.

The Mr. A. is Mr. Addington, brother of Hiley Addington, in the Opium-Eater's "Confessions" mentioned as an opium-eater.

The Opium-Eater entered himself some time back at the Middle Temple, with the view of being called to the bar, but he did not keep many terms.

On the subject of reading poetry, he observed that Wilson's character of countenance is generally very lively, but this leaves him the moment he begins to read poetry; his face then assumes a conventicle appearance, and his voice a methodistical drawl that is quite distressing. Southey mouths it out like a wolf howling. Coleridge lengthens the vowels and reads so monotonously, slowly, and abstractedly, that you can scarce make out what he says, and you lose the rhythm. Wordsworth sometimes reads very well.

It seems to me, from the manner in which the Opium-Eater recited a few lines occasionally which he had occasion to quote, that the reading upon which in his " Confessions " he piques himself would scarcely appear good to most people. He reads with too inward a voice ; he dwells much upon the long vowels (this he does in his conversation, which makes it resemble more a speech delivered in a debating society than the varitonous discourse usually held among friends); he ekes out particular syllables, has generally much appearance of intensity, and, in short, removes his tone and manner rather too much from the mode of common language. Hence I could not always catch the words

in his quotations, and though one acquainted with the
quotation beforehand would relish it the more from
having an opportunity afforded of dwelling upon it, and
from hearing the most made of those particular parts
for the sake of which it is brought forward, yet general
hearers would be left far behind, and in a state of wonder
at the quoter. I learned from him that he has several
works in hand. He is about to write a few notes to
Taylor's pamphlet,* for which purpose he is to have my
interleaved copy. He is to write for the *London
Magazine* an introduction to some English hexameters
which he has composed ; he is to write on the mode of
reading Latin ; on Kant's philosophy ; on Coleridge's
literary character ; on Richter ; to translate and abridge
some tales from the German ; to translate from the
same an introduction to the weather observations and
meteorological tables ; to sketch out a closing address to
the volume of the *London Magazine* ending December
next, and give No. 3 of the Opium-Eater's " Confessions "
for the February number ; to write a series of letters to
a young man of talent whose education had been
neglected ; to write on political economy.

The anecdote told by Hazlitt in the *London Magazine*,
vol. 3, is true. Wordsworth was the person, and Mrs.
Lloyd was the friend at whose house he snuffed out
one of the candles. The rest of the story, respecting
the order to the servant when the nobleman dined with
Wordsworth, is a fabrication for the sake of effect. The
Opium-Eater, to whom Lloyd told it, knowing from the
character of Wordsworth that it could not be true,
cross-examined Lloyd and ascertained its incorrectness.

* " The Restoration of National Prosperity shown to be immediately practicable." By the author of "Junius Identified " (*i.e.*
John Taylor). London, 1821.

Wordsworth would, in fact, scorn to be thought to
interfere with the domestic management of his establishment, and would despise any man who should do. He
would rather be thought, if possible, not to know there
was such a thing. Lloyd is the author of some novels : *
in one of these he gives a picture of Coleridge (under
the title of Edmund Oliver). His novels are all full of
excessive sentimentality, or rather sensitiveness—this
indeed is his character. He has been insane, and his
insanity originated from his extreme and intense
nervousness. He is quite harmless on those occasions.
He made his escape from the retreat or the asylum,
near York, and wandered about the country. The
Opium-Eater once met him in Westmoreland when
under one of these fits. They walked along for some
time together ; at length, in one of the loveliest and
wildest spots, near one of the most retired and wild of
the lakes, Lloyd suddenly stopped, and in great agitation asked the Opium-Eater if he knew who he was.
" I dare say," he continued, " you think you know me ;
but you do not, and you cannot. I am the author of all
evil ; Sir, I am the devil. By what inscrutable decree
of Providence it is that I was foredoomed from all
eternity to be this malevolent being, I cannot tell."

* He does not appear to have published more than one,
" Edmund Oliver," printed at Bristol in 1798, and dedicated to
Charles Lamb. It is a novel with a purpose, " written," says the
author, " with the design of counteracting that generalizing spirit
which seems so much to have insinuated itself among modern
philosophers." Godwin is the writer chiefly combated. It is
eloquent, impassioned, and although, as De Quincey says, somewhat too sentimental, on the whole a work of considerable merit.
' The incidents relative to the army," it is stated, " were given me
by an intimate friend." Coleridge is no doubt the person indicated,
but there seems no other ground for considering him to be introduced into the book.

He then cast his eyes upwards to heaven, and remained silent for a short time. "I know," he then said, "you will not believe me, but it is of no consequence: I feel satisfied that it is so." "I said to him," said the Opium-Eater, "I certainly had thought differently, and still did, but it would be more satisfactory to me to hear what his reasons were. He then said, 'I know who you are; you are nobody, a nonentity; you have no being. You will not agree with me, and you will attempt to argue with me, and thus to prove that you do exist; but it is not so, you do not exist at all. It is merely appearance, and not reality. There is, and there can be, but one other real being besides myself.' He then," said the Opium-Eater, "entered into a variety of arguments to convince me he was what he pretended. This was what I wanted. I had set his understanding at work. He reasoned and reasoned, and became more himself and more cheerful, and the fancy wore away by degrees."

"He is," said the Opium-Eater, "the very worst possible writer, though a man of talent in a particular way, in every style except one—that of a sort of Rousseauish feeling and sentiment. His novels are full of it." Taylor mentioned that he had had some MS. novels in verse of his, which were all of that class, and would not do for the magazine, for which purpose they were offered.

The Opium-Eater mentioned that when he called upon Murray in town, the latter had spoken to him of "your patron, Lord Lowther." "Now," said the Opium-Eater, "the word patron is a favourite word with me, from its association with those high and noble instances of patronage, about the age of Elizabeth, when great men took a pride and pleasure in fostering

ability, and lending their names and protection to
authors. This patronage was without humiliation or
servility : each party felt that he was receiving as well
as conferring a benefit. The poet in return for present
countenance and favours, had it in his power to transmit
his patron's name down with honour to posterity. He
made a sort of glory of this mutual obligation, and the
praise that he gave, though somewhat excessive, was the
poetic garb in which he decked the expression of his
own excited feelings. It was the illumination which
genius and enthusiasm always throw round their subject.
At the same time that they thus made their offerings or
expressed their gratitude to their noble friends, they did
not scruple to tell them that those offerings and those
thanks would be the means by which their names and
characters would be handed down to future times.
Shakespeare's sonnets to his patron are full of these
vaunts of conscious genius.

> ' And thou *in this* shalt find thy monument,
> When tyrant's tombs and crests of brass are spent.'
> ' Thy monument shall be my gentle verse,' etc.
> ' Yet be most proud of that which I compile.'

And others to the same purport; Spenser and Ben
Jonson the same.

" These addresses were grand and noble ; they carried
in themselves an excuse for their flattery. They had
a redeeming power about them which causes them to be
better and better liked the further the reader is removed
from the actual time of their composition. They were
very different from the gross and excessive adulation of
the wits of Anne's days. Dryden's dedications are
artful, elaborate, and energetic, but fulsome ; there is no
heart in them. The writer knew they were untrue when

he wrote them ; he wrote them for gain or its equivalent and they have about them, and suggest to the reader, the idea of insincerity and outrageous exaggeration. This style could not continue ; Dryden had carried it to its utmost extent, and it ceased after him. The dedicators of the next age rather insinuated than expressly assigned to those they addressed the virtues and perfections incident to humanity. But the same insincerity is apparent to the reader. The approved forms ran thus : 'If it was not notorious how averse your lordship is to have those qualities in which you far surpass not only your contemporaries, but also the greatest men of antiquity, made known to the world, I should consider myself blamable if in this address I were to pass over that nobility, etc., etc.'

" Even Addison has too much of this in the prefaces to his *Spectators*. But I was about to observe that, whether for this, or some other reason, the word patron has fallen into unrepute. And though I was convinced that Mr. Murray had no intention to offend me, yet I was satisfied that he did not use the word in its best, and if I may so say, its *Elizabethan* sense—and I felt that the use of it to any one at this day in the manner in which Mr. Murray used it, was, to say the least, unthinking. But Mr. Murray is quite a man of the world, and has a different behaviour for everyone, according to the idea he has of the relative importance to himself of the party. And I should imagine that the kind of reception one meets with from Murray would be a tolerably correct indication of the estimation in which one stands with people of a certain description with whom Mr. Murray is connected. His behaviour towards me was quite different from what it had been in Westmoreland, when he pressed me for an article, and insisted

G

that I should never come to town without calling upon
him, and enlarged upon the pleasure he should have to
see me. *But three hundred miles makes a great difference
in some people.*"

The Opium-Eater here went into an account of his
connection with the paper set up by the Lowthers, which
I have already briefly noticed, to show how little he was
of a client (to use an Horatian expression) of Lord
Lowther : whom, indeed, he had never seen above twice,
and then at election dinners.

The above anecdote I have set down, with the
disquisition on patronage connected with it, in the first
person, because, though not the very language of the
narrator, it contains the substance of what he said, and is
given somewhat in his manner, and in the order in which
he gave it ; and it will afford some idea of the general
tenor of his conversation, and of the richness of his mind,*
and of the facility with which he brings in the stores of
his reading and reflection to bear upon the ordinary topics
of conversation. But it can convey no adequate impression of the eloquence and scope of his language. The
subject was incidentally introduced by something said of
the *Quarterly Review ;* the incident had occurred some
time back, and the whole thing, though it assumes from its
air and coherence the character of a preconceived show-
off, was quite *ex improviso.* That it was really so will be

---

* De Quincey says himself of his talents for conversation :
" Having the advantage of a prodigious memory, and the far
greater advantage of a logical instinct for feeling in a moment the
secret analogies or parallelisms that connected things else apparently remote, I enjoyed these two peculiar gifts for conversation :
first, an inexhaustible fertility of topics, and therefore of resources
for illustrating or for varying any subject that chance or ⬛⬛⬛
suggested ; secondly, a prematurely awake⬛⬛⬛
to conversation."—*Opium-Eater,* ed. 186⬛

evident at once to those who are in the habit of asso-
ciating with him, and of hearing him, as it were, overlay
every little topic with rich discussion and valuable
information and reflection thrown in *quasi ex abundanti.*

Reynolds when in fine cue, and amongst friends, is
equally ready and lavish in his wit, sporting it extem-
pore on every subject, and with astonishing good-humour
and freedom from acrimony or personality.

23rd November, 1821.—I dined at Taylor's with Dr.
Darling, Perceval, and the Opium-Eater. In the course
of the evening the latter mentioned that the person he
alludes to in his " Confessions " as far exceeding himself in the quantity taken of opium is Coleridge. The
Opium-Eater was speaking to a surgeon in the north, a
neighbour of. Coleridge's, who supplied Coleridge with
laudanum, and who, upon a calculation made as to the
quantity consumed by Coleridge, found it to amount to
80,000 drops per day. The first time Coleridge went to
the house of this surgeon, he was not at home, but his
wife supplied Coleridge, and she saw him at once fill out
a large wineglassful and drink it off. She was astonished, and in much alarm explained to him what the
medicine was, as she imagined he had made a mistake.
Very soon afterwards he drank off another glassful, and
before he left the house he had emptied a half-pint bottle
in addition.

The Opium-Eater said that he himself once, at the
time when he was taking 8,000 drops per day, but when
he was not in the habit of measuring what he took, was
in some danger from the quantity he had taken. He
had been sitting for some time engaged in reading, and
had been helping himself to laudanum, almost unconsciously, and without reflecting how much he was taking,
when he suddenly found himself dizzy and heavy, and

G 2

very much inclined to sleep; he also perceived, as it were, the fumes rising to his brain. He exerted himself to get up and walk about : for if he had remained quiet, in one minute he should have fallen asleep in his chair. He then took an emetic and brought off much of what he had taken, and thus rescued himself from the danger.

The house in which the Opium-Eater lived, as mentioned in his " Confessions," rent free, and which is in a street leading out of Oxford Street, is in Greek Street, and the house is the corner house in that street, partly in the square, on the right hand as you go down from Oxford Street. The master had other offices elsewhere at which he carried on his game. He went by several names.*

The Opium-Eater tells a curious tale of his practices upon a foolish butcher who fancied he had a literary talent, and whose intellectual abilities his landlord for his own ends flattered in a most fulsome way, but so as nearly to turn the poor butcher's brain with vanity.

Sir William Jones was a man of much talent ; but he cannot be called a man of genius, for he wanted passion to attach him to one particular pursuit ; instead of which he was studying all subjects for a season in turn, and so he was never great in any one.

2nd December, 1821.—I dined at Dewint's with Taylor, Cunningham, and the Opium-Eater ; a Mr. Wilson, a Catholic gentleman and an antiquary, came in after dinner. Cunningham mentioned that a report had been spread in the north that Bloomfield had sustained considerable loss by the failure of Vernor and Hood. Taylor thought the rumour was entirely without foundation. Cunningham observed that Hogg, the Ettrick Shepherd, had set about a similar story respecting his own

* See page 34.

losses by the failure of a bookseller at Edinburgh, named
Gibson, who had published for him. Gibson happened
to hear the report ; and when he went to Edinburgh
and had traced the rumour to Hogg, he, to Hogg's great
surprise, made his appearance, and demanded of Hogg
his reason for such a misrepresentation. Hogg, with much
candour, answered, " Ah, sir, I thought you were *dead.*"

Cunningham spoke of Hogg as having much energy
and animation in his manner, considerable self-possession,
and a very ready knack at answering.

When Wilkie showed Hogg some of his pictures, the
latter looked over them one by one, and when it was
apparent that he was expected to say something, he
looked first at the works and then at the painter several
times, as though comparing them together, and then said,
" It's *weel* you're so young a man." The expression
bore two constructions. Wilkie took it as a compliment,
and bowed.

The Opium-Eater, in the course of a conversation on
versifying, and the sort of compensation in poetical
melody which requires a heavy or spondaic line after a
dactylic or lighter one, noticed Milton's excellence in
that respect, and quoted different passages in proof,
among which were the following :—

> " Thence to the famous orators repair,
> Those ancient, whose resistless eloquence
> Wielded at will that fierce Democratic,
> Shook th' arsenal, and fulmined over Greece
> To Macedon, and Artaxerxes' throne."
>
> (P. R. iv., l. 267.)

Oxford and classical learning, and the general ability
of University men next came on the carpet ; when the
Opium-Eater mentioned with surprise, as though it was
a sort of stigma upon the University, that a man like

Copleston who had so little in him, and had done so
little to distinguish himself, should be thought so much of,
and be so quoted with pride by Oxonians as an honour
to the University. "It seems," he said, "to be a virtual
condemnation by themselves of their University; for if
he be the highest, what must the lowest be; and what
must be the general standard!" The Opium-Eater was
himself of Oxford.

He then mentioned having had a presentiment, on
leaving his residence on a visit to London some time
back, that he should never again see a little child of
Wordsworth's, who was afflicted and had but the use of
one of its sides. It was a sweet little girl, about three
years old, and the Opium-Eater was much attached to
her. One night while he was here, he heard a dog
howling in a dismal manner at his door: it howled
three times, and the Opium-Eater with some curiosity
waited to hear a fourth howl, but in vain; the dog
passed on and was silent. This happened on some
particular day, either Christmas or New Year's Eve *
(which was named by him to Taylor), and he noticed
the time particularly. The effect was so vivid upon the
Opium-Eater's sensations that he at once began to consider which of all the persons he knew and loved might
most probably be in trouble or dying at that time; and
he thought that this little child was the most likely one of
whom he might expect to receive ill news. He waited
with some anxiety for the post on the day on which
intimation of anything that might have occurred at home
at the period he had noted would reach him in due
course. He listened to the postman and heard him in
the street, but he passed by his door without knocking.

* De Quincey's memory deceived him. The child died on
June 5, 1812.

However, in the course of the day he received by the second post a letter sealed with black wax. It was from Miss Wordsworth (Wordsworth's sister), who, knowing how partial he had been to the child, had written to him to apprise him of its death.

6th December, 1821.—I dined at Taylor and Hessey's this day, in company with the Opium-Eater, Reynolds, Lamb, Cunningham, Rice, Hood, Wainwright, and Talfourd. About one o'clock I accompanied the Opium-Eater home : we knocked several times, but no one answered the door, and he accepted my proposition of spending the night in my chambers. We accordingly returned to the Temple, and lighted a fire. The night passed away rapidly in most interesting conversation, and at eight in the morning I saw him home. In the course of the night he expressed a desire to try the effect of tabacco upon his stomach, for he observed he had been lately indisposed, so much so that he found himself obliged to increase his dose of laudanum to 200 drops per day, yet that day he had taken but 100 in the morning, but had omitted to take the like quantity as usual about four o'clock in the afternoon. The consequence was, that his stomach had been painful all the evening, and he thought this a fair opportunity for making the experiment. He smoked half a cigar, until he felt his head slightly dizzy ; but this soon went off, and he observed in about half an hour after that the smoking had quieted the irritation in his stomach. He smoked the half of another in the course of the night ; and he seemed to think it not unlikely that he might be able to substitute in a great measure the use of tabacco for that of opium.

The evening at Taylor's had passed very pleasantly to all but the Opium-Eater. Lamb, Rice, and Reynolds

were particularly lively and facetious ; jokes were
lavished sufficient to furnish a new Joe Miller.—"Mr.
Lamb," said John Taylor, " I shall be happy to take
wine with you.   Is that the hock you have before you ? "
" Hoc est," said Lamb.   Lamb on a former evening had
overthrown his glass by accident.   " Never mind," said
Taylor, " it is soon replaced."   " Ah ! " said Lamb,
shaking his head, " *oc-cidit !* "

Lamb, observing the Opium-Eater to be very still,
began a sort of playful attack upon him by way of
rousing him, and desired he would, as he knew of old he
could, be entertaining and facetious ; he also added
something in a jeering but good-humoured way about
Oxford Street.   The Opium-Eater seemed very unhappy at this, and assured Lamb and the company that
he was far from well, and it was totally out of his power
at that moment to enter into the conversation, and he
hoped they would not take it ill that he sat silent.
After Lamb and the rest were gone, the Opium-Eater
said to Taylor, Hessey, and myself, which he repeated
when he arrived at my chambers, that he had felt it out of
his power through indisposition to take part in what had
been going forward, and he hoped none of those who
had left them would attribute it to an improper motive.
He added, that if he *had* been in good health, he could
not have entered into conversation on any subject
connected with his opium-eating confessions, after the
manner and tone of levity and half-jeering in which
Lamb had made allusion to them.   " There are," said
he, " certain places and events and circumstances which
have been mixed up or connected with parts of my life
which have been very unfortunate, and these, from
constant meditation and reflection upon them, have
obtained with me a sort of sacredness, and become

associated with solemn feelings, so that I cannot bear without the greatest mental agony to advert to the subject, or to hear it adverted to by others in any tone of levity or witticism. It seems to me a sort of desecration and unhallowing analogous to the profanation of a temple, when the subjects are approached in conversation by any one unless in a feeling of sympathy and seriousness, and I would rather suffer the most excruciating bodily pains than the shock my whole nature feels at hearing these topics discussed in a ludicrous manner or made the ground of raillery."

Speaking of the characters of minds of different people, and indeed of various whole classes, he took notice that he considered the minds of the people in his own neighbourhood as being particularly gross and uncharitable. That they were fond of retailing anecdotes, however horrible, as true, without ever taking the trouble to ascertain their foundation, or caring at all whether they were true or not. This he attributes to the want of novelty and stimulus operating upon the vacant and inactive minds of people having no worldly cares to occupy them, rather than to any inherent maliciousness. The worst was that these tales, though they always cease to be current when any newer scandal is imported to supply their place, are yet liable at any time to be recalled from their temporary oblivion, and indeed are so ; and they often acquire more effect in their revived state than they had originally ; for at that time, though all repeated them, yet they were recent, and easily proved if true, and the very circumstance that every one had the same story, yet no one could vouch it, or personally knew anything of it, satisfied all the world that there was nothing in it. Yet when a story was revived, it was always mentioned with an *on dit* and

as having been well known and the common talk at the
time it happened, so that the rumour had thus more
chance of meeting belief than when it was first sent
abroad, and "the last state of the lie is worse than
the first." The Opium-Eater mentioned several stories,
entirely groundless, and carrying in their very horror an
assurance of their falsehood and absurdity.

8th December, 1821.—The Opium-Eater was reading at
Taylor's the notice in the *Literary Gazette* of Keats,*
introduced into a critique upon Shelley's "Adonais," a
poem on the death of Keats, and he expressed in the
strongest terms his execration of such a rascally and
villainous assault upon the memory of anyone scarcely
yet cold in his tomb.

The Opium-Eater mentioned that Wilson had sent
him Shelley's "Revolt of Islam,"† with a request that
he would write a review of it for *Blackwood's Magazine.*
This the Opium-Eater would not do, but he read it, and
was surprised to find in it more ability of a particular
sort than he expected, or indeed than he had conceived

* This remarkable piece of criticism appeared in the *Literary
Gazette* of December 8, 1821, and certainly merits the palm among
all the disgraceful reviews of the period for stupidity as regards
Shelley and brutality as regards Keats. It begins, "We have
already given some of our columns to this writer's merits, and we
will not now repeat our convictions of his incurable absurdity. . . .
Adonais is an elegy on a foolish young man, who, after writing
some volumes of very weak, and in the greater part of very indecent
poetry, died some time since of a consumption, the breaking down
of an infirm constitution having in all probability been accelerated
by the discarding his neckcloth. . . . We give a verse at random,
premising that there is *no story* in the elegy " (!).

† The review, written by Wilson, but as it now appears inspired
by De Quincey, was published in *Blackwood* for January, 1819,
and, with the subsequent notices of " Alastor " and " Prometheus
Unbound " in the same periodical, is by far the worthiest recognition that Shelley's genius received in his lifetime.

Shelley, whom he knew, and who had been his neighbour in the Lakes, to possess. He returned Wilson the book, with a letter stating his judgment of the work, and very soon there appeared a flaming article by Wilson in the magazine praising the book very highly. "Evelyn's Memoirs"—a weak, good-for-little book, which has been unaccountably much praised by weak people, and the praise thus lavished has been repeated over and over again by persons who take all their opinions upon trust. He was a shallow, empty, cowardly, vain, assuming coxcomb. It is not endurable to hear such a prig of a fellow, who ran away from England at the very time of danger, and remained in Italy looking at pictures and collecting butterflies during the time the war was going on, and who came back the moment all the fighting was over and the business done, abusing the fine spirits who died in the popular cause as rebels, etc. He was a mere literary fribble, a fop and a smatterer affecting natural history and polite learning, and yet his stupid memoirs are praised to the very echo. They are useful as now and then enabling one to fix the date of a particular event, but for little besides. The mind of a man is very generally seen in the use he makes of a journal. Evelyn's is very meagre and bad. You meet, for instance, with such matters recorded as that he dined with *this* person of quality, or called upon or was visited by *that* man of distinction, *without more*. Nothing that the party said in conversation is noted; nothing is stated as arising out of, or depending upon, the visit ; the purpose of setting the circumstance down at all seems to be merely to give an idea of the consequence which the writer imagines himself to derive from being considered an acquaintance of such men.

Taylor read a part of a letter from Clare, to whom he

had lately sent Wordsworth's poems, in which he says:
" I like Wordsworth better than Crabbe.   I can read the
one a second time over with added pleasure, but I am
disgusted with the other after it has been once read.
Still Wordsworth's nursery ballads inspire me with an
uncontrollable itch of parodying them; I did ease
myself by burlesquing one, which you shall have in my
next." The Opium-Eater wondered that he should
think of comparing Wordsworth and Crabbe together,
who had not one thing in common in their writings.
Wordsworth sought to hallow and ennoble every subject
on which he touched, while Crabbe was anything but a
poet. His pretensions to poetry were not nothing,
merely, but if they were to be represented algebraically,
the negative sign must be prefixed.   All his labours and
endeavours were unpoetical.   Instead of raising and
elevating his subjects, he did all he could to make them
flat and commonplace, to disrobe them of the garb in
which imagination would clothe them, and to bring them
down as low as, or even to debase them lower than, the
standard of common life.   Poetry could no longer exist
if cultivated only by such writers as Crabbe.   Wordsworth's aim is entirely the reverse of this: as to him
Clare seemed to fall into the general error, that he wrote
on subjects only fit for the nursery, and that his thoughts
and language were low and vulgar. " Now," says the
Opium-Eater, " I will not take upon me generally to
assert that no single low thought or expression occurs;
but I will say that I do not recollect any instance; and
that most of the passages usually quoted as instances of
this, are themselves proofs of the direct contrary.   And
the objection is generally made by persons of common,
low minds, who have not wisdom to perceive or
sympathy to feel the depth of his thoughts.   He is

accused of being too simple, when in fact he is too wise and too abstruse for them. He is thought to skim the surface while in truth he goes very deeply into the elements of our nature, too far indeed for many to follow him. People in general do not sufficiently attend to the principles upon which they act; and Wordsworth's apparent simplicity arises in a great degree from his acquaintance with the depths of the human heart and the secret springs that regulate and influence human feelings, thoughts, and actions. Thousands of persons will object to passages in Wordsworth because they do not understand the principles on which they themselves act, and on a knowledge of which the passage in question will depend, yet the same people will speak and act in other matters, though they do not themselves know it, upon the very same principle in the human mind upon which depends the expression they object to : and this may be proved to demonstration in various instances of their daily and hourly conduct. How many object to the simple and affecting ballad of the child at the tomb of its brother saying : 'Nay, we are seven.' Yet how deep must a man have gone below the thoughts of the generality, before he could have written such a ballad ! It contains the height of the moral sublime. Others dislike the description of the oxen, 'forty feeding like one.' Yet it seems most appropriately to convey the idea of the sameness and the continuity of employment of the whole herd. The ballad of the female beggar, too, has been called foolish.

> She had a tall man's height or more,
> No bonnet screened her from the heat,
> A long drab-coloured cloak she wore,
> A mantle reaching to her feet.
> What other dress she had I could not know,
> Only she wore a cap that was as white as snow.

In all my walks thro' field or town,
    Such figure had I never seen :
Her face was of Egyptian brown ;
    Fit person was she for a queen,
To head those antient Amazonian files,
Or ruling bandit's wife among the Grecian isles.

The last two lines are particularly grand and majestic."
Taylor then noticed that "what other dress she had I
could not know," was a botch ; it was unnecessary, and
set the reader's fancy rambling upon a point no ways
material. The Opium-Eater admitted this, and observed
that Wordsworth had a great difficulty in rhyming, and
this obliged him many times to insert needless exple-
tive words and sentences. Taylor thought that it was not
so much the simplicity of the language as the lowness of
the thought and the want of selection in the subjects
that led people to depreciate Wordsworth's merit.
The Opium-Eater upon this observed that the principal
complaints he had heard made against Wordsworth
were that his style was mean and low, and this reminded him of an observation which had occurred to
him upon the subject of *style*, which he believed had
never before been remarked in any book, nor indeed
did he observe any indication of its even having been
noticed, save from one German word which seemed to
point at the distinction. It had been supposed that
thoughts and words had some necessary, immediate,
and close correlation to each other ; that words were
the mere types and impressions of thoughts ; that the
one were the pictures of the other ; and indeed it had
been said that if a person has thoughts, he also has
necessarily suitable and commensurate expressions for
those thoughts given him at the same time, and may
at once and without difficulty give utterance to his
ideas in words. This seemed to the Opium-Eater not

strictly correct; he thought the phraseology, "That words are the *dress* in which thoughts appear," expressed the truth much more nearly than saying or implying that words expressed the actual thoughts themselves. He intended to touch upon and illustrate this subject in the first of the series of letters he was about to write for the *London Magazine,* * and which would begin with the subject of composition. It seemed to him that independently of the expression in which a thought was clothed, and as the substratum or groundwork supporting such expression, there would be found, upon analysis and separation of the different accidentalities of the idea, a simple plain and abstract thought, feeling, or conception ; that such thoughts, etc., were common to all men, but some did and some did not notice, cultivate, encourage, and express them. And the mode in which abstract thought was dressed up, the expression, figure, trope, or instance which was brought forward as representing, or rather expounding it to others, was an essentially different thing from the thought itself. A good thought might be very ill expressed. On the other hand, a poor or weak conception might be so adorned by the rich garb or exponential dress or image in which it was conveyed, that it should appear attractive, and its emptiness might thus escape unnoticed. This distinction between thought and the garb in which it was presented was not sufficiently attended to. The general complaint made against Wordsworth's poetry was that its style was low and mean, brought from the vulgar ranks of life, and deficient in interest, and childish. Now it might

* The "Letters to a Young Man whose Education has been Neglected;" in which, however, the relation of thought and language is not discussed.

be safely affirmed of Wordsworth's phraseology that it
is anything but mean—there is scarcely a mean word
that occurs in it. It is true that he often uses words in
their original and intense sense, where in common use
they have a slighter signification ; as in the instance of
the word *trouble*, in where it is employed in its original
and scriptural sense for great tribulation or anxiety, and
not, as in common conversation, for a lighter or more
transient inquietude, or slight molestation. But generally,
although his subject lead him to treat of the inferior
ranks of life, and to make those who walk in them
speak in their own peculiar manner and course of thought
and sentiment, yet he never admits their colloquialisms,
bad English, or vulgarities. Their diction is simple, but
pure and sensible, so that, so far as Wordsworth's style,
properly so called, is concerned, his detractors are
entirely in the wrong. Their complaint is then, in point
of fact, though they may not know it, against his
thoughts, not their garb. The former of these is
majestic, grand and only to be properly appreciated by
kindred spirits to his own.

At this part of the conversation (for on leaving Taylor
it was continued while I walked home with the Opium-
Eater), we had arrived at his lodging, where I took leave
of him about twelve o'clock. He had, however, said
nearly the whole of what he had to observe upon this
interesting subject. I should not omit to notice that
the Opium-Eater found throughout the whole of French
literature an universal weakness and poverty of thought,
and that when the French writers wished to be more
than usually grand, they loaded their thoughts with
glittering and tinsel expressions, but their conceptions
are poor, low, and imbecile. He inquired whether
Taylor knew if "B——" in Dryden's "Satires of Mac-

Flecknoe "* meant Burnet the historian of his own times —for the character there given was singularly applicable to Burnet. The Opium-Eater had mentioned to me a short time since his astonishment at the high opinion which seemed to be entertained generally of Burns. He allowed him ability of a particular description, some fancy, much power of catching and expressing generous sentiments in free and easy language, but nothing that could entitle him to rank high as a great poet. His "Mary in Heaven" was false in sentiment, and very commonplace and factitious. His "Cotter's Saturday Night" had nothing of the high poet in it, and the subject was suggested by a poem of Fergusson's, the thoughts in it were common to most persons, and there was nothing great in the manner of treating them. His "Tam o' Shanter" was one of his best works, but that has been greatly over-praised.

28th December, 1821.—The Opium-Eater was asked by Taylor about his college and Oxford, and whether he had taken a degree there. He said that he had not, and the circumstances were rather peculiar; and, as reports contrary to the real state of the case had got abroad, he would state the transactions exactly as they occurred. The college to which he went was Worcester College. At that time it was in very bad repute. There were no very good tutors, and the young men there were greatly low in point of attainment, and very free and irregular in their habits, owing to the lax discipline that prevailed. As soon as the Opium-Eater arrived there, he was invited by many of the men of his

---

* There must be some mistake in Woodhouse's report. No "B——" is introduced into "Mac-Flecknoe," nor is Burnet alluded to. He is satirized as the Buzzard in "The Hind and the Panther."

H

own standing to their parties, which he joined, but he
found them to be a drinking, rattling set, whose conversation was juvenile, commonplace, and quite unintellec-
tual. He invited them once or twice in return, and then
dropped the intercourse, and in a short time he came to
be looked upon as a strange being who associated with
no one, and he was left to himself, and to do in fact just
as he pleased. Upon some occasion it was necessary
that a declamation should be written and delivered in
Latin by some one of his college, and it fell to him to
do it. He accordingly composed and delivered the
oration, and as he had written it with some care, and
was a tolerable master of the language, it excited
considerable attention. These things were generally
passed by without much notice ; but he could perceive
by the interest which was taken while he was declaiming,
and by the buzzing and whispering, that it was much
better than had been expected, and that it had caused
some sensation in the auditors. Immediately many
persons high in the University came up, shook him by
the hand, and congratulated him. Soon after this he
found himself noticed by the head of the college, and
several of the students ; he received invitations, and soon
discovered that *all* the University men were not of the
same description as those with whom he had at first
associated. His tutor also paid much attention to
him, and excited him to try for honours. This he
refused to do. In fact, from what he saw of the examinations at Oxford, he looked upon them as so much a
farce, and so unfair a standard to try a person's general
ability and proficiency, that he had determined not to
attempt to gain distinction or even to take a degree,
which to his mind could convey no honour worth
seeking for. His intention at this time was to travel in

Germany, and he should not have wished even to belong to the college, but because the name of having been of Oxford would have been of service and an introduction to him abroad as a scholar. His purpose was merely to matriculate and reside there for a time, but many persons incited him to try for honours. A friend of his (named Millar) offered also himself to try for honours, if the Opium-Eater would go up also with him, and his tutor (of the name of Jones) was particularly anxious that he should do so, thinking probably that it would be of great service to himself to have the credit of turning out two scholars from that college who should have distinguished themselves. It was his wish to serve his tutor that principally weighed with the Opium-Eater to consent. Another inducement was an order that had been just issued that the answers in the Greek examination should be given in Greek. Here there seemed something to be done. He determined instead of giving in any particular books, to give up Greek literature generally, and he felt conscious of going through the examination triumphantly. He *read* (as it is termed) very hard for two months before the examination. But about a week before it was to take place, the order for giving in the answers in the Greek examinations in that language was rescinded, and it was directed that they should be given in English. This completely destroyed all stimulus in the Opium-Eater's mind ; he no longer cared to go through an examination which would only show that he in common with others had acquired knowledge of a particular description, but would not leave him room to show his general proficiency. He thought of declining to go up, and it was only the earnest wishes of his friend Millar and his tutor that induced him so to do. He entertained a contempt for

the general acquirements of his examiners, for the sort
of examination to be gone through, and especially for
that trickery in the examiners of trying students in some
particularly difficult passages or points in which they
would make themselves perfectly at home, without any
attempt to ascertain the real ability of the person under
examination in the language. He had, for instance,
studied Aristotle's " Organon " throughout, and he
meant to have given up that book in logic. He had had
not merely to master the construction of the language,
and to understand the meaning of the author, but also,
such was the condensation and depth of the matter, to
think deeply and ponder over every passage, and almost
every word, so as to imbue himself with the wisdom of
the author. Now there was in use in Oxford a manual
of Aristotle, and selection of parts of him, which was
generally taken in the examination, and, as he was
pretty confident that his examiners had never looked
into the large work itself as he had done, he felt sure that
though they would pretend to examine him from the large
book, they would in fact confine themselves to such
parts of it as were contained in this manual. Again,
they would frequently put before the student particular
parts of the Greek tragedians which were manifestly
corrupt, or at best only to be made sense of by some
strained interpretations of scholiasts and commentators.
These he had never thought it worth his while to attend
to. The Agamemnon of Æschylus was one of these, and
he felt little doubt that he should have this put into his
hands by the examiners. Had he been ever so well
prepared in this respect the utmost his knowledge
would have amounted to would be what a great
number of people had written and conjectured upon
the difficult passages. He counted the lines of the

play, and reckoned the number of minutes to the examination, and he found that there would not be time even to read the play itself properly through. This circumstance, and the thought of the possibility of failing, and in a matter of so little real importance, and which went so very little way as a fair trial of ability, yet more disinclined him to the examination.

The first day of the examination, which was merely in Latin, happened to be on a Saturday. It is the custom to take five or six persons a day. On the average they last two hours each person, but the examiners sometimes bestow more upon the examination of one and less upon that of others. The Opium-Eater underwent a very long examination. He was first put to translate Latin into English, and afterwards to render English at sight into Latin. And he could perceive from the whispers, the silence, and various other indications, that he was considered a proficient, and was likely to pass a splendid examination. This was intimated to him afterwards from various quarters. On Monday he was to be examined in Greek. But all his contempt for his examiners, his thought of the possibility of failing from the unfair mode of examination (as though a lover of Shakespeare should be tried exclusively by his intimate acquaintance with the difficult and corrupt passages of the " Pericles " or " Titus Andronicus "), and the conviction that from the alteration in the language in which the answers in the Greek examinations were to be given, no opportunities of distinguishing himself was afforded, came upon him at once. On the Sunday morning he left Oxford, and has never been in the place since except upon one occasion for about half-an-hour. When the time came he was *non inventus*. Many different reports

were abroad on the subject,* which he had heard himself.
A lady once archly said to him, "I have heard of
such a thing, Mr. de Quincey, as a person's heart failing
him."

Others said that he was disgusted at the mode of
examination and the ignorance of the examiners, and
that he declined honours because he felt that to undergo
such examinations could confer no honour. "And this,"
observed Taylor, "is near the truth, and the matter may
be left with this impression." "However," said the
Opium-Eater, "I have stated exactly how the matter
was, and my opinion of Oxford examinations is just as
it used to be."—*Ex relat. J. T.*

29th December, 1821.—This evening I saw the Opium-
Eater into the mail; he was about to return to Westmoreland.

Allan Cunningham had gone off by another coach for
the North the same evening, It was a subject of regret
to both that they had not travelled together.

The Opium-Eater always disliked in modern composition what is termed Ciceronian Latin—that style in
which twenty or thirty words are used to express what
might be as well or better given in five or ten. The
declamation he gave at Oxford was framed more after
the style of Cæsar in his " Commentaries " than after

---

* Mr. Grinfield, De Quincey's early friend, at this time a
member of Lincoln College, says : " I rather incline to believe that
he had some distrust of his own presence of mind, feeling that his
intellect was somewhat impatient of grappling with the smaller
points which are demanded in a university examination." Dr.
Goodenough, of Christ Church, who was one of the examiners,
declared to a member of Worcester College : " You have sent us
the cleverest man I ever met with ; if his *vivâ voce* examination
to-morrow correspond with what he has done to-day, he will carry
everything before him."

that of Cicero. It was studiously clear, simple, and short ; and it was probably the novelty of avoiding all floridness in the composition that caused it to excite so much notice.

NOTE ON RICHARD WOODHOUSE.

RICHARD WOODHOUSE, barrister of the Temple, himself wrote nothing for publication, but mingled with the brilliant literary circle which, about the year 1820, gathered around Messrs. Taylor and Hessey, publishers of the *London Magazine*. To Keats in particular he was devotedly attached : and, bating some unjust though not unaccountable prejudice against Leigh Hunt, he may be reckoned the most judicious as well as the kindest of his friends. His affection for the unfortunate poet and compassion for his blighted life were expressed with a grave and touching manliness : and to him were the heart-rending communications of Severn from Italy most commonly addressed. The proofs of these facts have unhappily perished in the conflagration which in 1883 destroyed the premises of the publishers of this series. One precious volume escaped, the note-book, which establishes that from September to December, 1821, Woodhouse enjoyed De Quincey's intimacy and recorded his conversation. It is highly to his credit that he should have so quickly discerned the splendour of this new light, which to the world at large had shone only in a single magazine article. His was no undiscriminating hero-worship, but the same intelligent recognition of genius which he had already manifested in his loyal devotion to Keats. Nor can his fidelity as a reporter have been inferior to his perception as a critic. The reader of his notes will have no difficulty in distinguishing all the characteristics of De Quincey's style as a writer, and no less the peculiarities of his conversation as indicated by Carlyle, Hill Burton, Mrs. Gordon, and others who have not, like Woodhouse, afforded us the materials for our own judgment. We seem conscious of the silvery accents, the courteous deference, the exquisitely refined phraseology, the subdued yet almost exaggerated earnestness, the circumstantiality and subtlety, the copious flow of polished speech never lapsing into twaddle or swelling into harangue, which, if they could not wield a democracy, could hold a half-astonished, half-amused aristocracy of intellect by a spell like the Ancient Mariner's. The reader's imagination must indeed be enlisted to fill up some portions of this picture impaired by the absence of the speaker and the inevitable brevity of the reporter. But none can question that the actual discoursing De Quincey is brought nearer to us than ever before, and that his discourse is the counterpart of his writings.—DR. GARNETT's *Introduction to the " Confessions."*

A SOUVENIR OF OXFORD DAYS.

I HAVE been able to rescue a relic of great interest concerning a period of which we know so little in De Quincey's career—his college days.

The Latin theme here given was found among the papers of the late Dr. Goodenough of Christchurch, who was one of De Quincey's examiners at Worcester College, and had expressed a high opinion of his ability as recorded in the preceding "Notes of Conversations."

Whether this theme is the "declamation" specially referred to by Richard Woodhouse, or some other college exercise, is matter of doubt. The original is written on a leaf of post quarto in the beautifully clear handwriting of De Quincey. In earlier days this was larger and much more sloping than in middle and later life. The mature style is shown in the *facsimiles* given of two " unpublished letters " in this volume.

The leaf is endorsed " Quincey," apparently in the handwriting of Dr. Goodenough.

For the English rendering I am indebted to the courtesy of Dr. R. Garnett, the Keeper of the Printed Books at the British Museum.

" Non id, quod magnum est, pulchrum est ; sed, quod pulchrum, magnum."

Velle maxima obstacula, quæ ansibus obstant, superare et per scipsum jurare esse superaturum—non est nisi

magni ; refugit enim ab omni arduo minoris animi timida
imbecillitas : at plerumque in consiliis nefariis maxima
oriuntur obstacula ; unde non raro, in factis maxime
facinorosis, animi emicuit lethalis 'splendor populis in-
cutiens terrorem ; et aliquando summa anima in facinore
maximo luride subridens exultavit : hinc illustrium aliquot
prædonum fulgente scelere oculi posteriorum adhuc
perstringuntur.　Non est ergo necesse magnum esse
pulchrum.

Sed patet omne pulchrum esse necessario magnum :
vera enim virtus ortum habet ex ingenita vi mentis qua
ad altius quiddam affectandum incitatur, ideoque magna
est in origine ;—posita est autem maxima ex parte in
rigida effrænati impetus disciplina (quæ est maximum
imperium) et est ideo magna in seipsa ; finem vero
assequitur in cultores suos naturæ alicui sublimiori
affines efficiendo, et magnam ergo se præstat in effectu.

Quamvis igitur plerique, cum non sint ipsi magni, veræ
magnitudinis fines sæpe prave dijudicârint et hinc gestis
multis notissimis falsum nomen impresserint,—sunt tamen
aliquot nefanda facta quæ revera sunt magna, nulla vero
evidenter pulchra quæ non simul magna.

[*TRANSLATION.*]

" A thing is not fine because it is great, but is great because it is
fine.　(Or, less literally, Merit, not magnitude, is the measure of
greatness.")

The desire to overcome the greatest obstacles which
impede adventurous undertakings, and the resolution of
overcoming them by one's own unaided efforts, are the
property of nothing less than greatness ; for the timid
weakness of an inferior mind recoils from whatsoever is
arduous.　But the greatest obstacles commonly arise in
the execution of nefarious designs ; whence not unfre-

quently in deeds of the greatest turpitude a deadly splendour has shone forth from the mind striking terror into the nations, and sometimes an elevated soul has exulted with a lurid smile in the commission of some peculiarly atrocious action: insomuch that the eyes of posterity are yet held spellbound by the dazzling crimes of some illustrious robbers. A great action, therefore, is not necessarily a fine action.

But whatsoever is fine is necessarily also great; for true Virtue has her birth in that innate force of the mind whereby she is incited to aim at something yet higher, and therefore is great in her origin: but also chiefly consists in the rigid restraint of unbridled impulse (which is the greatest of all dominion), and is therefore great in herself; but attains her end in rendering her votaries akin to some more exalted Nature, and therefore proves her greatness by the effects which she produces.

Although, therefore, the mass of men, not being themselves partakers of greatness, have often misconstrued the definition of true glory, and hence have misnamed many most celebrated actions—yet there are some wicked deeds that may truly be termed great; but there are no manifestly fine actions that are not at the same time great also.

DR. COTTON ON THE OXFORD LIFE.

[In a lengthy article published in the *Quarterly Review*, vol. 110 (1861), there occurs the annexed passage, concerning which the reviewer observes :—" We are indebted for the following particulars to the kindness of Dr. Cotton, the Provost of Worcester College."]

OF his Oxford life he has left us few memorials. He appears to have resided there from 1803 to 1808 ; that is, from his eighteenth year to his twenty-third. But of his own obligations to that University he says not one syllable. Whether he read or whether he idled we are left to conjecture. And this is the more singular, because the two favourite pursuits of De Quincey are also the studies most prized in the University of Oxford, namely elegant scholarship and metaphysics. The modern examination system also was introduced during these years, and we should have been glad to hear what De Quincey thought of the reform, and what he heard said about it among older men than himself. But his Oxford life is an unwritten chapter of the Autobiography.

It is curious indeed that it should be so ; his career at Oxford having been, according to the testimony of contemporaries, highly characteristic of the man, and one which nobody who took the public into his confidence so freely as De Quincey did, need have shrunk from describing. He was admitted a member of Worcester College, and matriculated on the 17th of

December, 1803 ; and his name remained upon the
college books for seven years, being removed from them
on the 15th of December, 1810. During the period of
his residence he was generally known as a quiet and
studious man. He did not frequent wine parties, though
he did not abstain from wine ; and he devoted himself
principally to the society of a German named Schwartzburg, who is said to have taught him Hebrew. He was
remarkable, even in those days, for his rare conversa-
tional powers, and for his extraordinary stock of information upon every subject that was started. There
were men, it would appear, among his contemporaries
who were capable of appreciating him ; and they all
agreed that De Quincey was a man of singular genius
as well as the most varied talents. His knowledge of
Latin and Greek was not confined to those few standard
authors with which even good scholars are, or were,
accustomed to content themselves. He was master of
the ancient literature ; of all of it, at least, which belongs
to what is called pure literature. It appears that he
brought this knowledge up to Oxford with him ; and
that his university studies were directed almost wholly
to the ancient philosophy, varied by occasional excursions into German literature and metaphysics, which
he loved to compare with those of Greece and Rome.
His knowledge of all these subjects is said to have been
really sound ; and there can no doubt that he was
capable of reproducing it in the most brilliant and
imposing forms. It was predicted, accordingly, by all
who knew him, that he would pass a memorable examination ; and so indeed he did, though the issue was a
somewhat different one from what his admirers had
anticipated. The class-list had lately been instituted ;
and there seems no reason to doubt that, had De

Quincey's mind been rather more regularly trained, he
would have taken a first-class as easily as other men
take a common degree.   But his reading had never
been conducted upon that system which the Oxford
examinations, essentially and very properly intended
for men of average abilities, render almost incumbent
upon every candidate for the highest honours.   De
Quincey seems to have felt that he was deficient in that
perfect mastery of the minuter details of logic, ethics,
and rhetoric, which the practice of the schools demanded.
With the leading principles of the Aristotelian system
he was evidently quite intimate.   But he apparently
distrusted his own fitness to undergo a searching oral
examination in these subjects, for which a minute
acquaintance with scientific terminology, and with the
finest distinctions they involve, is thought to be essential.
The event was unfortunate, though so agreeable to De
Quincey's character that it might have been foreseen by
his associates, as by one of them it really was.   The
important moment arrived, and De Quincey went
through the first day's examination, which was conducted upon paper, and at that time consisted almost
exclusively of scholarship, history, and whatever might
be comprehended under the title of classical literature.
On the evening of that day Mr. Goodenough of Christchurch, who was one of the examiners, went down to a
gentleman, then resident at Worcester College and well
acquainted with De Quincey, and said to him, " You
have sent us to-day the cleverest man I ever met with ;
if his *vivâ voce* examination to-morrow correspond with
what he has done in writing he will carry everything
before him." To this his friend made answer that he
feared De Quincey's *vivâ voce* would be comparatively
imperfect, even if he presented himself for examination,

which he rather doubted. The event justified his
answer. That night De Quincey packed up his things
and walked away from Oxford ; never, as far as we can
ascertain, to return to it. Whether this distrust of
himself was well founded, or whether it arose from the
depression by which his indulgence in opium was invariably followed, we cannot tell. So early even as his
Oxford days, De Quincey, we are told, was incapable
of steady application without large doses of opium. He
had taken a large dose on the morning of his paper work,
and the re-action that followed in the evening would,
of course, aggravate his apprehensions of the morrow.
Be that as it may, he fairly took to his heels, and so
lost the chance, which, with every drawback, must have
been an extremely good one, of figuring in the same
class-list with Sir Robert Peel, who passed his examination in Michaelmas, 1808, which was, no doubt, the
era of De Quincey's singular catastrophe.

RECOLLECTIONS OF THE GLASGOW PERIOD.

By COLIN RAE-BROWN.

AT various times, and in several publications—issued within the last ten or twelve years—incorrect statements have appeared regarding De Quincey's *last* visit to Glasgow.* It is now high time that a faithful record of it (so far, at least, as the *cause* and *date* of it goes) should be plainly set forth; and the following details are made up from notes still in my possession.

At the close of 1846, the projectors of the *North British Daily Mail* offered me an engagement as business manager of the contemplated "First Scottish Daily." I accepted the offer, and entered upon my duties immediately. Amongst the first of the arrangements I set about was that of an office in Edinburgh. By this time, the proprietors of the *Mail* had purchased the copyright of *Tait's Magazine*, and it was considered most advisable to secure the continued services of De

---

* Misled by a printer's error—the substitution of "1848" for "the close of 1846"—Dr. Japp, in his 1890 edition (Hogg : London) of "De Quincey's Life and Writings," says :—"De Quincey was again in Glasgow in 1848." Dr. Japp's previous statement (in his 1887 edition of the same work) was quite correct, viz. :—"He returned (from Glasgow) to Lasswade in the end of 1847, and lived there without intermission till the beginning of 1852."

Quincey as a leading contributor, and also to endeavour
to get him to reside in Glasgow—for a time—so that
he might be closely identified with the "future" of the
well-known Whig-Radical organ.   I was accordingly
instructed to arrange for a meeting with De Quincey
in Edinburgh, and to offer him certain terms *re* contributions to *Tait*, and occasional special articles for the
Mail.   That meeting took place early in December,
1846.   I may here mention that *Tait* was transferred
to Glasgow during the month just mentioned, and that
the first issue in the "Second City" was that of January,
1847.   In order to assist in the production of the first
"Sanct Mungo" number, De Quincey reached Glasgow
in the course of the preceding month.   The *Mail* did
not appear till the 14th of April, 1847.   De Quincey
at first hesitated a good deal, but in the end agreed to
the terms proposed ; while he stipulated, nevertheless,
that his stay in Glasgow was not to exceed six months,
and that apartments of a modest kind could be secured
for him at the *highest altitude* possible in the northern
part of the city.   " I had some painful experiences,"
he went on to say, "of life in Glasgow several years
ago, when I was victimised to within an inch of my life
by the sulphuretted hydrogen—or some such noxious
exhalation—which was then discharged into the atmosphere by the so-called 'Secret Works' at the 'Town-
head.'   But if I could get tidy apartments not very far
from this objectionable manufactory, the great length
of the chimney-stack would allow the wind to carry the
pestilential smoke quite over and away from me."   I
promised to set inquiries on foot as to suitable accommodation in the locality indicated, and also to let him
know the result by an early post.   Throughout the
interview—it was my first meeting with him—I had

been more closely engaged in intently studying the individual than in listening to his mildly expressed denunciations of the "Glasgow vapours." If I describe him as being, physically, of the type of Cardinal Manning, I am giving something nearly akin to a true flesh and blood portraiture. De Quincey stood somewhere about five feet or thereby, and was very sparsely built; while the pale and delicately transparent brow and cheek seemed almost ethereal; but when the latter were visited, as they often were during conversation, by a slight roseate tinge, it rendered the ever mobile and intelligent face more interesting still. Prior to this interview, I had formed no idea whatever of the "English opium-eater" in the matter of *physique*. Nevertheless, with such men as Christopher North and other stalwart Edinburgh celebrities of the day in my mind's eye, I never for one moment imagined that the man now beginning to "bulk forth" so largely in the intellectual world would turn out to be of such diminutive stature and frail construction. But what most riveted my attention to the speaker was the refinement which characterised every action and every expression, combined with an exactitude of pronunciation which was the very reverse of pedantic. His extreme gentleness of manner, almost that of a retiring yet high-bred child, made me at once feel—Here is the very essence of charity and good-will to his fellow-man. I was charmed with my reception, no less than with the cordial politeness of his gracious "Good-bye," and truly went on my homeward way rejoicing.

Determined to act up to his request in the matter of apartments, I set about the search personally, and was able in the course of a few days to inform De Quincey that I had secured exactly what he wanted in the upper

I

flat of a tenement in the "Rottenrow," a quiet, humble thoroughfare in the highest quarter of Glasgow, exactly at the point he had indicated, and so situated that the aforesaid "noxious vapours" would be blown quite over and beyond the spot. Then I was able to add that the mother-in-law of the tenant, a quiet, fairly-well educated widow, of some sixty years of age, seemed to keep house in a manner that might be termed scrupulously clean. Within a week after I had so written, De Quincey was comfortably deposited under the care of Mrs. Tosh, and (save for its enforced short duration) neither he nor I had ever any occasion to regret the selection of his whilom domicile (now designated "Dean Place").

We had scarcely been seated at a comfortable tea on the evening of his arrival when he inquired of me whether the landlady's surname, "Tosh," was not also used as a familiar Scottish adjective. "I cannot remember its precise significance in the least, but it will, as you West Country people say, keep 'running through my head.'"

"No landlady," I replied, "could have been more appropriately named. 'Tosh' is a very common Doric expression for 'neat, clean, tidy, etc.,' and your worthy dame is all that and something more."

The printing-office and the editorial chambers of the *Mail* and *Tait* were situated at a distance of about a mile from De Quincey's lodgings, and we had very often to despatch messengers there for delayed "copy." He was in the habit of bringing such down to town in detached portions, a practice which, joined to his somewhat irregular habits of rising, frequently kept half-set articles standing and printers idle. On one occasion— it was close on the 28th of the month, the date when the following month's magazine was supposed to be

ready for the wholesale houses in London and Edinburgh—a most important article of De Quincey's had
been partially set up, and our boy-messenger had twice
returned from the "Rottenrow" with the same message
from the landlady, "the old gentleman had no got 'oot
o' his bedroom yet!" The editor was dreadfully put
about. Coming into my room, he said, "I wish you
would drive up and see De Quincey about the remaining
copy. You are the only one that seems to have much
influence with him. I am absolutely getting to my
wit's end, as we must go to press some time to-night."
I sent for a cab and drove up to the "Rottenrow"
lodgings. As I had expected (having come to know
about the "opium-eating"), I found, on entering De
Quincey's room, that he was either uncommonly sound
asleep or in a state of stupor. He lay stretched out on
the heathrug before the parlour fire-grate (his bedroom
entering off that apartment), clad in an old dressing-
gown, with no stockings on his feet, and merely a pair
of thin, loose slippers over his toes. "I'm sure the puir
body's deid!" the landlady exclaimed, as I bent down
to ascertain whether he was really still alive. An examination, which did not occupy more than five seconds,
showed me that he breathed heavily, and I was able to
assure the worthy old woman that all would be right
when he awoke; at the same time I insisted that she
should not, as she had proposed, "dash cauld water on
his face," but leave him to awake naturally. Looking
about amongst his scattered books and papers on a
small side table, I soon discovered the "tail of the
copy" I was in search of, neatly tied up with red tape,
and addressed to the "Editor of *Tait's Magazine.*"
Careless to slovenliness in many things, especially in regard to bodily attire, he was scrupulously exact in others.

I 2

As I was leaving the lodgings Mrs. Tosh said, in a half-whisper, "There maun surely be somethin' raaly wrang wi' my lodger. He doesna eat as muckle in a week as my wee oo (grandson) eats in a day. D'ye think he's in his richt mind?" Having thoroughly assured her as to the perfect sanity of "Mr. Quinsey," as she termed him, I hurriedly drove away with the much-desired copy.

The following day—a Wednesday, I think—was one of those on which De Quincey and I generally partook of a mild lunch at the "Rose Tavern," in Argyll Street, still the leading thorougfare of the business part of Glasgow. From whatever cause, he never once alluded to the "copy" which I had taken away, nor to the inconvenience which delay had caused us. Afraid of hurting susceptibilities which I knew were of a very tender nature, I maintained a discreet silence on the subject. On that occasion our conversation was directed to a new edition of Burns (in *de luxe* form) which had just been announced. "Ah!" De Quincey remarked, while his eyes visibly dilated, "the Ayrshire Colossus is still expanding outward and upward, in spite of all his detractors. If some of my Lake friends had had more critical insight, or more liberality, their immature deliverances on the achievements and future position of our Ayrshire poet would have savoured more of the characteristics of genuine criticism and true prophecy."

This remark was one of the few which I took the liberty of making more than "a mental note of." "Burns-worship" was then becoming one of my great hobbies. Of another subject of conversation that day I also made a brief memorandum. It had reference to a placard recently put up on the gates of one of the largest workshops in Glasgow, and which read as

image
not
available

As we walked back to town a slight drizzle (which we
experienced a little of during our outward walk) seemed to
have developed into a thorough, almost blinding "Scotch
mist." This led to a disquisition on the British climate,
that portion of it which prevailed in the West of
Scotland coming in for De Quincey's most effective
adjectives. "The damp and fogs of the late autumn
and winter will never," he remarked, very gravely, "be
cured ; but why the municipal authorities of all our
large manufacturing towns do not erect or encourage
the erection of Winter Gardens, covered over with glass
—such as Chaucer foreshadowed—I never can conceive.
Both instruction and amusement—the latter consisting
principally of music—might be combined in such insti-
tutions, and that at low—what is called popular—prices.
Why don't you newspaper people set an agitation going
in this direction ? There can be no doubt of a pecuniary
success, provided the management be energetic. As it
is, a poor, hard-worked artisan must either share a
stuffy, ill-lighted and worse-ventilated apartment all
the evening, along with his wife and children, or go—
where ?—to the nearest public-house. The whole
system is rotten that does not provide something better
for the spare hours of our toiling millions."

Of this deliverance I made an extended note as soon
as I reached home, and shortly afterwards (and frequently since) wrote on the subject.

Since that date we have had Crystal Palaces and
Exhibitions in succession on both sides of the Channel
and the Atlantic, but, as far as I know, nothing in the
shape of permanent covered-in Winter Gardens for our
ill-cared-for masses.

What we require is popular music, innocuous variety
entertainments, and plain refreshments, at a little

more than cost price, with an almost nominal admission
fee.

De Quincey was not destined to remain long under
the watchful, motherly care of Mrs. Tosh.   Her little
grandson was suddenly struck down by scarlet fever,
and we had to make immediate arrangements for transferring our valued contributor and his few belongings to
another domicile.   "Ah," he answered, putting his hand
to his forehead, "that reminds me that I have been
paying the rent of apartments in Renfield Street for a
number of years.   Many valuable books and papers
are or should be there still."   As he thus spoke, I stared,.
almost agape, in downright amazement.   That he
should have omitted to furnish me with some details
regarding his former lodgings, when he and I were
conversing about Glasgow and its drawbacks a few
weeks previously, was more than I could conceive
possible.   And yet I never once allowed myself to
think that he had intentionally withheld such particulars.   I also consider that any "rent" paid for so
long a period can only have been a nominal charge for
"storage."   As it turned out, he had actually kept on
these apartments from 1843, though by far the greater
part of his time had been passed since that year in and
near Edinburgh.   So back to Renfield Street he went.
But the more I came to know of De Quincey, the less
I wondered at the strange peculiarities which characterised his every-day existence.   In short, he was regular
in his irregularity, and oblivious of the consequences.
The following little episode is an instance of the scant
attention he paid to the exigencies of common life—
especially to matters of £ s. d.

We were leaving the printing-office on a Monday
afternoon, some three or four weeks after his arrival

from Edinburgh, when he said—"I think I shall draw
a few pounds in advance of the money which will be
due to me at the end of the month."

"I should think you must have some £20, or thereby,
lying at your credit already," was my reply. "You can
have it all if you wish. But you told me on Saturday,
when you drew £5, that you thought the money would
be better to accumulate in our hands."

He stared as I spoke, as if utterly bewildered, and at
length broke out into a speech of pathetic appeal:
"Well, well, what can I be thinking of?—You really
must excuse me—but where can the money be?" So
saying, he nervously thrust his right hand into his
trousers' pocket and fished out a sadly crumpled envelope—the same into which I had placed five one-pound
notes only a few days before. "I beg a thousand, ten
thousand pardons. I believe I am becoming the most
stupid of men." Such was the deliverance which the
discovery elicited, and it was accompanied by the most
gracious and deferential of parting salutes. As he left
me, I saw him thrust the envelope and its contents well
down into their former receptacle. It was wonderful at
times to observe what he *did* bring forth from that
seemingly capacious pocket—bits of red tape, two or
three stumps of black-lead pencil, pieces of twine, etc.

As is well-known to all who have made the story of
his life a study, De Quincey was no Sybarite. Food,
solid or liquid, was to him quite a secondary consideration, in common with all other purely sensual require-
ments. On the other hand he was no Anchorite—far
from it. Nothing rejoiced him more than to see all
around him, more especially children, enjoying themselves to their hearts' content. No more lovable man,
no man with such powers of attraction, ever walked

God's earth. To see and know was to love and venerate him. Humble to a fault, and simple as a child, there was, nevertheless, a true nobility of nature and a more than merely polished refinement interwoven with his every act and expression. Such were inherent to and irremovable from his nature.

He continued to reside in Glasgow, and to contribute to *Tait* and the *Mail* up to October or November, 1847, returning then to his cottage at Lasswade.

image
not
available

letters and in public life, the desire to record such intercourse never overcame me, save in this one instance.
This of itself may be taken as a humble testimony to
the singularly attractive and impressive character of De
Quincey's talk. The notes were taken at the time
merely and solely for the refreshment of my own
memory ; if it ever afterwards occurred to me that they
might be of other use, I always felt that they could be
so used only after a considerable lapse of years. With
the lapse of thirty years or thereby reasons against
publication have lapsed likewise, and there now seems
to me nothing to prevent those scanty jottings being
given to the world of De Quincey's admirers, to be taken
for what they are worth.

The notes extend over a period of seven years—
1852–59—the last years of De Quincey's life. They
were mere memoranda pencilled on scraps of paper,
sufficient to refresh an originally vivid and retentive
memory, until, fearing its failure to keep hold of
connecting links, I found leisure fifteen years ago to put
the scraps into shape and write them out clearly and
fully. In this state they have been seen and read over
by one or two of my friends who knew and admired De
Quincey ; I think only by John Hill Burton, Alexander
Russel, and John Brown—all now, alas! no more. I
have recently felt it my duty to submit them to Mr. de
Quincey's surviving daughters, and their approval to the
present publication has been most heartily accorded.

The notes appear here, with one or two trivial
excisions, exactly as they were written out in 1870; I
have thought it better to relegate to the foot of the page
anything like explanation or addition.

J. R. FINDLAY.

1885.

PERSONAL RECOLLECTIONS.

—◦—

MY friend Mr. John Hill Burton had often promised to introduce me to Mr. de Quincey, knowing that I took great interest in his writings, although at that time I was acquainted with them mainly through such stray articles as I had read in magazines.

On the 10th January 1852, Mr. Burton and I walked out to where Mr. de Quincey was residing, with his three daughters, in a cottage at Mavisbank, a sort of upper suburb of Lasswade. We were received by Miss de Quincey and Miss Florence.[*] Before reaching the house Mr. Burton had warned me that it was twenty chances to one whether we would see De Quincey, as he was very shy of strangers, or visitors of any sort, and that I might consider it a great favour if he made his appearance. Miss Florence ascertained that her father was visible, and in a very few minutes he entered the room—a man, once seen, never to be forgotten. His appearance has been often described, but generally, I

[*] Miss de Quincey (Margaret) married in 1853 Mr. Robert Craig, who settled as a farmer in Tipperary. She died in 1871, leaving one son, now a captain in the Royal Artillery, and a daughter, now married. Florence married in 1855 Colonel Baird Smith, R.E., who died in 1861, leaving two daughters. Emily, the third daughter, I did not have the pleasure of seeing till a subsequent visit. See Appendix A.

think, with a touch of caricature.* He was a very little man (about 5 feet 3 or 4 inches); his countenance the most remarkable for its intellectual attractiveness that I have ever seen. His features, though not regular, were aristocratically fine, and an air of delicate breeding pervaded the face. His forehead was unusually high, square, and compact.† At first sight his face appeared boyishly fresh and smooth, with a sort of hectic glow upon it that contrasted remarkably with the evident appearances of age in the grizzled hair and dim-looking eyes. The flush or bloom on the cheeks was, I have no doubt, an effect of his constant use of opium ; and the apparent smoothness of the face disappeared upon examination. The best description of his peculiar appearance in this respect is one given by Sir Walter Scott in reference to General Platoff, whom Scott met at Paris, and from whom, he tells us, he took his portrait of Mr. Touchwood in " St. Ronan's Well." " His face, which at the distance of a yard or two seemed hale and smooth, appeared, when closely examined, to be seamed with a million of wrinkles crossing each other in every direction possible, but as fine as if drawn by the point of a very fine needle." Mr. de Quincey's eyes were dark

* The " Thomas Papaverius " description in " The Book Hunter," the best known—and the best—of these, certainly errs on this side. It recalls the features, the complexion, the expression and aspect of its subject much as vigorous and highly-coloured caricature portraits—in *Vanity Fair*, for example—recall noble and honoured faces and figures. We acknowledge and smile at the likeness, with a secret grudge at the perverted power of the limner.

† As the hair got thinner on the upper part of the head the brow assumed a more arched aspect, as seen in Mr. Archer's drawing, which gives a very good idea of De Quincey's ordinary appearance in his later years—a familiar rather than an intellectual version, however.

in colour,* the iris large, but with a strange flatness and
dimness of aspect, which, however, did not indicate
any deficiency of sight. So far as I ever observed he
saw distant objects tolerably well, and almost to the
very end of his life he could read the smallest print
without spectacles. I remember on one occasion he
talked about George Gilfillan's pen-and-ink portrait of
himself, in which the Reverend George spoke dis-
paragingly of his eyes, declaring that De Quincey never
looked people straight in the face. He resented keenly
the imputation that he had anything approaching to a
squint, still more keenly, in his own humorous style, the
insinuation, which he declared George intended, that he
had also a " moral squint." He had certainly neither
the one nor the other ; he looked quite straightforward
at one ; but it was often difficult to catch his eyes from
the hazy expression diffused over them. They had the
dreamy look often observable in students or in short-
sighted people.†

No one who ever met De Quincey could fail to be
struck, after even the briefest intercourse, with the

---

* The Scotch word " blae " would best express the shade.

† Persons suffering from such weakness of eyesight are liable to
be accused of declining to look an interlocutor fully in the face,
simply because their doing so involves a painful strain on their
eyes in the attempt to adjust the focus to the distance between the
speakers, especially if one eye be weaker than the other. This
seems to have been De Quincey's case ; but Gilfillan's description,
which appeared originally, I think, in *Tait's Magazine*, and was
reprinted in his " Gallery of Literary Portraits," 1845, goes further
than this. He says : " His eyes, they sparkle not, they shine not,
they are lustreless : can that be a squint which glances over from
them towards you ? No. It is only a slight habit one of them has
of occasionally looking in a different direction from the other ;
there is nothing else particular about them ; there is not even the
glare which lights up sometimes dull eyes into eloquence."

extreme sweetness and courtesy of his manners. He had the air of old-fashioned good manners of the highest kind; natural and studied politeness, free from the slightest ostentation or parade; a delicacy, gentleness, and elegance of demeanour that at once conciliated and charmed. As Mr. Burton was well acquainted with the family, and had much to say to the young ladies, De Quincey and I were left for the most part to carry on a sort of side conversation between ourselves, a position which at first I found sufficiently embarrassing. Here I was, a novice, set face to face with one of the greatest masters of conversation—of a special kind of it at least —of his day, with the talk drifting about to all sorts of subjects, for none seemed to come amiss to him. In any attempt to transcribe, or rather describe, his conversation, the chief difficulty would be to fix—perhaps to account for—a certain evanescent charm which every one felt, but which can be only remembered, not transmitted. It was in fact an exquisite and transient emanation from the intellectual and moral nature of the man, enhanced in its effect by the rare beauty of his language, and the perfectly elegant construction of every phrase and sentence that he uttered. The comparison which the American poet and critic and diplomatist, Mr. James Russell Lowell, makes of good style to good breeding is admirably applicable alike to De Quincey's literary style and to his personal manner. Lowell speaks of "that exquisite something called style, which, like the grace of perfect breeding, everywhere persuasive and nowhere emphatic, makes itself felt by the skill with which it effaces itself, and masters us at last with a sense of indefinable completeness." He did not quite, as Burton had told me he would do, talk magazine articles, but the literary habit was notable, though not in the least obtrusive, in all his talk. One effect of this was somewhat trying to an inexperienced listener, for when in the flow of his conversation he came to the close of one of his beautifully rounded and balanced paragraphs, he would pause in order to allow you to have your say, with the result sometimes of rather taking one aback, especially as the subject of conversation often seemed to have been brought, by his conduct of it, to its complete and legitimate conclusion. The listener was apt to feel that he had perorated rather than paused. In his mode of conversing, as in everything else, his courtesy of manner was observable. He never monopolised talk, allowed every one to have a fair chance, and listened with respectful patience to the most commonplace remarks from any one present. The fact that any one was, for the time, a member of the company in which he also happened to be, evidently in his eyes entitled the speaker to all consideration and respect. But he had a just horror of bores, and carefully avoided them. We talked, among many other things, about Macaulay, and about his prodigious power and love of talk. De Quincey remarked that such passion for speaking was usually the sign of a weak and shallow mind, but that Macaulay was a remarkable exception to this rule—that he was the only man of real power and substantial acquirements of whom he had ever heard, who was possessed by " an actual incontinence of talk." Even Coleridge, regarded as the greatest talker of the day, would not always talk, whilst Macaulay seemed ready to pour forth a flood of disquisition and information at any given time. With Coleridge there was always one difficulty, and sometimes two. It was sometimes a great difficulty to get him to begin to talk ; it was always so to get him to stop.

On our leaving, Mr. de Quincey accompanied us to the door, and whilst he was standing in the little garden-plot in front of the house I observed that his feet had been thrust stockingless into an old pair of slippers. And here he was, a man of sixty-three years of age, and apparently of extreme feebleness, thus standing bare-headed in the raw air of a January afternoon. We remarked that he would catch cold, and were hurrying away, but he begged us not to be the least uneasy on his account, for he never did take cold ; it was one of the many advantages of opium that it preserved him against all such trivial accidents. His dress, to an allusion to which I have thus been drawn incidentally, was at all times peculiar. His clothes had generally a look of extreme age, and also of having been made for a person somewhat larger than himself. I believe the real cause of this was that he had got much thinner in those later years ; whilst he wore, and did wear, I suppose till the end of his life, the clothes that had been made for him years before. I have sometimes seen appearances about him of a shirt and shirt-collar, but usually there were no indications of these articles of dress. When I came to visit him in his lodgings, I saw him in all stages of costume ; sometimes he would come in to me from his bedroom to his parlour, as on this occasion, with shoes, but no stockings, and sometimes with stockings, but no shoes. When in bed, where I also saw him from time to time, he wore a large jacket—not exactly an under-jacket, but a jacket made in the form of a coat, of white flannel ; something like a cricketer's coat in fact. In the street his appearance was equally singular. He walked with considerable rapidity (he said walking was the only athletic exercise in which he had ever excelled) and with an odd one-sided, and yet

K

straightforward motion, moving his legs only, and neither his arms, head, nor any other part of his body—like Wordsworth's cloud—

"Moving altogether, if he moved at all."

His hat, which had the antediluvian aspect characteristic of the rest of his clothes, was generally stuck on the back of his head, and no one who ever met that antiquated figure, with that strangely dreamy and intellectual face, working its way rapidly, and with an oddly deferential air, through any of the streets of Edinburgh—a sight certainly by no means common, for he was very seldom to be seen in town—could ever forget it.* He was very fond of walking, but generally his walks were merely into town to his publisher's office (Mr. Hogg's, then in Nicolson Street) and back again to Lasswade. Till he was nearly seventy he took this walk —one of twelve miles—without inconvenience.

At this introductory meeting at Lasswade it was arranged by Miss de Quincey that Mr. Burton and I should come out to dinner ten days afterwards, and on Monday, 19th January, we again walked out. The family party was on this occasion augmented by his third daughter, Miss Emily, but Mr. Burton and I were the only strangers. At dinner we talked on ordinary topics, in which small and table talk De Quincey was always as ready to join as in the most abstruse discussion. He took an interest in, and kept himself up with, all the current topics of the day ; knew the latest accident and incident reported in the newspapers, as well as the minutest occurrences recorded in the lives of distinguished

* See Mrs. Baird Smith's description of her father's mode of dressing, p. 361, vol. i., of "Thomas de Quincey : his Life and Writings." By H. A. Page. Two vols. London, 1877.

characters of past generations.* When the ladies left, Burton and De Quincey got upon talk about old authors, and on questions of history and classics that were beyond my depth ; so that sometimes for considerable intervals I was left stranded on the shore, with this double tide of erudition and speculation ebbing and flowing before me. Among other things we had some conversation about ecclesiastical matters—about the habit that every ecclesiastical set, every church or corporation, has of abusing and denouncing its rivals, and of the ingenuity with which each could fasten upon the other Scriptural symptoms of reprobation. De Quincey remarked that this was really not a difficult matter. " I think," said he, " it would be a very easy task for any one possessed of ordinary powers of research, and some knowledge of the great Antichrist controversy, by the exercise of moderate ingenuity to fix down all the marks of Antichrist—of course you don't for a moment suppose that I in the slightest degree believe in the popular notion and theory of Antichrist—but certainly all the popular signs and characteristics of Antichrist might be very readily fixed down upon the Presbyterian Church of Scotland." The placidity of manner and tone with which he enunciated this, and other startling propositions, corresponded well with the

* He read the newspapers sedulously ; and Dr. Warburton Begbie, in his notes on De Quincey's last illness, says : " Whether seated in his chair or lying in bed, I equally found him attempting to read without spectacles, which he never employed. The *Scotsman*, if not in his hands, was very near him, and he highly prized it, styling it a wonderful newspaper, exhibiting a versatility of political, chiefly, but of varied talent, such as, he believed, had never been surpassed." As this passage is omitted from the version of Dr. Begbie's notes given by Mr. Page (see Life, vol. ii. p. 295), I have a natural and, I hope, excusable, pride in printing it here from the original manuscript.

description which Bayle gives of an eccentric philosopher who was burnt in Paris in 1573, for " privately dogmatising upon Atheism," and who, says Bayle, " although he maintained his heterodox opinions until death, always pronounced them with a sweetness and gentleness of manner, and from a mouth made up for the delivery of the most refined phraseology." We had some speculation as to the terrific denunciations which would follow the publication of a treatise on this subject and in this tone, from a man able to exercise such perverse ingenuity as he described—none better fitted to do so, as I ventured to hint, than himself. Once, after some pause in the conversation, De Quincey and Burton began to talk at the same moment. Burton, of course, at once gave way. This, however, De Quincey would not permit, and after a prolonged struggle in politeness De Quincey carried his point by bargaining that, when Burton had said his say, he would be prepared to follow with the remark he had been stopped in making. Burton having accordingly at some length delivered himself, asked De Quincey to take his turn. But by this time oblivion had covered up what he had intended to say, leading him to indulge a humorous lamentation over his lost idea, regarding which he said all that he could be certain was, that it was unquestionably a brilliant and original one, which might have shed light upon some of the great questions that perplex the world ; though now, to the lasting loss of humanity, the spark had gone out for ever.

In the course of the evening a curious episode occurred. The perfect quiet of the rural roadway or lane was suddenly broken by the sound of children's voices singing. The whole household went to the door, and found in the little garden plot a party of " guisers," who, their song finished, were sent away with some small gratuity. Whilst the little group, including the ladies and the maid-servants, were gathered in the doorway looking at and listening to the children singing, De Quincey stood silent, and appeared to have lapsed into a sort of dream, which abstracted state continued for a few minutes after our return to the dining-room. He had evidently misunderstood the character of his visitors, and instead of rightly regarding them as village children on an evening frolic, fancied that they were in actual distress, and making a somewhat peculiar and more than usually clamorous appeal for charity. Silence was strikingly broken by his exclaiming, "All that I have ever had enjoyment of in life, the charms of friendship, the smiles of women, and the joys of wine, seem to rise up to reproach me for my happiness when I see such misery, and think there is so much of it in the world."

After we had rejoined the ladies, in talking about our having to walk home in the dark, there were some jokes about the possibility of our being attacked and garrotted. We both remarked that we would be poor subjects of plunder, when De Quincey said that we would certainly not be such profitable subjects as a young gentleman whom his son had lately brought out to visit them, and whom they had made very uneasy on the score of the risks he ran. He was covered, De Quincey said, with magnificent jewellery—hung over with chains, rings, breastpins, etc. De Quincey speculated upon the pleased surprise with which any party of garrotters would regard the capture and plunder of such a gilded youth. They would have rejoiced, he said, as did the pirates of old when they came across, not an ordinary prize, but a Spanish galleon. The young ladies played overtures and other pieces on the piano, one of which De Quincey particularly praised, saying that it soothed him like a delicious anodyne. Miss Florence remarked that it was a poor compliment to the music to say that it sent him to sleep. He explained to her, with burlesque excess of particularity and politeness—the humour of which he himself evidently enjoyed as keenly as the amused auditors—that it was really the highest compliment he could pay to it, for he meant that the music was giving the greatest spiritual gratification, and being to him, for the time, the highest good, as making him, usually so miserable, temporarily happy ; and therefore fulfilling its purpose, though not, perhaps, in the ordinary way or according to rule.

On our leaving, Mr. de Quincey, though the night was dark and the road tortuous, insisted upon accompanying us to Loanhead, in order that he might show me the ultimate point to which the Lasswade coach would carry me in the direction of his house, "when next I did him the honour to come out to see him." On the way I asked him if he ever visited his old friend Professor Wilson, who was at that time residing in bad health with his brother in Dalkeith. He said he had not. His reason for not going to see him was, he said, that he understood Wilson, from the nervous condition of mind into which he had fallen, did not care to see visitors ; was not, indeed, able to receive them. "I have, however, intended for a considerable time to write to him. I have not yet accomplished my purpose, but I shall probably make it out to-morrow." He continued, "The misfortune of the case, and the consideration which retards me from writing, is that I have two motives for doing so—one an interested motive, the other a disinterested one. And when these two go together, the former, like Pharaoh's lean kine, swallows up the latter, entirely annihilates it, and leaves only the

interested one standing in its native and loathsome lean-
ness. I have, you will believe me, the most sincere
desire to ask after my old friend John Wilson's welfare,
but years ago he did me a service which I in some sort
now require to have renewed. The circumstances were
that, among many wanderings, I had settled for some
time in Glasgow. I had left there a number of books
and manuscripts of some value to myself, although not
perhaps of very much to any other person. Subsequently, when residing in Edinburgh, I wished to place
those articles out of the risks of such accidents as
arrestments and the like. Being acquainted with no one
in Glasgow who could aid me in such a difficulty, and
knowing Wilson's connection with the west of Scotland,
I naturally applied to him, and received from him a
letter of introduction to a Glasgow bookseller. On
presenting the letter this gentleman expressed in the
strongest terms his willingness to do anything whatever
to oblige his friend Wilson. Of course, reinforced by
such aid, I felt as if I had come into the possession of
Aladdin's lamp, Wilson's friend being the genius who,
thus called up, was ready to relieve me from all my
troubles—a man who said to his servants, Come, and he
cometh ; go, and he goeth ; do this, and he doeth it ;
and who furnished me with all the necessary means for
recovering and transporting the books and manuscripts.
They were deposited in safety, and I returned home in
triumph. This was some years ago, and my present
dilemma is, that I have totally forgotten not only the
name of the street and the appearance of the place in
which they were deposited, but also the name and
address of the gentleman to whom Wilson gave me the
introduction. My unfortunate chattels, therefore, instead
of being rescued from destruction, are plunged into a

deeper and more hopeless oblivion than ever. This,
you will see, is what I want to know from Wilson, not,
of course, where the books are placed, but the name of
the gentleman to whom he introduced me, and I shall
certainly write to him one of these days." *

On another evening (10th November, 1853) on which I
went to Lasswade again with Mr. Burton, Mr. R. M.
Craig, who soon after married Miss de Quincey, was of
the party ; and this was the only occasion of the many
times I saw De Quincey, at all hours and under varied
circumstances, on which he did not shine—that is to say,
he was languid and dull. He was probably suffering
from mental stress and want of sleep, or possibly from
the reaction supervening on one of his terms of extra
addiction to opium. We had little talk with him during
dinner, and he made almost no effort to join in, or keep
up the conversation. In the evening, however, he
brightened up a bit, and we had some good discussion
about Dr. Johnson. Johnson's contradictoriness, and
his remarkable want of knowledge of, or adherence to,
first principles, were strongly dwelt upon by De Quincey.

---

* Those are no doubt the papers afterwards restored to him by
the ingenious intervention of Mr. Hogg: see Page, vol. ii. p. 8.
My memory even now (1885) retains assurance that in this case I
report almost word for word De Quincey's phrases. I do not
know that in all cases where I have in like manner reported him I
could be quite so certain, but must be content, like Mr. Woodhouse,
to give the substance of what he said "somewhat in his own
manner," with the view of affording "some idea of the general
tenor of his conversation, and of the richness of his mind, and of
the facility with which he brings in the stores of his reading and
reflection to bear upon the ordinary topics of conversation." But
I feel, as Mr. Woodhouse says he did, "that it can convey no
adequate impression [either of those qualities, I may add] or of the
eloquence and scope of his language." Those felicities were indeed
too delicate and transient to be so caught and transmitted.

The only writings of Johnson's which seemed to him to
indicate any appreciation and hold of first principles
were the law papers which he drew up for Boswell.
Johnson evidently did not appreciate, did not comprehend, the high philosophic powers of Burke for example ;
even as such powers were indicated in Burke's " Treatise
on the Sublime and Beautiful," a subject that would
naturally interest Johnson.

Talking about the Scotch accent and language, and
remarking how pleasant a dialect Scotch was if spoken
without vulgarity on the one hand or affectation on the
other, I instanced Lord Cockburn as one of the best
speakers of Scotch that I ever heard. De Quincey
demurred a little, on the ground that Cockburn prided
himself rather too much upon it, and that there was in
his Scotch the slightest shade of that affectation which
had been deprecated. Remarking on the light in which
the Scotch tongue was regarded by the English, I
complained of the unconcealed contempt with which the
vulgar English regarded any indication of Scotch pronunciation, and expressed a fear that the same dislike
extended pretty well up in society. This De Quincey
and Miss Florence vehemently denied, maintaining that
in good English society they never heard the speaking of Scotch, unless it were obviously tainted with
vulgarity, remarked on otherwise than as giving
additional interest to the person using it.

On Sunday, 25th June, 1854, in the course of a walk I
met De Quincey at the Dean Bridge at the close of the
afternoon service. He told me that he was staying in
town, and that he had taken advantage of the quiet of the
Sunday afternoon for a walk, but that he unfortunately
miscalculated his time, and, seeking for solitude, had found
himself in the midst of a crowd of gay and fashionable

people returning from church, or walking after church.
With his usual politeness he insisted upon walking back
towards town with me, in spite of the crowds. He did
so to the west end of Princes Street. I returned again
with him to the end of the Dean Bridge. He insisted
upon going back with me ; and so we walked back and
forward five or six times. He began conversation by
telling me that he was extremely desirous of sending to
one of my sisters—who were by this time acquainted
with him and his daughters—a copy of the newly
published third volume of his works.* He had been
unable, however, he said, to ascertain whether we spelt
the name Findlay with or without a "d," and that this
"d" difficulty had prevented him inscribing, as he
intended to do, the volume ; for of all the petty breaches
of good manners that he desired most to avoid, was that
of either mis-calling or mis-spelling any one's name.
He considered it unpardonable in the case of any one
with whom you have any pretension to acquaintance-
ship ; and his want of precise knowledge had proved an
insuperable obstacle to his carrying out the intention
referred to. He had consulted his publisher on the
point, but he could not give him any certain or trust-
worthy information. He had not supposed, he said,
that young ladies would be at all interested in the
biographical portion of his book, of which the two first
volumes mainly consisted, but the third being more of a
narrative, might, he thought, amuse them. I told him
that they had read all the three with great interest, but
that, nevertheless, they would attach a high value to his
proposed present ; which, of course, never came.† He

* "Selections : Grave and Gay," etc. Hogg.
† This arose, I believe, from real incapacity to carry out his
intentions in such matters ; a sort of paralysis of the will suspending

explained that he had left Lasswade partly to be near books and libraries to complete his fourth volume more conveniently, but partly also for change, and from a desire which perpetually haunted him to fly from himself. "I often," he said "feel an almost irresistible inclination to rush away and bury myself among books in the heart of some great city like London or Paris." I asked for his daughters. He said he had not seen nor heard of them since he left Lasswade, some three weeks before. He never wrote letters, and did not wish to receive any; therefore he had no means of knowing how they were, unless he walked out to ask for them, which he intended to do very soon. Passing across the Dean Bridge, he remarked upon the peculiar beauty of the view—the mixed elements in it, the noble city view, imposing mansions on the one side, and trees, hills, and the sea in the distance, and yet apparently in immediate proximity. It was a *rus in urbe*, or, more properly, it was a town in the country. Once, in walking with him in moonlight on George IV. Bridge, before it was so much built up as it is now, he spoke enthusiastically of the dark masses on the west side of the Bridge, crowned by the broken bulk of the castle with all its romantic associations.*

---

the action that ought to have followed the intent—a condition all nervous people can more or less understand, as being so far subject to it themselves. It is aggravated by anything like a dilemma or a choice of courses; in those cases the impulse, faint enough perhaps to carry action into one course, gets hopelessly dissipated in the contemplation of more than one; though I suspect that De Quincey rather enjoyed being subject to such dilemmas.

* This moonlight walk arose out of a highly characteristic trait. He had dined with me at George Square; he preferred an early hour, and our small party had sat down to dinner at five or six o'clock. The two or three guests, all equally fascinated and de-

We got, somehow or other, into a sort of sad, and
almost too personal, mood of converse, in the course of
which he spoke in that tone of despondency into which

lighted with his talk—only my uncle,* Russel, and Burton probably
—had left us one by one : my uncle for the country, where he was
staying, I inhabiting alone his house in town ; Burton, unceremoniously enough when he thought fit to go ; and at last Russel,
about eleven o'clock, he having his work at the *Scotsman* office for
next morning's paper, as I had also. After fully an hour more had
slipped away I was obliged to tell De Quincey that I too must go.
Then came elegant apologies, undoubtedly sincere, and we left
together, my desire being to see him safe home to his lodgings in
Lothian Street. No, he would accompany me through the silent
midnight streets that fine summer evening. So we walked backwards and forwards for probably another hour between the High
Street (where the office of the *Scotsman* then was) and Lothian
Street, till at last the inevitable "good night" was spoken. I got
to my post to find my work for the night all but finished by
Mr. Russel, who immensely enjoyed the "fix" in which he had left
me, and was much surprised at my having, by any device or
exercise of moral courage, got out of it. As De Quincey said of
Coleridge that the first difficulty was to get him to begin to talk
and the second to get him to stop, so of De Quincey the first
difficulty was to induce him to visit you and the second to reconcile
him to leaving. He would have sat up talking all night on this or
any other night as readily as he did one night with Mr. Woodhouse
(Mr. Garnett's edition of the "Confessions," p. 212 : in that case also
after a long sederunt at dinner), quietly happy in the exercise and
interchange of thought, and oblivious of the lapse of time. He ate
almost nothing (we were always careful to have some light soft food
prepared especially for him), he drank nothing, even under "social
pressure," beyond one or two wineglassfuls of extremely weak
brandy and water, and out of his own lodgings I never saw him
touch laudanum. He seemed on such occasions truly, as he calls
himself in his "Confessions" or "Autobiographical Sketches," "an
intellectual creature," independent of the ordinary wants and conditions of humanity. Something of congenial company—once he

* Mr. John Ritchie, proprietor of the *Scotsman ;* Mr. Russel
being its editor.

he occasionally fell, of the melancholy that attached to
looking back upon life ; how small is the benefit which
people in the course of it obtain from experience which
they really only acquire when they have little further
use for it ; and how mortifying it is to reflect how very
different a man's course might have been had he known
at the beginning what he knows at the end of it. For
himself, he said, so "stale, flat, and unprofitable" was the
retrospect, that he turned away from it "shuddering and
ashamed."

I told him that Dr. Robert Lee * had expressed a
desire to be introduced to him, and asked if I might take
the liberty of bringing him to call.   He said he should
be delighted.   " I have long known him," he said, " from
his public appearances, have admired his learning and
liberality, and had I not been the miserable, incapable
creature that I am in all such matters, I should certainly
have sought an introduction to him long ago.   I should,
therefore, be extremely grateful to you if you will so far
trouble yourself in the matter as to be the medium of
bringing us together."   I remember, either on this or on
a subsequent occasion, speaking to him of Dr. Lee's
pulpit appearances, and asking him if he would not come
to hear him preach.   He said that he never went to

---

was in it ; for it was not a necessity to him ; it sought him, not he
it—with speculative and pleasant talk, so beguiled for him hours
that might otherwise have been weary and heavy-laden that they
glided on unregarded by himself, and only reckoned by his companions as too short to have had crowded into them so much
worth remembering that each memorable opinion or expression
was but too apt to jostle the other out of recollection.

* Minister of Old Greyfriars' Church, Edinburgh. He was a
leader of liberal thought and practice in the Church of Scotland,
and as usual was denounced and persecuted in its courts, his great
merits and services only now coming to be fully acknowledged—
fifteen years after his death.

church ; on which I remarked that probably he had not
persisted so long in doing so as another friend of mine
who declared that he went to church until it became a
sin to go.   He said he feared that he could not entertain
the idea of returning, even to hear Dr. Lee, for the
irksomeness which he had often endured of sitting
listening to a man groping and fumbling, where he saw
a clear way to leap, was so intolerable that he could not
subject himself to the slightest risk of a repetition of such
mental agony.

Mr. Burton, hearing that De Quincey was in town,
asked him to supper, and requested me to call at Lothian
Street for him on my way from George Square to Ann
Street, Stockbridge—where Burton then lived—and if
possible to bring him with me.   On calling on the
evening in question (28th June, 1854), at De Quincey's
lodgings, I found he had left a message for me, to say
that he would meet me on the Dean Bridge.   There
accordingly I found him, and on expressing my satisfaction at seeing him so far on his way to Mr. Burton's, he
begged that I would not infer from the fact of his being
on the way that he was going there.   Naturally enough
at such an odd remark my inclination was to laugh, and
to try a little banter ; but for this his tone was too grave
and sincere.   "I have come out," he added, "to try
whether the delightful air of this fine summer evening
will do anything to dispel that intolerable languor and
deep-seated suffering that distract me, and to which I
have been a martyr for days."   I tried to persuade him
that as there was no party—only my uncle and another
friend—a little society might probably help him towards
attaining a more cheerful state of mind.   But he would
not be induced.   He said he felt so wretched that he
could not face any one—that there were times when he

fled from his best friends, and that this was one of them. Besides, he said that if he went he would be compelled, by a desire to bring himself up to something like the common level of humanity, to take some stimulant, a little wine or spirits, and that for such indulgence, even to an amount which in any other person would be not only ordinary but trivial, he should afterwards suffer the pangs of hell. " Oh, my God," he exclaimed, " the miseries I have been born to endure ; what tortures I have suffered, and what tortures am I yet doomed to suffer !" I was greatly pained and distressed. Nothing, he said, but a large dose of laudanum gave him relief ; that he took such a dose to enable him to get through a burst of work occasionally, but that he dare not repeat it too often, and so in the intervals he had nothing for it but to endure.

We wandered, as usual, into all sorts of subjects, and amongst others he spoke of Dugald Stewart, whom he did not estimate highly, referring to the slight notice he took of Kant as evidence of his not being at all alive to the magnitude of the revolution which Kant's system of philosophy was calculated to effect. With considerable persuasion I got him to go so far as the north end of Ann Street, which I was enabled to do the more readily as he said he recollected that Wilson lived in that street in his early days. I had drawn him thither with a vague hope that if Burton had been on the outlook we might have pulled him in after all. But, unfortunately, no such chance occurred, and we parted at the end of the street, he insisting that I should not make myself late by going back with him.

On Saturday, 29th July, of the same year, I called on De Quincey at his lodgings in Lothian Street, to ask him to come round to my uncle's to supper next evening,

when we expected Burton, who had been disappointed
by his previous non-appearance. We had some talk
about Burton and his prodigious power of working.
" He seems," says De Quincey, "to hunger and thirst
after opportunities of working, a feeling which I am
perfectly incapable of comprehending." We talked of
Burton's appointment as Secretary of the Prison Board,
and De Quincey remarked that he was well acquainted
with his predecessor, Mr. Ludovic Colquhoun. He knew
the family, and had often been asked to Mr. Colquhoun's
or his father's to dinner ; and, though he never went, he
had frequently called to apologize for not having gone.
We talked about his (De Quincey's) articles on Pope,
Shakespeare, and Goethe, in the seventh edition of the
Encyclopædia Britannica. On my telling him how much
pleased I had been to find my own preconceived notions
of Goethe confirmed by his high authority, and by the
good reasons he gave for such opinion, he went pretty
fully into the whole question of the nature of Goethe's
genius. Among other things he mentioned that Wordsworth, who was apt to take extreme opinions upon such
subjects, regarded Goethe as little better than a quack.
Wordsworth he said, never read books, but somehow or
other" Wilhelm Meister "had fallen in his way, and he had
gone through it till he came to the scene where the hero,
in his mistress's bedroom, becomes sentimental over her
dirty towels, etc., which struck him with such disgust
that he flung the book out of his hand, would never look
at it again, and declared that surely no English lady
would ever read such a work.

Invited to return to see him, I called from time to
time ; half an hour's conversation with him was a
privilege I valued too highly to risk drawing upon it
too often. He was ready to talk on any subject ; the

day's news ; the articles in the *Scotsman ;* recent books ; our common friends ; anything that came uppermost ; for he was in converse a man of the world, and no mere pedant or bookworm. At times he would play, as it were, with trivial topics in talk ; treating them with a sort of mock importance. For example, in this way he once entered into a long dissertation on the troubles of dressing. Shaving, especially, he said, was a grand difficulty. After collecting the best information on the subject, he had purchased a set of first-rate razors, but he had been told that they could not be kept in order without continual stropping, a task to which he could not think of subjecting himself ; besides which there was the necessity for keeping a soap-box, an article of furniture he utterly abhorred. Some years after he solved the difficulty by allowing his beard to grow. The first time that I saw him in this state, the under part of his face covered with thin grey hair, he explained to me that his hirsute condition was not owing to his having joined the "mustache movement," as it was called. He hoped that I would acquit him of any such utter imbecility as that. It all arose, he said, from the old difficulty of razors. He could not be troubled shaving himself, and he could not endure any other person shaving him. The intolerable smell of a barber's fingers in every case in which he had attempted to undergo the operation, had filled him with disgust so great that he could barely muster courage and politeness to endure its being carried out.*

* Once when he had walked in from Lasswade to dine at George Square he was shown into a room to wash in which was a fixed basin with hot and cold water, an arrangement not so common thirty years ago as now. Turning on the water, I left for a moment to fetch a towel, and on my return found Mr. de Quincey standing in an attitude of paralysed perplexity a little way off from the

L

On one occasion (24th November, 1854) I called to ask for him, he having sent word that from illness he could not come to supper at George Square as he had promised to do. He stated that he had made an effort to write an explanatory note, but was unable to do so, and had been obliged to content himself with a message. His foot, he said, had been affected by his having been taking large doses of opium ; " in fact," he said, " my leg is quite black, from the foot to considerably above the knee." He treated lightly my expressions of regret at such an alarming appearance, saying that he had had it before, and knew how far it would go, and how it could be got quit of.* The best cure, he said, would be to take six months' walking ; on which I said that his case was like that of St. Denis :—" *Ce n'est que le premier pas qui coûte.*" How was he to begin this regimen ? He

---

nearly brimful basin. His alarm was lest the basin should overflow and deluge the room, an evil which I explained was provided against. He justified his fears by calling attention to the rapid inflow of the water, and made the most amusing comparisons of himself to the hero of the German story " Undine," overwhelmed by waters which he had conjured up but could not control. I daresay he must have used to me in his description of his plight some such phrases as that very characteristic one in his " Logic of Political Economy," in which he speaks of water bearing no value in a country like this " except under that machinery of costly arrangements which delivers it as a permanent and guaranteed succession into the very chambers where it is to be used." His language naturally and unavoidably shaped itself into such stately phrases. If any auditor were tempted to smile at their occasionally somewhat inappropriate pomp and elegance, he would have readily joined in the laugh—though, indeed, he rarely laughed at all—and would have amplified the illustrations and heightened the humour of the occasion.

* In an unpublished letter, of date March 9, 1846, he speaks of an abrasion on his heel having "brought back that dreadful *purpura* from which I suffered so much for three years."

answered that by his leaving off opium, even for a few days, his leg would so far recover as to enable him to go out; "but," he says, "I cannot do that, for without opium I can't get on with my work, which the publishers are urging me to complete. The work must be done; the opium can't be left off; therefore I cannot begin to walk, and the leg must take its chance."

He remained in these lodgings from 1854 until his death five years afterwards; his temporary residence thus becoming permanent, with, I believe, an interval of not more than five or six months at Lasswade. This was extremely characteristic; in fact he had walked into town from Lasswade to these lodgings, where he had been some years before, without any preparation in the way of luggage or otherwise; and he explained to me if it had not been that his landlady, Mrs. Wilson, being a conscientious and careful woman, had preserved for him a quantity of clothing which he had left on his former sojourn, he would have been in sad straits as to dress. Into such straits he occasionally lapsed afterwards, for I remember his frankly telling me that on one occasion he could not go out to walk because he had not a pair of trousers. Of course it was sheer carelessness on his part; even the vigilant supervision of his daughters was insufficient to keep him, in these matters, in anything like the condition of ordinary mortals.

Thus far I have brought my recollections into something of consecutive and connected order; for the rest, I must be content to present them rather disjointedly; or, at least as mere notes or memoranda.

30*th July*, 1854.—De Quincey came to supper with us in George Square on Sunday. We were *en*

L 2

*famille ;** the only other guest being Burton. We spoke of
the different habits of men in drinking different liquors.
He said he used to be fond of gin and water, and drank
it till Byron's Life was published, when he gave it up,
because he did not wish to be accused, however falsely,
of imitating Byron even in that. He was much amused
by my account of a scene between Sydney Dobell,
Professor Piazzi Smyth, Mr. Augustus St. John, and
Leitch Ritchie, which I told him I had witnessed.†
The incident had occurred a short time previously (4th
February) and was this :—Leitch Ritchie had asked
some friends to supper at his house (32, Danube Street,
Edinburgh), to meet Mr. John Augustus St. John, author
of several books of travel, a fine looking man of between
sixty and seventy, who had lost his eyesight from
ophthalmia in Egypt. Among those who arrived early,

---

* My grand-uncle's family consisted of his niece, my mother,
my two sisters, and myself ; and an old habit was kept up by the
household of having a small supper on Sunday evening at the
highly unfashionable hour of nine o'clock, at which one or two
friends usually dropped in. To my uncle, who was at that time
nearly eighty years of age—he died in 1870, having almost completed his ninety-third year—Mr. de Quincey took a great liking,
admiring and commenting on his great physical and mental vigour
in advanced age, and on his independence and strength of judgment.
Though nearly fifteen years younger than my uncle, De Quincey
looked the older man of the two, and, both having personal memories
of events of earlier date than we of a second or third generation,
they found many topics of mutual interest apart from literature and
politics. My uncle's natural courtesy and kindness of disposition
likewise attracted De Quincey, as it did Thackeray, who always
spoke of him as "that kind old gentleman."

† Mr. Leitch Ritchie was at this time editing *Chambers's Journal ;*
Mr. Robert Chambers was one of this party. His brother, William
Chambers, spoke of Leitch Ritchie to Thackeray as "the most
gentlemanly literary man we (*i.e.* the Messrs. W. and R. Chambers)
had ever had to do with," a saying which Thackeray repeated with
an expression of supreme scorn.

was Mr. Piazzi Smyth, Professor of Astronomy, Edinburgh University. He has an impediment in his speech which sometimes altogether prevents utterance for a few moments. Leitch Ritchie himself, again, was extremely deaf. The deaf man, the blind man, and the stammering man, were all the company who had arrived, except Dr. Findlater* and myself, when the door opened and Mr. Sydney Dobell was announced. Dobell rushing into the room, as soon as Leitch Ritchie mentioned in a vague way, "Mr. Dobell—Mr. St. John," seized by the hand, not Mr. St. John, but Professor Smyth, and began a speech he evidently had cut and dry. "And is it possible that I hold by the hand one who bears the illustrious name of St. John!" Smyth in vain attempted to assert his identity ; his tongue refused its office. Leitch Ritchie, not hearing Dobell's hushed tones, looked on bewildered. It was the blind man, Mr. St. John himself who came to the rescue, saying, "It is I whose name is St. John." Whereupon Dobell turned to him and began "Oh, then, is it possible, etc." Findlater and I not being sufficiently familiar in the house, and knowing none of the parties except Smyth and Ritchie, had not felt it right to interfere, but remained amazed and amused spectators. Of course Dobell's speech fell very flat, and, besides, St. John further set him down, though gently, by telling him he had no connection with the Bolingbroke family. De Quincey said the complication was as complete as anything the older dramatists ever fancied. He said that walking —a long walk—gave extraordinary depth and spirituality of expression to ladies' eyes. Mr. Burton towards midnight hinted that he was waiting for him to give the signal to rise. De Quincey protested *he* had been waiting for him, Burton. Burton said he could

* Editor of *Chambers's Encyclopædia*, etc.

not think of rising before him. We all talked away for
a time, and Burton again spoke of going. "Oh, no,"
says De Quincey, "since you give *me* the privilege of
fixing the time I shall not be coerced, and, even to show
my independence, shall have a little more brandy and
water and conversation."*

19th September, 1854.—De Quincey dined with us at
George Square—with Russel. I called for him at his
lodgings in Lothian Street at a quarter before five. He
drew my attention to his being ready before the time,
pointing to the clock. The weather had been very fine,
but the sky was beginning to get cloudy and gray, and I
said that I feared a change. De Quincey said, "Yes, but
it will be gradual. All the great operations of nature
are slow, and the grand dome of fine weather which has
hung over us for weeks is not to be lightly or suddenly
broken up." Some rather dirty little children were
lingering in the common passage of the stair as we came
out to the street. He smiled his sweet pensive smile,
and patted one of them on the head—she, poor little
thing, rather shrinking from the attentions offered by so
weird-looking a patron. He turned to me, and we
smiled together.

At dinner Mr. Russel asked him why he lived in town
at this season when he had such a nice place in the
country. He said, "The convenience consists in this ;
that there seems less criminality in disappointing printers
when they send only in the next street, than when they
come seven miles." I asked him about his daughters.
Miss Florence had been expected from Ireland on Friday,
and he had been out at Lasswade on that day, but had

* Sometimes De Quincey preferred to come after dinner, rather
than sit through a meal of which he could partake so little. See
page 155.

not waited to see her. "She was expected at six, and I left at five." In course of some talk about Professor Wilson, Mr. Russel remarked on his pension, and on his having had to go to the Whigs for it. De Quincey spoke of its disproportionate amount—£300, one-fourth of the whole sum annually allowed for literary distinction to be absorbed by Wilson. We spoke of Wilson's thin-skinnedness. Quillinan's poems were reviewed by *Blackwood* as " Poems by a Heavy Dragoon." Quillinan in retaliation parodied in verse Lockhart's description of Wilson in " Peter's Letters." One of the lines was :—

"And catch a pig, although its tail be soaped."

Wilson's resentment was intense. Mrs. Wordsworth asked Wilson some time afterwards, when he happened to be in the Lake district, if he would object to dine with Quillinan. He fired up and exclaimed, "Oh, no, I'll dine with the Devil if he be asked to the same party." De Quincey remarked as a bad feature in Wilson's character his love to be surrounded by parasites—persons who were lower in position than himself, and who ministered to his vanity. He ridiculed the sickly, false sentiment of his works, and their evidently insincere and vulgar, over-wrought religionism. His works—his tales at least—were a jest among the Wordsworths. De Quincey spoke of Wilson as a lecturer. He had heard him once or twice. All dignity and impressiveness as a lecturer were destroyed by his drawing his forefinger down the side of his nose at the end of almost every paragraph. De Quincey's imitation of the action was very droll. He said that the hearer began to anticipate it whenever he saw Wilson coming to a pause, and the fulfilment of the expectation raised a sense of the

ridiculous even in Wilson's grandest passages.   His perverse emphasis—on "this," and "and," and "of," and
other insignificant words—was also very distressing to a
sensitive ear.

We asked De Quincey about Wordsworth's personal
appearance.   His figure, he said, was bad, and his walking "sidling," he did not keep his own line of path.
Wordsworth thanked God that there was only one man
in England he would go out of his way to see, namely,
Belzoni.   De Quincey remarked on the beggarly idea of
renown Wordsworth entertained in regarding as nothing
all the intellect and worth of England as compared with
a man seven feet high, who could walk about with a
living pyramid on his shoulders. · Wordsworth's scorn of
public opinion was excessive.   It was not superciliousness,
but an almost inhuman scorn.   This was a natural reaction of the abuse he suffered early.   He (De Quincey)
had, he said, on one occasion to show the honours of the
vale of Grasmere to a French visitor, and was greatly
diverted by Wordsworth's and the Frenchman's almost
unconcealed contempt for each other.   Wordsworth's
feeling was on account of the French revolution, and
from a neglect and scorn of strangers in general ; and
the Frenchman's feeling arose from his having derived
all his ideas of Wordsworth from the *Edinburgh Review*,
and regarding him as the very imbecile of literature.
"Nothing," De Quincey remarked, "could be more
unfortunate than the titles given to Wordsworth's larger
poems.   The argument of the 'Excursion' has nothing
to do with the accident of the excursion that gives its
name to the poem.   Then the 'Prelude' as a name
equally inappropriate.   He designed it as the opening of
a great poem, but as the great poem was never finished,
the 'Prelude' stands as an opening to nothing.   The chief

weakness of the 'Excursion' lies in the commonplace nature of its religious sentiment—nothing higher than what you might hear intelligent old women talk on such subjects."

Of Mrs. Crowe as a writer he expressed great admiration, especially as to her power in arranging plots. Her machinery was coarse—a murder—but the ingenuity with which in "Men and Women" she distributes the suspicion of the murder between four or five persons was most masterly.

He spoke highly of Southey ; his strict honour and good-nature, and mentioned his feeling of humiliation in having his articles in the *Quarterly* altered by Gifford. De Quincey said Lamb was one of the most loving and delightful of men ; Southey one of the most estimable.

We talked of Hannah More. De Quincey's mother built a house near Hannah More's for the express pleasure of enjoying her society. De Quincey himself, though not admiring her, was of course compelled to tolerate her. The Mores were six maiden sisters, the youngest sixty, and the eldest eighty. Miss More's manner was very ladylike and refined, and her sisters were very nice women, "but eaten up with the cant of Methodism." Remarking on Sheridan's giving Wilberforce's name instead of his own when found lying drunk, De Quincey went on to picture Wilberforce's horror at having in succession all the seven deadly sins fastened down upon him by similar imputations. Hannah More was ignorant of Wordsworth's merits as a poet till she was struck with the extracts from the "Excursion" given in the *Edinburgh Review*. She could not believe that these noble Miltonic lines had been written by a man whom the reviewers had been assailing for years. "Of course," said De Quincey, "I had too mean an opinion

of Miss More's intellectual powers to have condescended
to indicate Wordsworth's abilities to her."

Of Moore's *Byron* he spoke as a miserable piece of
biography, slovenly and slight. With the materials
Moore might have made an admirable Life.

On one occasion we had a conversation on the chances
of long life. De Quincey said it had been observed that
people had not the same chance of long life if one or
other of their parents had not attained it. "Now, as my
mother survived till she was nearly a hundred, I fear that
I shall be compelled to drag out existence to a protracted
period, and I look forward with horror to being left helpless, a burden and trouble to others." I reminded him
that as his mother had retained all her faculties, he had
the best hopes of doing so also. "True," he replied,
"but she was one of the most temperate of beings, living
a pure and gentle life. Now, I have tampered so much
with opium, and tried my mind and health in so many
ways, that I cannot look for a like immunity from the
natural ills of age" I referred him to my uncle as an
example of cheerful and contented old age, with full
possession of all the faculties.

2nd December, 1854.—Called on De Quincey at Lothian
Street, and found him seated in bed, dressed in a flannel
vest with sleeves, and his bed covered with books, papers,
etc. He apologised for so receiving me ; said he seldom
rose till four or five ; for though uncomfortable everywhere, he was less uncomfortable in bed than anywhere
else. I asked him if he had heard from his daughters.
He said not lately, and that he could not expect to do
so, for he had not written to them, or rather he had never
despatched his letters to them—for he *had* written many
—and that there were probably thirty or forty pages of
unsent notes to them lying somewhere about his room.

I mentioned Ferrier's " Institutes of Metaphysics," just published.   De Quincey said he had the highest possible opinion of Ferrier's powers of thinking ; but that he could not from Ferrier's letters comprehend his system, and was anxious to see his book, in the hope that it would make the matter clearer.*

We spoke of the remarkable change that had recently been gradually wrought in toleration of freedom of thought on religious subjects.   De Quincey said he tried thirty years ago to get a bookseller to accept a translation of Strauss, but that everybody shrank from it.   "But now, Strauss is not only translated but patronised, talked about, and introduced into society, like a tiger into a drawing-room."   He spoke of a professor of heterodox opinions in this country having been in the position of a man seeing a crowd with angry eyes on every side of him.†

2nd March, 1855.—Misses Florence and Emily de Quincey were at an evening party with us last night, and they were to stay over to-day.   I asked Mr. de Quincey, who was staying in Lothian Street, to come down to dinner at five, or in the evening.   He sent word that he would come at six ; then a note.   It was as follows :—

" *Friday, 2d March.*

"MY DEAR SIR,—It struck me, as a casuist, that an answer almost rude, which should not keep your messenger waiting, must be preferable in your eyes to any answer more entirely ceremonious, that should occupy

* When Ferrier was a candidate for the Chair of Moral Philosophy in Edinburgh, De Quincey wrote a testimonial for him ; a highly characteristic production—a disquisition in the form of a testimonial—which may be seen by the curious in the collection of such documents in the Advocates' Library.

† See Appendix B.

the time of your servant at an hour when perhaps it
would be most in request.   The rudeness I should have
left to heal itself.   But it strikes me suddenly that I may
have left room for a misconstruction, or rather for a
suspicion upon your part of a misconstruction upon mine.
By saying that I would come down at six, it is just
possible that I may seem to have misread your dinner-
hour, as being six instead of five.   This is not the case.
I meant to say that I would come immediately *after*
dinner ; which *now*, on revising my plan, I will assume
to be nearly seven.   Having no paper accessible at this
moment, I use a fragment of your own note.—Ever, my
dear Sir, your obliged,

"THOMAS DE QUINCEY."

He came and remained talking with my uncle and the
rest till eleven.   I had to leave early for my night's
work.   Talking of Wordsworth's *Guide to the Lakes*, De
Quincey said that on its original publication he offered
Wordsworth an account of the origin and character of
the language of the Lake district, which unlocked all its
peculiar nomenclature ; but "Wordsworth, who never
liked to be obliged to anybody for anything, declined it
in his usual haughty and discourteous manner, and it
was ultimately published in a Kendal newspaper." •

2nd May, 1855.—Called on De Quincey at Lothian
Street.   Found him in his room, with a small glass half
filled with liquor of the colour of pale port, and a phial
of undiluted laudanum beside it on the table, which was
covered as usual with books and papers.   He complained
of pain in his left arm which, as he described it, seemed
like rheumatism.   It prevented his sleeping, and, un-

• No doubt in the *Westmoreland Gazette*, of which De Quincey
was himself editor in 1819.

fortunately, he said, laudanum had no effect on it. I advised him to try chloroform, applied externally, which led to some talk about chloroform. Then of vaccination, and the immunity it afforded from the curse of small-pox. I remarked on the fewer persons marked with small-pox now to be seen in the streets. He said that it was still more noticeable some years ago in contrasting English-men with foreigners, who were marked in far greater proportion. I mentioned Pope's allusion to small-pox, as one of the greatest curses of life, classed by him with old age, in the "Rape of the Lock," and De Quincey expressed surprise at his not recollecting the couplet. He spoke of small-pox as a disfigurement, and said it was difficult to imagine a more horrible moment than that in which a once beautiful young woman, who had suffered from the frightful disease, looked in her mirror again for the first time. Fortunately, he said, human life seldom presented in its course such fearful trials of fortitude.*

17th November, 1856.—Called on De Quincey in Lothian Street about five. Found him at tea; his room littered with MSS., books, etc.; small glass of laudanum in one hand, teacup in other. I called to ask him to dine with us, to meet Thackeray, on the following Saturday. He said he would do his best to come, but had work on hand which he must have finished this week, and also that he had not been out of his house since May.

Talk of his revised "Confessions," just published. On my alluding to a note referring to Coleridge's opinion on the famous passage in Job, "I know, etc.," and to Dr. Robert Lee being engaged in a controversy with the *Witness* newspaper on this point, he asked me if Dr. Lee

* See Appendix C.

knew of Coleridge's opinion. I told him I had sent
Dr. Lee the volume of his Selections, in which the
passage is commented on, and that he was much pleased
with it. De Quincey said that the last conversation he
had had with Coleridge was about this very passage.
Coleridge had in his writings declared against the
commonly received opinion about it ; but De Quincey
having heard he had retracted, questioned him about it.
Sara Coleridge, his daughter, "full of talent, learning,
and piety—rather too much of that indeed"—had
induced him to retract, or to appear to do so, because the
opinions he expressed were disagreeable to the pietist
connection in which she moved. But the impression
De Quincey's conversation with him left was that
Coleridge had not done so sincerely, but only for peace.
"For myself," said De Quincey, "I should as soon
expect to find something about the blood of Christ
blurting out in the pages of Livy or Plato as an allusion
to immortality in this old Arabian writer."

On the Saturday a little note came from De Quincey
as follows :—

"MY DEAR SIR,—On Wednesday evening I was
obliged to attend a party, from which I returned with a
most distressing affection of the chest ; and since then
the greater part of every day has been passed in bed.
To-day up to 3 o'clock I endeavoured to struggle with
it, but have been obliged to go to bed. I am ashamed
to have caused you any trouble ; but in deep sincerity I
am wholly disabled even for sitting up.—Pray believe
me your obliged

"THOMAS DE QUINCEY.

"*Sat. 22nd November.*"

When I told Thackeray that we had hoped to get

De Quincey to come to meet him, he said he felt much flattered, and that nothing would have pleased him more than to have met a man whose writings he so much admired. I handed him the note of apology; he praised in his quietly enthusiastic way the extreme neatness of its style, and penmanship, and antique courtesy of its tone.

Two other notes referring to invitations are characteristic enough to be recorded. They are of dates 29th January and 30th January, 1859. I was anxious to get De Quincey to meet our friend Mr. Carruthers of Inverness, who remembered him in old times; and wished to renew the acquaintance. The reference in the first letter to "Miss Jean Stark" is to his landlady's sister, whose attention and devotion to him partook of

"The constant service of the antique world,"

and showed strongly his power of attracting and enchaining interest in all who came in contact with him.* His allusions to Mr. Russel's articles explain themselves; and his final congratulation to the *Scotsman* is in reference to Miss Isa Craig (now Mrs. Knox) having just gained the prize of 50 guineas for the Centenary Burns Ode offered by the Crystal Palace Company.

LETTER.

"You will find somewhere below, and buried in a heap of words, that, to my great regret, I shall not be able to join your party to-day.

"MY DEAR SIR,—I beg your pardon for what must have seemed inattention in acknowledging no sooner

* See Page's Life; and Masson's "De Quincey."

your kind invitation for to-day.   But literally I *could*
not. What you were told yesterday, viz., that I had
gone abroad to walk, was a romantic fiction, ' pure and
simple,' of Miss Jean Stark's.   And certainly, when her
'hand was in,' she might as well have asserted that I
was botanising on the Himalayas—which would have
been conclusive, needing no more words—whereas now
she has left to you the labour of reading, to me of
explaining, that in order to meet the anxiety of my
publisher (who knows, or who fancies, a special benefit
from publishing in January), I *was* last night, and *am*
through this day, entangled in the very final arrears and
valedictory *P.S.* of my 10th vol.   The word 10*th* makes
me ashamed ; but it is Boston that is answerable,
Yankee Boston.   I am, as it happens, unable at this
time to walk ; *that* might have been remedied by a cab ;
but there is a more complex hindrance from the
grievous defect (or default, or how shall I express it ?) of
an amanuensis—my youngest daughter, who otherwise
is my right hand, being unavoidably absent in Tipperary ;
and thus it is that I am embargoed triply in this anchorage of No. 42 L. Street.

"Whilst waiting to hear from the Press, let me
mention that I have some half-dozen 'plaints' against
Mr. Russel as regards statements of fact.   One, a
bagatelle, arises this morning as to Lord Ripon.   1stly,
His exact nickname was *Prosperity Fred.*   2dly, This
name was given to him by Cobbett. So far I am sure ;
at least *positive*—which means *obstinate.*   3dly, I think,
but am not *viciously* certain, that the name had no
special reference to any prediction ; rather, I should say,
to his retrospects ; to the general flattering haze with
which he invested his budgets, or prefatory abstracts when
introducing his budgets as Ch. of the Exch.   Was it not

Prosp. Fred who made the discovery that Taxes ' fructify ' in our pockets ?

" It must be a great satisfaction and a just ground of pride to the *Scotsman* establishment that a foster child of their own evocation, a daughter of their own encouragement, should have had this distinguished success —being herself crowned amidst her own act of coronation—reaping whilst she thought only of sowing.

" I halt suddenly but unavoidably ; for the Fiend is up from St. Andrew Sq. seeking whom——

" Ever most truly yours,

" THOMAS DE QUINCEY.

" *Sat. 29th Jan.*"

The second note is as follows :—

" *Sunday, 30th Jan.*

" MY DEAR SIR,—Nothing is more distressing to me than the being compelled by uncontrollable accidents to decline what I should naturally regard as an invitation alike flattering and friendly. Nine days hence you will yourself understand from a letter which I will then write to you, how impossible it was for me to do otherwise.

" Mr. Carruthers I had a special interest in meeting about 20 years ago ; if I do not greatly mistake I met him—not *at* Prof. Wilson's house—*but in his company.* Since then Mr. Carruthers has written, with results known to the Antipodes (who, however, continue little the better for the information constantly reaching them) on the Biography of Pope. Consequently, having myself also troubled those waters—tho' only enough to stir up the mud—I have a personal as well as a general interest in *him.* So I should have made an effort, you may be sure, to meet him.

M

"That fair *Incognita* who condescended to leave the letter of invitation, connected herself in the strangest fashion of cross-readings with the final words of my dreams ; which dreams she broke up ; so that in fact I have a message for her from the land of dreams, true and false.

"Yours ever; excuse the writing ; it has suddenly (3.30) grown dark as Erebus."

It will be seen that in the sudden darkness of the winter afternoon he had omitted to append his signature ; and it is, I daresay, needless to add that the explanatory letter, to be written "nine days hence," never came to hand. The "fair *Incognita*" was simply the maid who had handed in my note.

For a year or two before he died, Mr. De Quincey rarely moved out of doors. I called on him from time to time, but have no notes of those later interviews. Once Miss Jean Stark reported that he regretted he could not see me, as he was particularly engaged ; and the next time I went he was profuse in apologies, stating that he had been in a chaos of books and manuscripts and clouds of dust, searching for a missing document of some importance. The confusion of this sort in which he lived was marvellous. After his death Mrs. Craig told me that the mass of letters and notes, many un-opened, to be gone over was bewildering. In the heterogeneous heap, too, stray pound notes and packages of small coin, in silver and copper, were so numerous as, when collected, to form a considerable sum. Some of the notes were between the leaves of books ; the parcels of coin had probably been handed to him as change, laid aside, and forgotten. The task of looking over lent books, and returning them to their owners, as far as these could be discovered, was also a heavy one.

During his last illness he sent for me, and I saw him several times. On the last occasion I remained only a few minutes, as he was extremely feeble ; yet in all his weakness his wonted courtesy prompted him, on my rising to leave, to deplore that, from inability to rise, or even to turn fully in bed, he was unable to ring, and that so I was left to show myself out. His youngest and only unmarried daughter, Emily, was with him at this time, and she promised to let me know if I, or any of our family, could be of any service. We did not therefore risk disturbing them by sending or calling often, and indeed, having had experience of his surprising recoveries from previous illnesses, we were not fully alive to the gravity of this one. Most unfortunately, two notes which Miss de Quincey posted to me failed, through being imperfectly addressed, to reach me in time. On the afternoon of the 8th December, 1859, a rumour reached me that De Quincey was dead, and I hastened to Lothian Street, in some hope, however faint, that rumour lied. " Is what I hear true ? " I said to the kind landlady, Mrs. Wilson, who opened the door. Without answering she ushered me at once into the chamber of death. On the simple uncurtained pallet, whence in that last interview he had smilingly, with all those delicately polite regrets, said goodbye, the tiny frame of this great dreamer lay stretched in his last long dreamless sleep. Attenuated to an extreme degree, the body looked infantile in size—a very slender stem for the shapely and massive head that crowned it. The face was little changed ; its delicate bloom indeed was gone, but the sweet expression lingered, and the finely-chiselled features were unaltered. I was profoundly impressed ;

the more so, perhaps, that, as it so happened, I had never seen a dead person since I was a child of seven years old. In the next room I found his tearful and agitated daughters—Mrs. Craig, who had arrived a day or two before, and Miss Emily. They spoke much of the patience and resignation with which he suffered ; of his gentleness and considerateness to the last. He grudged giving them the slightest trouble, even when he most required attendance. On one occasion when they were moving him in bed, and lifting his feet, he, using a grand generalisation in a spirit of the most profound humility, and snatching, as it were, at a sacred sanction for his exacting the care he needed, said, " Be gentle, be tender ; remember that those are the feet that Christ washed."

Ascertaining that there existed no adequate portrait of Mr. de Quincey in his later years, I suggested that a cast of his face should be taken. This was done by Mr. (now Sir) John Steell, R.S.A. ; and from this cast, aided by other materials, this eminent sculptor produced, in the shape of a noble marble bust, a permanent record of the strikingly intellectual and refined lineaments of " The English Opium-Eater."

APPENDIX A.

PAGE 124.—MRS. BAIRD SMITH with her daughters and Miss
de Quincey now live in London. To all the three daughters
no small share of their father's attractive intellectual qualities
descended ; to the eldest, perhaps, in somewhat fuller measure,
especially in so far as a certain fluent facility and felicity of
expression in talk and writing reflected, in a softer and
feminine fashion, the celerity of conception and copious stores
of reflection and information so notable in her father.

Mrs. Baird Smith's contributions to Mr. Page's Life * of her
father sufficiently indicate her fine literary faculty, and Miss
Emily, in the same pages, displays a like gift.

It may be permitted here to make some mention of the
services of Colonel Baird Smith ; service faithful unto death.
The brief record on his tomb in Calcutta Cathedral is as
follows :—

Colonel Richard Baird Smith, of the Bengal Engineers, Master
of the Calcutta Mint, C.B., and A.D.C. to the Queen, whose career,
crowded with brilliant service, cut short at its brightest, was
born at Lasswade on December 31, 1818. He went to India in
1836. Already distinguished in the two Sikh Wars, his conduct
on the outbreak of revolt in 1857 showed what a clear apprehension, a stout heart, and a hopeful spirit could effect with scanty
means in crushing disorder. Called to Delhi as chief engineer,
his bold and ready judgment, his weighty and tenacious counsels,
played a foremost part in securing the success of the siege and
England's supremacy. The gathered wisdom of many years spent
in administering the Irrigation of Upper India, trained him for his
crowning service—the survey of the great famine of 1861, the

---

* " Thomas de Quincey : his Life and Writings," by H. A. Page.
Two vols. London, 1877.

provision of relief, and the suggestions of safeguards against such calamities. Broken by accumulated labours, he died at sea, December 13, 1861, aged scarcely forty-three years. At Madras, where his Indian career began, his body awaits the resurrection.

There may be added, in correction of a misapprehension as to his share in the work at Delhi, the following from Colonel Malleson's " History of the Indian Mutiny of 1857."

"Major Baird Smith, an honour even to the corps of engineers . . . . was chief engineer of the army before Delhi, and brought to the performance of his duties the large mind, the profound knowledge, the prompt decision, which had characterised him in his civil work. Neither the shock and pain caused by a wound, nor the weakness and emaciation produced by a severe attack of camp scurvy, aggravated by diarrhœa, depressed his spirits or lessened his energies. Refusing to be placed on the sick list, though assured that mortification would be the result of a continued use of this wounded leg, *Baird Smith clung to the last to the performance of his duty.* The advice which he gave to General Wilson proved that never was his courage higher, never were the tone and temper of his mind more healthy, than when, bowed down by two diseases, and suffering acutely from his wound, he seemed a livid wreck of the man he once had been. It was to such a man that Wilson appealed. The answer was clear, emphatic, and decisive. Baird Smith was for action, for prompt and immediate action."

APPENDIX B.

Page 155.—His daughters were at this time in Ireland, and though very ill he was reluctant to hurry them home. His condition seemed so serious that I felt it a duty to force his hand so to speak, and of the results he gives the following account in a letter to Miss Florence :—

December 8, 1854. MY DEAREST FLORENCE,—This morning— viz., Monday, December 4—came into my hands your letter and Emily's appendix. I had, however, previously possessed myself of a pen, and was in visionary conceit tracing out, whilst yet unaware of any communication from Tipperary, that letter which now, three hours later, I am actually writing. The fact is, I am alarmed at the premature explosion of a train which I had laid on Saturday (December 2nd) for drawing your attention in a leisurely way to Mavis Bush. The match has ignited the train far sooner than I had counted on. And thus it is possible enough that you may be thrown into needless hurry. It had happened that on Saturday, the 2nd, Mr. Findlay called, as sometimes he is kind enough to do, and on my explaining the general course of my correspondence with you—viz., that I write a letter—parboil it, as you may say, *i.e.*, half-finish it, then order it, in the House of Commons phrase, " to lie on the table," during which repose several strata of other papers gather over it within a few days or hours, so that very soon it is "snowed up," and finally it withdraws into darkness. Hearing this, I say, Mr. Findlay kindly undertook to apprise you, or M. or E., how the matter stood, and that the time was drawing near when I should want various papers (now at Mavis Bush) for the fifth volume. This service I counted on his fulfilling about four or five days later. But behold! yesterday being Sunday, the very next succeeding day he called with a *Times* newspaper, and at the same time left a note informing me that he already *had* written—viz. not to any one of you three, but to Mr. Craig. I am anxious, therefore, as the train is actually fired, to intercept any evil consequences. I announce, therefore, that, if you could set off ten or eleven days from this, *i.e.*, about the 18th day of December, you will meet the most clamorous of my purposes. You see there are counter-perils to weigh off against the perils of procrastination. I declare it will be a lesson to me for the rest of my life not to hurry.

The *Times* contained a review of his works. A month after this he was again alarmingly ill—See Page, vol. ii. p. 94.

APPENDIX C.

Page 157.—There is a lapse here in my notes which may be appropriately supplied by a notice by De Quincey himself of one of his visits to my uncle's house. In a letter addressed to his daughters of date July 31, 1855, the following passage occurs :—

Last week, viz., on Thursday, the 26th of July, I dined by invitation with a small party—*men* only—at Mr. Ritchie's in George

Square. Mr. Ritchie and his family have been very kind in their attentions to me. But, to finish my story of the dinner-party,—on entering the drawing-room, inquiries buzzed about me as to your whereabouts and intentions with regard to the homeward route, &c. ; and upon my answering that I had reason to look for you (speaking nautically) "*in all August*" somebody said, "We understand, Mr. de Quincey, you are going to lose another of your daughters." This arose naturally out of a previous inquiry about M. and the chances of her coming over to England ; but it took me so far by surprise that I did not know how to treat it, for I was not certain as to F.'s own wishes on this point. However, I said, smiling, that such a rumour was certainly current. "Aye, but it's more than a rumour," said Mr. Russel, the editor of the *Scotsman;* and then it came out that on the morning of this very Thursday a son of Lord Dunfermline's, one of the Abercrombies who is now by accident on a visit to Edinburgh, had announced the news as highly probable. He is our British Minister at Turin ; and it had so happened, that when Colonel Baird Smith was studying the system of irrigation in the King of Sardinia's Continental dominions (Piedmont, &c.), he was invited to take up his quarters in the hotel of our English Legation, which he did, and thus became intimately acquainted with Sir Ralph, for I believe that this son of Lord D.'s is the one known as Sir Ralph A. So that here is at once an end to all further secrecy, it you had any wish for it. On this occasion, by the way, as previously at Mr. J. B.'s, I found all persons loud in the praise of Colonel Baird Smith.

Sir Ralph, it may be noted, was the only son of the first Lord Dunfermline (James Abercrombie, Speaker of the House of Commons) ; he succeeded his father as second Lord Dunfermline, and dying without male issue, with him the title became extinct.

DAYS AND NIGHTS WITH THOMAS DE QUINCEY.

By JAMES HOGG.

OUR FIRST INTERVIEW.

IT was in the spring of 1850, forty-five years ago, that I first made the acquaintance of De Quincey at Edinburgh; the same day on which he first met my father. It happened thus: At that time I was serving my apprenticeship as an editor on *The Weekly Instructor*. For four years I had been my father's associate in the management of that periodical—a task which gradually devolved on me entirely as regards the editorial work.

The magazine was for a time "composed" (to use the technical phrase) in one part of Edinburgh and printed off in another—at a suburb called Canonmills. There had been a serious break-down of machinery, which threatened to interfere with publication, and engineers were summoned to repair the accident.

I was in our office, near the college, when I was told that a gentleman waited to see me who had enquired earlier in the day where my father could be seen, and now returned with a message from him.

On going forward I saw De Quincey for the first time, but could not gather who the visitor was. He informed me, in a quiet, gentle way, that he had been to this

office in the forenoon, but on finding that my father had
gone to Canonmills, had walked down there.

He produced from one pocket of an " Inverness " cape
a small roll of manuscript, and from the other a little
brush with a handle. Opening the roll and carefully
brushing each sheet as he handed it to me, he added
that he proposed to contribute to *The Instructor*, and
had arranged concerning this manuscript. So saying,
he handed me the leaves of " The Sphinx's Riddle."
Then he produced from his waistcoat pocket a scrap of
paper on which my father had hastily pencilled an
instruction to hand Mr. de Quincey a sum named. I
instantly realised the position and the *status* of the new
contributor.

Seeing he looked tired, I invited him to walk in and
rest in an inner room beside my desk. There I at once
complied with his wishes as to money, and received him
with a sympathy and respect which I think won his
grateful regard. I did not need to be told anything
about " the English Opium-Eater."

In those days I was in the swim amongst a number
of enthusiastic collegians—young literary aspirants,
lawyers, and medicos—all pressing forward in various
walks of life.

Although these ardent spirits did not exactly realise
Sydney Smith's humorous description of the early
Edinburgh Reviewers, as "cultivating literature on a
little oatmeal" (a motto proposed and condemned
because it was too near the truth)—still, there was a
good deal of "plain living and high thinking" amongst
a group of young men who, later on, won both fame
and pudding.

We studied Dante and Goethe, talked Carlylese,
reviewed the reviewers, and were always ready for some

literary exploit—discussing, without hesitation, any subject under the sun, and appraising "celebrities" according to our own sweet fancy. Nothing came amiss. It was all very glowing and somewhat dogmatic, but with a fine flush of genuine enthusiasm and buoyancy which has made marks here and there over the world. I was thus well primed as to the famous "Confessions," and delighted to have an opportunity of chatting with their distinguished author.

De Quincey, as he rested, began to expatiate on the subject of the paper which he had just placed in my hands. "The Sphinx's Riddle," it will be remembered, he treats as a "double riddle," and in it are some of the most impassioned passages he ever wrote. For the moment, the ancient mystery on which his mind had been dwelling seemed to possess him. Time slipped away as he discoursed with fervour on the grandeur and gloom of that old-world story, and more than an hour elapsed before he arose, refreshed, to resume his homeward walk. We took to each other from that first moment of acquaintance.

PERSONAL CHARACTERISTICS.

I have often been asked, both orally and by letter, whether I could give anxious admirers some idea of De Quincey's most remarkable facial characteristics, and wherein lay the peculiar charm of his manner which common report has certainly not exaggerated.

This is an extremely difficult question to answer. I may say, however, that no one who has sat for hours close beside him, as I have so often done, could fail to be struck by the strange depth of the eye. It seemed fathomless. I have never observed this in so high a degree in any other person. Then there was the gentle, refined, fastidious manner, chording so well with the beautifully chiselled features. Lastly, there was the soft, rhythmic utterance, as if the procession of words had long been duly marshalled—all fit for duty. However fantastic the thought that was being expressed, the exquisite cadence lent a singular charm to the most grotesque idea.

De Quincey was a keen, omnivorous reader of the newspapers, and often dwelt upon reports of scenes, pathetic or brutal, which moved his pity or indignation. As he commented on such things the slight frame would quiver and the melodious voice would vibrate with a richer and more organ-like swell, often inexpressibly touching.

When in good "form" De Quincey had a recurring vein of exquisite jocularity; he was fond of a sort of refined "rigmarole."

I could generally foretell when he was about to indulge in this pastime. He would give himself a sharp pinch in the arm, as if he were an organist pulling out some stop. Things political in the newspaper, absurd police cases, whimsical wills, and such like material, he would take up and polish off in a bantering fashion.

De Quincey once suffered weeks of perfect agony as the result of his unfailing politeness. We are told that " the lofty Essex doffed his bonnet to the meanest apple-woman at her stall." In this same spirit De Quincey was always thoughtfully, studiously polite and kindly to every one ministering in the slightest degree to his wants. Miss Stark, the very tall and rather shy sister of his widowed landlady at Lothian Street, had never been able quite to throw off, even when she had arrived at mature years, an excessive nervousness of manner. She was greatly devoted to De Quincey, studying, to the best of her ability, all his little whims ; whilst he on his part did all in his power to mitigate the almost painful anxieties of his attendant. This led to the catastrophe.

Having rung the bell during his solitary dinner, he had in a dreamy mood been quite oblivious of the act, and inattentive to a gentle tap at the door. He had just taken up a morsel of potato when he observed the wistful face of Miss Stark in the doorway. She had feared some sudden indisposition. Startled at his own forgetfulness, unwilling alike to replace the food on his plate or keep his anxious attendant any longer waiting for orders, he bolted the potato. " Like the Spartan boy, I swallowed it," he told me afterwards.

The consequences were exceedingly painful. The potato was extremely hot, and the whole passage to the stomach was severely scalded. So acute was the pain that for weeks he dreaded the act of swallowing either food or drink. I was very apprehensive of some serious result, such as ulceration, and begged him to allow me to obtain medical advice. But no, this he would not permit. With a smile he again and again referred to " the Spartan boy," bore the brunt of his extreme politeness with the most exemplary patience, and gradually threw off the ill effects.

An amusing specimen of the interest De Quincey took in small people generally I once witnessed in these same lodgings. A handy little girl, niece, I believe, to the landlady, was accustomed to officiate in aid of Miss Stark, as it was observed that De Quincey liked the child. They called her Ellen at the place, but De Quincey discovered that she had been christened Helen.

One evening as she brought in tea in the twilight, De Quincey, who sat dreaming in the glow of the fire, suddenly opened his eyes, and thus solemnly addressed the little maid :

"My dear child, let no one on earth defraud you of your noble name. You bear one of the grandest names that woman *can* bear. You are not Ellen, but *H*elen. Think of your ancestress of Troy, and never allow any human being to call you other than Helen." With a strong aspiration of the " H " the oracle ceased.

The poor child nearly dropped her cups and saucers as she opened her eyes wide and stared fixedly during this strange admonition. Although tolerably well accustomed to Mr. de Quincey's ways, no doubt she went out and reported that the old gentleman had at last " gane clean daft."

Of all the subjects which exercised a permanent fascination over De Quincey, I would place first in order Thuggism in India and the Cagots of Spain and France. The Thugs gave rise to endless speculation. There was a good series once on the subject in one of the leading magazines (*Blackwood's*, I think) which afforded him material for ever-recurring study. The far-reaching power of this mysterious brotherhood, the swiftness and certainty of its operations, the strange gradations of official rank, and the curious disguises adopted—all these exercised an influence on his mind which seemed never to wane. Every authentic detail he examined with the closest attention.

In like manner the Cagots—the lepers of France and Spain—excited his deep pity. Many times he would draw word-pictures to me of the sad, touching scenes which must have been witnessed by half-scared worshippers—the wistful, wasting figures preparing to enter church by the Cagots' door, of which specimens are still to be found in the Pyrenean churches.*

Interwoven with these two subjects there arose sometimes, on the spur of the moment, wailing passages of almost unearthly beauty and pathos, unsurpassed by anything in the " Suspiria," and never reduced to writing by either of us. I can only now remember the weird power of these strange glimpses of his inner life, as the melodious voice of my companion seemed to lift me, by some magic, far away from the dimly-lit room to behold scenes which no Dante has ever described.

If only I had taken notes of some of these things when memory was green! Need I say that I regret such lost opportunities? Sometimes in the night-watches stray, fleeting memories drift across me, but I feel unable to catch the whole so as to present a faithful report.

However large the table might be at which De Quincey sat when at work, he invariably wrote at the very extremity of one corner if a square one, or as far as possible from the centre if of other shape. The remainder would be piled with manuscripts, newspapers, and books in admirable disorder. I suppose, like many literary men with their "papers," he had some secret arrangement in the way he put some of these things down. Any sudden attempt to move them in the least seemed to impart a little nervous shock to the owner.

At Lothian Street Miss Stark had to be very careful,

---

* I was forcibly reminded of these old conversations by a recent visit to that ancient and beautiful edifice—the Priory Church of Christ Church, near the New Forest. There we still see the Lepers' Chapel, and the orifice in the massive wall through which the officiating Priest conveyed the consecrated bread on a cleft stick to the poor sufferer in Pre-Reformation times—whose outstretched hand alone was visible to him.

when the time approached for a meal, to obtain special permission as to what she might touch out of the
queerly-assorted heap.

De Quincey would gaze with a sort of anxious, affectionate, almost frightened look upon his MS. treasures,
sometimes merging into a smile if I ventured on a jocular
remark about these valuables.   This would be followed
by a grave reminder that in order not to delay the press,
it was *absolutely* necessary (here a variety of amusing
contingencies would be stated) that any slip, or note, or
matter not yet forwarded to the printer, should be perfectly within reach of his hand at a single moment's
notice.   Perchance, if by any misfortune or error he had
to commence a laborious search for such " missing link,"
the effort might be too great for his strength, and in the
consequent reaction the manuscript or proof in hand
might be irretrievably injured.

However solemnly this might be delivered, he would
almost invariably look up with just the faintest smile
and twinkle of the eye, as much as to say, " Do you
really believe it all ? " or, " Will it not be all the same a
hundred years hence ? "

Another very grotesque thing was the famous *brush*,
often carried about in his pocket.   This was a most
important part of the literary equipment, nearly as much
so as the pen, ink, and paper.   It was an instrument
about ten inches long all told, the fine bristles about two
inches in length, and with a short handle.   In some
respects it seemed to fulfil the office of a fan with a lady.
In pauses of conversation he would solace himself by
taking a page of manuscript from the table and carefully
brushing it, holding the paper first one way, and then
the other.   After a thorough scrubbing in perhaps three
positions, the leaf was carefully replaced beside others,

with an air of satisfaction and an evident increase of serenity.

This process was generally gone through with every separate leaf of manuscript which he might happen to give me for the press. One by one they were taken up, put through the positions, and one by one committed to my hands, with a grave upward glance to see how I was getting on.

I used to be very patient, for it was all very amusing. He did not mind a bit my evident desire to have some sport about the practice.

Sometimes a page bearing a special smudge, or one showing an unusual amount of interlineation, seemed to require particular treatment. After it had received extra polish, and still remained in his grasp, the brush upraised for another flourish, I would suggest, "That one will do now." When this happened, he always gave in gently and in the most gracious manner, with a single final touch.

KANT AND HIS GARTER MACHINE.

During the progress of his works through the press, when the author was at Mavis Bush Cottage, I had to be a frequent visitor, either with proof-sheets, or on some matter connected with the enterprise.

After dining with the family, or going over press matters with De Quincey alone, he would often insist on walking with me from Lasswade to Edinburgh—a distance of some five or six miles. As we did not start, perhaps, until 11 P.M., or later, and walked at a slow, steady pace, it would often be nearly 1 o'clock A.M. before we reached the Newington toll-bar, which was our

N

general point of separation. De Quincey would then walk back alone. At first I felt anxious, fearing some danger might arise from these solitary rambles—perhaps a passing weakness which might make him succumb to cold, with no one at hand to assist. But when I found how greatly he enjoyed such excursions, and, moreover, was in the habit of taking them alone, I ceased to demur.

I may say that I had one faculty—I was a good listener. In these long, slow, swinging walks, sometimes by moonlight, sometimes by starlight, sometimes stumbling against each other in the blank darkness, I heard "all things in heaven and earth" passed in review.

One thing which often came up in these rambles was Kant and his apparatus in lieu of garters.

De Quincey, as is well known, was the first real English exponent of the Kantian philosophy, and he was well up in all the personal peculiarities of this singular being.

Kant, amongst other studies in the art of taking care of himself, avoided ordinary garters. He permitted no ligature to be placed on any part of his body, fearing to hinder in the slightest degree the circulation of the blood.

He found it necessary at the same time to keep up his stockings. Accordingly he had loops attached to them, and outside each hip he wore a contrivance which may be called a box windlass (as I understood it). These affairs somewhat resembled an angler's reel with a spring, which secured the line at any given point.

Behold Kant then expounding his philosophy to a select circle of disciples. Like the famous counsel who could not state his argument without twisting a bit of twine, Kant worked the windlasses as he talked. The idea of this grotesque practice so tickled De Quincey that he often dwelt on the odd sight which it must have been to observe the master "paying out the cable," or hauling in "the slack," by aid of this curious machinery.

I remember nothing which afforded De Quincey such frequent and intense amusement. The darker the night, I observed, the more surely did Kant and his garter-machine come above-aboard as we swung along.

After some quizzical remarks on German metaphysics generally, off went the quiet, melodious voice, with its clear, resonant *timbre*, into some queer byway of scholarship. There would be a flash of some long-forgotten spark of wit, some curious passage would be quoted, which the retentive memory had treasured for half a century, and Kant and his garters would be forgotten until next time.

OUR LANTERN.

This article to which my father alludes in his "Reminiscences" (Page's Life), was an amusing apparatus.

Near Mavis Bush there was a streamlet, some feeder or offshoot of the Esk. It lay on the route to Edinburgh, at a rather twistical sort of corner, the ground at that part being of an up and down character. On dark nights, with no glimmer of moon or star, it was easy enough for a pedestrian with all his wits about him to wander into this water and get an unpleasant wetting. This had happened to De Quincey on several occasions on his late and solitary peregrinations, and after much cogitation a "bull's eye" was procured. But this proved an irksome and faithless friend.

On the journeys when De Quincey accompanied me

to Newington toll-bar, we did not use it whilst together, joint wisdom being supposed equal to piloting us safely round the dangerous point.   The lantern was the reserve force for the homeward journey.   It was lit as we parted at the toll-house, and off De Quincey marched.

I could spy the beam of light, like some far-off glow-worm, as I looked backward on the long straight road. But that vile lantern *always* went out just as the traveller approached the trying spot.   After being carried for miles, it proved totally useless at " the supreme moment," as De Quincey put it.   I suggested a larger reservoir, a little more oil, etc., as a ready solution.   No ; he had got tired of such a worrying companion, and preferred to face the difficulty aided only by that natural instinct of which we are all supposed to possess some share, whether savage or civilized.

DE QUINCEY ON OPIUM.

As may be supposed, during those memorable years I listened to innumerable disquisitions on the power of the drug—its pleasures and its pains.   It seemed to be a mental relief to retrace in the hearing of a quiet, patient listener the far back steps, from the first moment of indulgence on to that later moment which gave rise to the sad exclamation, " Thrice I rose and thrice I fell ! "

He was never tired of declaring to me the opinion noted in the Collected Works, that the medical faculty would wake up at last to a sense of the beneficent power of opium in cases of incipient consumption, before the physical derangement has gone too far to be arrested. He dwelt continually on its sovereign power for maintaining *insensible perspiration*, so invaluable when premonitory symptoms give warning of phthisical danger.

During the rigour of the bitter Scottish winters I suffered a good deal in the chest. The keen, cutting east wind of Edinburgh exposed me to frequent and severe attacks of catarrh, so that for weeks I continued in a state of misery from this cause. De Quincey pitied me much, and as he took his own dose, liquid or solid, often told me that my enemy could be attacked and the discomfort speedily alleviated by some small doses.

I had, however, an invincible dread of the potent drug, and never once tasted it. Seeing my feeling about the matter, he ceased to offer any advice on the subject. I had to fight it out on the orthodox gruel principle. One distinguished old Edinburgh practitioner, then President of the College of Surgeons, whom my father consulted for my benefit, curtly and gruffly said, "Take his dinner off him!" Ever afterwards I looked on that man as a despot. I took the "grand cure" which so many Scotsmen find efficacious. I migrated southward, and left Edinburgh for London.

THE UNEDUCATED BUG.

One very droll thing rises to my memory which, I think, is too good to be lost. Over-sensitive people, like the spinster who desired to have the "legs" of a table called "limbs," are invited to skip this passage and imagine a blank space.

There is a certain unpleasant insect known to the British householder called—*a bug*. Once De Quincey spied one in his room, and it filled him with unspeakable alarm—so he said.

I was called upon once, twice, thrice, perhaps oftener, to consider seriously with him the terrible possibilities of the danger with which he was thus suddenly confronted. "The Vision of Sudden Death" in *The Mail-Coach,* or living in a Swiss village about to be buried by an avalanche—these and such like things were mere trifles, ordinary accidents of life, when compared with the new and awful calamity which threatened.

"Suppose," he said, "that this wretched insect has a companion, and that this companion, relative or otherwise, should, unknown to me, force its way to the canopy of my bed. And suppose that I may be asleep, and in an unguarded moment—a moment of dreams—I should suddenly open my mouth ever so little (which, by-the-way, is quite against my usual practice), and suppose that this poor foolish bug, whose education has most probably been grossly neglected by its parents, should at that instance of time be right overhead, and in a careless moment relax its hold and—*tumble!* Oh, horror, can you imagine anything more revolting ?"

This charming, impassioned picture, so powerfully drawn by the hand of a master, at first nearly sent me into a fit with laughter. I believe this was part of the effect which was intended to be produced, for he seemed to enjoy the merriment, recalling me quickly, however, to the extreme gravity of the case.

"Well," I said, "the thing of course is possible, and when I go home I shall get out De Moivre ' On Chances,' and work out the problem for you. Given one bug only, the chances are enormously in your favour. Of course, if there should be a procession of bugs out on their travels, like so many Canterbury pilgrims, I admit at once that the case would be very different indeed. It might become serious. However, let us hope that this fellow you saw was what the Germans call 'a wandering bird,' an adventurous traveller, perhaps. Or perhaps he may have been a pariah, an outcast from his fellows, and as such entitled to your profoundest sympathy and protection. Don't you think that is possible?"

He admitted that I had calmed his fears, and possibly things might not turn out so badly as at first sight appeared probable. For a few weeks we had an occasional debate on this interesting subject. It soon branched into a higher department—Buffon on the dreams of animals, or the nature and amount of education which the inferior animals (insects, birds, etc., everything in creation, in fact) bestow upon their offspring. It was a wide and fruitful topic for discussion which was thus started by the advent of the solitary and unwelcome traveller.

WHAT WOULD THE BAKER SAY?

When De Quincey was most depressed, there was one talisman I held by which, judiciously used, I could nearly always "lift" him. This was "The Baker" in the famous essay on "Murder Considered as One of the Fine Arts."

We had somehow gradually established a queer sort of freemasonry about this character. It is difficult to define it. Perhaps I may put it that we had elected to consider him a handy man at a pinch—a man quite free from shilly-shally—always decided in his views, and with a certain ready activity in asserting them.

When the fits of depression came on, and in cold weather they were often long and severe (De Quincey

sometimes said to me that he had never been thoroughly
warm all his life), I watched my chance.

When I saw that things were at the worst, when some
peculiarly moody, morbid observation showed the mental
tension and physical misery, I used to remark, rather
suddenly and shortly, " *What would the Baker say ?* "

The effect was perfectly magical.   The drooping head
was raised, the pallid face slowly wreathed into a half-
amused smile, which seemed to convey : " Well, that is
a good idea.   We have not yet considered what can be
said and what can be done from that point of view."   It
seemed to act as a mental tonic.   After a short pause
he would start some subject—something often which I
saw he expected would make me disputatious.   Gradually he warmed to it, and as I kept "the ball rolling "
by a few brisk rejoinders, or some fresh " feelers " which
were not difficult to find, away he went—full speed.

The original subject soon became two ; by-and-by it
branched and became half a dozen.   The torpor and
depression seemed to disappear as the active, awakened
brain found expression through the tongue, and in two
or three hours I would leave him quite a new man.   He
would afterward most gratefully acknowledge the benefit
which had accrued in this fashion.   On the next interview I would generally remark, " The Baker did you
good the other evening."   This received a cheerful assent, either in words or by a meaning smile.   I never
used the charm except when we were quite alone.   A
third person, I think, would have spoilt it.

PASSION FOR THE VIOLIN.

Whilst De Quincey, as his writings show, was profoundly impressed by the majesty and blare of the organ, his favourite instrument was the violin. Hundreds of times I must have heard him dwell with impassioned force upon the *capacity* of the violin as a musical instrument.

"There is an *infinity* about the violin," was his favourite expression on the subject.

On many occasions he delighted me with his recollections of famous performers who were only a name to me.

Mingled with the old London operatic memories, which always seems to afford him such intense pleasure, there appeared to stand out clearer than all else the recollection of the chief pieces played by every great violinist whom he had heard.

This passion for the violin led him on one occasion, and one only, so far as I can remember, to break through the rule he had laid down in these latter years of avoiding all public entertainments. Remenyi, the famous Hungarian violinist, came to Edinburgh to perform at the Theatre Royal. I had observed the announcement in the newspapers, but thought nothing of it, having previously heard the master in London. De Quincey observed to me one evening :

" Remenyi is coming. Did you ever hear him ? "

"Yes," I replied. " I think he is the greatest performer on the instrument I have ever heard."

Next day he again brought up the subject, so I hazarded the remark—

" Should you like to hear him ? "

" *Very much indeed,*" he answered, "if I could only go quietly, and without being troubled to see people."

" Oh, yes," I said ; " we shall get a quiet box, and you need not be bothered seeing anybody."

" If you *would* have the goodness I should be *so much obliged to you,*" was the grateful response.

I secured a box of which one side was well screened from the house, permitting at the same time a full view of the performer as he stood on the stage.

I never saw De Quincey exhibit such evidence of rapturous enjoyment as he did that evening. He lay back for a long time in the dark corner, as if in a trance. I took care not to disturb him either by speech or movement.

When the programme was far through and there was a short interval, a momentary curiosity to see the audience caused him to change chairs with me. In a few minutes, however, observing a row of glasses levelled at him (from the " press " box, I think), he beat a hasty retreat, and did not again venture to stir from the quiet corner in which I had at first installed him.

For weeks that performance was a source of ever-recurring pleasure. The exquisite nervous organization seemed to *feed* upon the recollection of the glorious sounds, and I was gratified by numerous critical comparisons with by-gone masters of his favourite instrument.

DE QUINCEY AS A PRACTICAL MAN.

During my editorship of *Titan*, to which he was a frequent contributor, De Quincey often astonished me by his shrewdness in the affairs of everyday life, and his keen sense of what would be popular in magazine management. That a man who was generally regarded at that time as a mere "dreamer of dreams" should see so clearly the practical chances of a given course, was a surprise. It may be puzzling also to many who have read Charles Knight's dashing account of the rather shiftless habits of De Quincey at an earlier day.

On any mere *literary* question there would, of course, have been no ground for anything but respect as to his judgment. But I here speak distinctly of the *business* aspect of matters. When he chose to take the trouble, he saw "farther into a millstone" than most people gave him credit for.

One piece of sound advice he sometimes gave me (would that I had taken it oftener!); it is embodied somewhere in his works: "Don't fire over the heads of this generation. That won't suit your purpose."

He was often my counsellor, particularly as regards articles which would run into a series. His ripe experience and sound judgment were often invaluable to me in such cases.

THE CARLYLES.

Many, many times De Quincey referred, with the most touching, almost tearful, earnestness, to Mrs. Carlyle and her kindly care of him during a severe illness. Mrs. Carlyle had nursed him, if I remember rightly, at their own home, and he ever afterward retained the most profound feeling of gratitude for her motherly kindness, combined with the highest possible opinion of her character and intellectual power. More than once, while dwelling upon her qualities of heart and head, he

exclaimed, " She was, indeed, the most angelic woman I
ever met upon this—God's earth ! "

Some little time before the fourteenth volume of the
books came out (the close of my father's series), I was
about to transfer myself to London.   De Quincey said :
" If ever you meet Carlyle, will you tell him from me—"
and he charged me with a solemn and moving message.
I dare only say that it referred to Mrs. Carlyle.

Years passed before I delivered what then had become
a message from the grave.

At intervals I had some correspondence of a cordial
character with Carlyle.   This originated when I had
begun to assume the active editorship of the *Instructor*
in order to assist my father.   A series of " Celebrities "
had been planned for the magazine, giving biographical
and critical sketches, accompanied by steel engravings,
which were executed by the late Frank Croll. ￼

For this series I desired a portrait and sketch of
Carlyle.   I communicated with him on the subject, and
asked whether he would sit for a photographic portrait.
In a serio-comical reply he growled about portraits
generally, and expressed a great disgust at sitting to
anybody, winding up, however, by saying that he would
do so if I wished.   Accordingly I arranged a sitting at
Mr. Mayall's, and a daguerreotype was taken which
satisfied Carlyle.

At a later date, after I had founded *London Society*
(which I edited for twenty years), I conceived the idea
of a certain series of articles, and laid the plan before
Carlyle, with an offer which he was pleased to say was
" an abundantly liberal one."   But although he liked the
notion of my series, he explained to me how the work
he had in hand precluded him from making the attempt,
as he felt his strength already severely taxed.

Time passed on. I had often thought of calling on my correspondent, but the pressure of my work had always thrown something in the way.

At length one forenoon in April, 1876, whilst making arrangements for a visit to Germany, I was passing down the Embankment, and suddenly paused, conscience-stricken. The thought struck me, " There is that message from De Quincey never delivered. If I do not make haste, I may never have the chance." I wheeled round, and made my way to Cheyne Row.

After sending in my name, I learned that Carlyle was at home. He sent down a message to let me know that he was dressing, and that if I could wait a little he would be glad to see me. By-and-by he appeared, apparently very nervous and feeble.

At first I let the conversation drift hither and thither, but gradually bent it to De Quincey and their old working days. By this time Carlyle had become animated, and seemed to gain nervous power. I then told him I had a message to him from an old friend now no more. I gave De Quincey's words as faithfully as I could.

As I spoke, Carlyle started, quivered, and the tears sprang to his eyes. It was some little time before the tremor ceased. Slowly, sadly, tenderly he murmured little ejaculatory recollections of those old days, and after the first thrill of emotion, it seemed to do him good.

We sat long, as he questioned me concerning De Quincey's latter years, when I had been so much with him. He seemed much pleased to learn about the signal success of the Collected Works.

By-and-by the card was brought in of a German professor from Breslau, who had previously forwarded an introduction from Ranke, the historian.

I rose to go, but Carlyle pressed me to stay, so we
were joined by the professor, a lively, genial German,
evidently well steeped in Carlyle's works.

The German had "battle on the brain." He was full
of the great Frederick's engagements. There was one
battle the strategy of which he was specially anxious to
discuss with Carlyle. On the subject coming up, Carlyle
pulled himself well together (considering the lassitude I
had so lately observed), and proceeded to illustrate the
matter with surprising vigour. He asked the professor
whether he had ever seen Arthur's Seat (the hill so
called) at Edinburgh. The professor had. So it was
worked in as a help in considering the German battle-
ground, which both appeared to know well.

After the professor's departure we had more talk.
Arthur's Seat had called up old Edinburgh days to us
both—Carlyle's residence at Comely Bank, etc. I
amused him by telling that when a boy I had often
gone with some companions to the hill-top about sunrise
on May-day to gather May dew. I suggested that we
should require to be fairly well paid to undertake such
a job now. To which he responded (hands crossed on
his staff as he sat beside me, with his feet on the fender),
with the deep " Ay, ay," which I found was his favourite
rejoinder.

These Edinburgh reminiscences recalled another
" mutual friend " and his own early days.

The late Rev. George Johnston, D.D., of Edinburgh,
was a distinguished minister of the United Presbyterian
Church. His first charge was at Ecclefechan, where he
became acquainted with Carlyle and his father, the
latter being, if I mistake not, a member of his congrega-
tion. When I left Edinburgh this old friend said to me,
" When you come across Carlyle, don't forget to tell him

that George Johnston, of Ecclefechan, desires to be kindly remembered." I did so, and this seemed to carry Carlyle back to the old Dumfries days,* concerning which he made some musing observations.

I was able to tell him how wildly enthusiastic a number of my fellow-students became (when I was at college at Edinburgh) concerning "Sartor Resartus" and "Murder Considered as one of the Fine Arts." The combination of Herr Teufelsdröckh and Toad-in-the-Hole seemed to tickle him.

There was some talk about the age of Ranke, which differed from that of Carlyle, I think, by a year or so. This led me to mention that I was about to start for Leipzig, in order to spend a week at the great Easter Fair, which annually brings together so many publishers and booksellers from all parts of Europe. Again Carlyle responded : " Ay, ay. We're a wandering people ; but it's good to go and see one's fellow-creatures."

This hit at "wandering people" was an allusion to our being brother Scotsmen.

I remember well the parting scene. Carlyle drew himself up to his full height and planted himself firmly on his feet as I prepared to leave. I said : " Now, my

* Dr. Johnston told me a characteristic anecdote of the elder Carlyle—his dogged determination, or obstinacy, whichever it may be called. He was once suffering from a serious illness which confined him to bed. He was a very troublesome patient both to his medical attendant and those who were nursing him. He constantly desired to get up, although warned that he would injure himself, perhaps seriously, by any such attempt. Nothing, however, would pacify him. One day he said, grimly, " I'll gar mysel' dae't " (I will force myself to do it). So, before he could be stopped, he flung himself out of bed and fell flat on the floor. After being picked up he managed to stagger a few steps about the room, and then allowed himself to be put to bed, and was rather more manageable afterwards.

wife has never seen you. Some day perhaps, when we are near this, you will allow me to bring her to have a little chat with you ? "

" Ay, ay," said Carlyle. " I am little able now, as you see, to meet people ; but "—and he smiled—" if she cares to see the old monster, why, come."

With a sort of presentiment, as we cordially shook hands, he said, " Farewell ! "   We never met again.

DE QUINCEY'S FEELING CONCERNING THACKERAY AND DICKENS.

I cannot more truly or effectively state the exact feeling of De Quincey concerning these two famous men than by telling the following story. It will dispose, once for all, of some loose, speculative writing which I have seen on the subject from the pens of those who had no opportunity of arriving at exact knowledge.

When Thackeray came to Edinburgh to lecture (I think it was the series on "The Four Georges") he expected to meet De Quincey, and looked forward to the event with great pleasure.

Mr. John Ritchie, the proprietor of *The Scotsman* (which may be called *The Times* of Scotland), was well acquainted with the De Quincey family, so also was Mr. Findlay, his nephew, the present proprietor.*

An invitation was sent to De Quincey, hoping he would join a dinner party at which the author of *Vanity Fair* was to be present, also some Edinburgh celebrities. To this a very courteous reply was received, declining in terms of studied politeness. I believe indisposition was

* See pp. 158-9.

the reason alleged, and that truly, for I remember De Quincey was not very well at the moment. Thackeray was greatly disappointed. He had counted on meeting the weird author of the "Confessions."

Mr. Ritchie made another kindly attempt to bring the two together. A second dinner party was put in motion, and Mr. Findlay called personally to urge De Quincey to favour them with his company. Whether he received some contingent promise in the matter, I forget.

It happened that on the very evening fixed for this second dinner party, of which I was then ignorant, I met De Quincey at Lothian Street, with a bunch of troublesome proof-sheets which we proceeded to examine together.

I suppose we had gone on some two hours working and talking when De Quincey fell into one of those dreamy pauses, with closed eyelids, which I never disturbed, knowing that he would soon tell me what had crossed his brain. By-and-by he looked up, and said : " Well, I suppose about this time they may, perhaps, be expecting me again at George Square."

I guessed the case in a moment. " What ! " I said, " is there another dinner party, and are you going to disappoint them again ? "

" Well, you see," he replied, rather apologetically, as if desirous to debate the case with me, " I have not been quite well, as you know ; and then my dress suit is not here ; it is lying at home " (Mavis Bush Cottage).

I thought it a great pity that Thackeray and De Quincey should fail to meet, so I did my best to induce him to go. "Come," I said, "what nonsense talking about dress suits ! You know very well they would be glad to have you in the jacket." By this I meant the huge warm flannel affair, built with a very high collar,

O

according to his own design, which constituted his
favourite working costume, and in which he was then
sitting. "But," I proceeded, more seriously, "your
ordinary walking dress is here, and George Square is
very near. There is a cab-stand outside. If you will
only dress in that " (pointing to a coat which lay on a
chair), " I will drive you round in a twinkling. You are
quite in time yet. Let the proofs wait."

For a moment I thought that he wavered, moved by
my earnestness. But the eyelids closed again, and
another dream-pause followed. I waited patiently, and
by-and-by he said : " No ; much as it troubles me to see
people, if it had been Dickens, now, I might have gone
—I should have gone ; but not Thackeray. There is a
benignity in everything that Dickens has done."

This was said with that quiet resolution which showed
me he had made up his mind. So I abandoned the
attempt, and we resumed our task at the proof-sheets.
This lasted until about midnight, and as all the household had gone to bed, De Quincey came with a candle
to assist me in gaining footing on the staircase leading
from the flat.

As I began to descend I could not resist having a
Parthian shot about the party. "Now," I said, "if you
had only done as you ought, you would have had dinner
by this time, and been digesting it over a good talk with
Thackeray."

He gave a little shrug, and made a droll little "*moue*,"
which seemed to convey, "Well, you're quite right ; I
know I am a very naughty boy."

I leave the incident without comment. The memorable words about the " benignity " of Dickens struck me
forcibly, and remain imprinted most distinctly on my
memory.

CHRISTOPHER NORTH.

Professor Wilson was one of the few whose society De Quincey enjoyed. Sometimes, when below par, he rather shrank from encountering the exuberant spirits of the leonine Kit North. However, he always spoke of him with a certain affectionate regard.

I have already referred in the notes on Carlyle to the series of biographical sketches carried on in the *Instructor*. My father and myself were anxious to have Professor Wilson included. De Quincey kindly promised to write the sketch, but for a long time the portrait was a difficulty.

Messrs. Ross & Thomson were the leading photographers in Edinburgh at that time, and again and again they held themselves in readiness to take the renowned Christopher. He always professed willingness, but the difficulty was to catch him, and then Ross & Thomson doubted whether they could get him to keep quiet long enough.

At last one fine day Frank Croll, who was to be the engraver, with a couple of "mutual friends," captured the professor, and landed him safely in Ross & Thomson's studio. By a little management they got him to keep steady, with his hand on his staff, for a short time, securing an admirable portrait. He was told so.

"Well, we'll see. Get one ready to-morrow, and when lecture is over I shall have a look at myself."

As good as his word, he came flying in next day to our office, which was nearly opposite the University.

"Where's that thing you've been taking of me?" he exclaimed to me.

I showed him the photograph, which he held out at arm's length.

"Ah, that's the fellow, is it! I shouldn't like to meet him on a dark night! *And what's more, I shouldn't like to buy a horse of him!*"

With this humorous criticism of his effigy, he laughed and departed, the staff swirling and the big shirt collar flapping.

This reminds me that pedestrians often thought it prudent to give him rather a "wide berth" as he crossed the North Bridge to his daily lecture. The whirl of the staff as he strode on, ejaculating portions of the coming discourse, might have sometimes been more than awkward.

One winter De Quincey was very poorly indeed, and opium, which generally brought relief in cold weather, failed to alleviate his unpleasant symptoms. A constant gnawing sensation was felt in the region of the stomach. I have no doubt this was a real sensation, induced by the long-continued use of the drug. At the same time remembering Dr. Copeland's remarkable article on the power of the mind in bringing on symptoms of disease, it is quite probable that the intensity of the suffering was increased by a remembrance of the dreadful passage in the original preface to the "Confessions," wherein he mentions that "Mr. Addington, an Under-Secretary of State and brother to the first Lord Sidmouth, described to me the sensations which first drove him to the use of opium in the very same words as the Dean of Carlisle, viz., 'that he felt as though rats were gnawing at the coats of his stomach.'"

De Quincey at length conjured up the idea that some living creature occupied the stomach, and on waking up at intervals, proceeded to gnaw the coats of it. He was in a very morbid mental condition, and the physical weakness was considerable.

We did all that we could to get him out of this sombre notion, which preyed greatly upon his mind, and for hours at a time paralysed all exertion.

One day, while in this state, De Quincey called upon Professor Wilson, who soon observed that he was in a very prostrate condition. De Quincey commenced with plaintive eloquence to tell him all about the doings of this horrid creature in his stomach ; that he was being consumed by inches ; was a doomed man, and so forth.

Christopher diagnosed the case at a glance. With great solemnity he said : "De Quincey, I am really surprised and shocked. You are generally the most considerate of mortals, but this is a case of downright cruelty to animals. You say he gnaws you. Why shouldn't he ? Feed him, man,—feed him, and he won't bother you. The poor fellow is hungry. Come, let us give him some hare soup at once." He rang the bell, ordered the soup, and compelled De Quincey to swallow it.

The professor's prescription was a capital tonic. The whole scene gave the poor patient a wholesome fillip. He began to regain his better health, the unpleasant symptoms gradually died away, and we heard no more of the creature in the stomach.

NATHANIEL HAWTHORNE.

Numerous pilgrims from America, when on the European tour, called at Mavis Bush Cottage. This being at no great distance from the classic spots of Hawthornden and Roslin Chapel (with its famous 'prentice's pillar), enabled them to kill three or four birds with one stone.

De Quincey appreciated highly the interest in himself

and his works which was evidenced by these calls. At
the same time they were a source of serious pain to him.
He was most carefully supported in every way by the
graceful, thoughtful hospitality which his daughters
exercised toward all these enthusiastic visitors, but the
strain of being called on to appear before strangers at
moments when he was either in need of physical repose
or desired perfect quiet in order to elaborate some
literary effort—all this was often very trying to him.

Another evil attendant on this strain, on which he
often comically commented to me, was that he had no
son at home who could drink wine with guests. Ladies,
of course, he remarked, could not be expected to be
proficients in this accomplishment, and as for himself,
when he made the attempt he was almost sure to be ill
afterwards.

The correspondence also from America—from warm
admirers of the author's works, entailed no small amount
of labour on the part of De Quincey's daughters in their
courteous attention to such epistles.

Amongst this correspondence nothing gave De
Quincey greater pleasure than the letters received from
Nathaniel Hawthorne. The two famous men had much
in common. De Quincey, on countless occasions, expressed to me his high opinion of Hawthorne as an
author, and the satisfaction he derived from the letters.
As usual, the correspondence was kept up by his family.
Whether De Quincey ever replied personally, I have
forgotten. Thinking over the singular interest attaching
to these letters I endeavoured, lately, to ascertain whether
any of them are in existence. On this point Mrs. Baird
Smith finds herself unable to help me. We fear that they
perished in a rather hurried "sorting," or rather burning
of papers which took place after De Quincey's decease.

CLARE MARKET.

Amongst the passages in which De Quincey has been supposed to be playfully "throwing the hatchet," "romancing," or whatever you may call a stretch of imagination concerning slender elements of fact, that which bears on Clare Market and his proffered assistance to poor people in their marketing is often supposed to be one. I firmly believe that it is a simple record of fact.

On many occasions he dilated to me concerning his mode of life and the incidents which befell him while residing at No. 4, York Street, Covent Garden, where he wrote the "Confessions."* He told me of his solitary walks at night, his studies of the working poor in and around Drury Lane and St. Giles's, and his close knowledge of the concentrated misery of these quarters of London.

What these places were then I learned from the sombre Rembrandtesque pictures which he drew of the life he had so closely studied. What it is still, after daylight has been driven into so many "rookeries," many of us know.

Clare Market was one of his favourite hunting-grounds. Sometimes, also, I think, but not so frequently, the region of the New Cut, at Lambeth.

His Saturday evening pilgrimages to Clare Market were frequent. He was a keen observer of human nature in the buying and selling which went on in that London hive, watching the investment of part of the hard-won wages on a Sunday dinner, that oasis in the life of the working man. His especial commiseration was excited by the poor, fragile, worn-down wives, often with a child

* The late Mr. H. G. Bohn showed me this room, which formed part of his warehouse. It was destroyed some time ago when certain structural changes were carried out by his successors, Messrs. George Bell & Sons.

in their arms and several at their feet. To such as these he would now and then, if he thought it would be useful, offer a kindly suggestion concerning a morsel of meat or a supply of vegetables to be purchased. Such suggestions he assured me were generally received by the feeble, hesitating, ignorant women with grateful thanks. They readily divined the good intention, the perfectly disinterested action, of their singular but gentlemanly adviser.

The Story of the "Confessions."

It was long before De Quincey could be induced by the persuasion of his family and his friends, combined with the united efforts of my father and myself, to " pull himself together" and encounter the task of revising his writings for the issue of a collected edition of his works from Edinburgh.

It certainly was what Abraham Lincoln would have called "a big job." His precarious health and periods of deep depression as well as the varied difficulties which cannot be explained shortly—all rendered it a matter of formidable labour and some perplexity. For a time these mixed considerations threatened to crush all hope of the enterprise. Gradually, however, the prospect cleared, and the material help afforded by the American edition at last led the way to a contract with us for the series of fourteen volumes which ultimately saw the light.

The first volume of "Selections, Grave and Gay" (Autobiographic Sketches), was far advanced—nearly the whole of it being printed off, when announcements heralding the series were inserted in the London papers.

Here commences a story which I now tell for the first time in print—as concisely and with as little egotism as the case permits. Being the only one of the chief actors now alive, it appears to me to have become my duty, as the survivor, to place the facts on record in this volume. For this purpose I put them circumstantially, adding the names of those immediately concerned. The struggle was notably an interesting episode in the history of the " Confessions "—it was practically the turning-point as to whether the public would ever obtain the author's revised edition of his works.

To proceed — no sooner had the advertisements appeared giving notice of De Quincey's intention than my father received a letter from the late Mr. John Taylor, then the surviving partner in the firm of Taylor & Hessey who were the proprietors of *The London Magazine* in which the "Confessions" originally appeared. In this letter Mr. Taylor claimed the absolute copyright of the "Confessions," and peremptorily forbade the use of them in any edition of the author's works.

This sudden unlooked-for embargo was a very serious affair. Mr. Taylor declined either to enter upon the grounds of his claim or to consider any possible arrangement in the matter.

De Quincey at first said, thoughtfully, but somewhat dubiously, that he had not parted with the " Confessions " in any formal manner. At the same time gravely and serenely, indeed half-humorously, he said, " Well, if the ' Confessions ' really are not mine, there is an end of everything. We cannot proceed without them ! " It seemed a happy deliverance from a great deal of laborious, tormenting work which he had faced with reluctance and would be glad to get rid of.

In the deadlock thus caused my father consulted his solicitor, but did not get much comfort there. The utmost that Mr. Taylor vouchsafed was this:—" I have the authority of two counsel of eminence for stating that the copyright of the ' Confessions ' is my property."

My father's solicitor advised, after consulting Scottish counsel, that, probably, De Quincey had forgotten some letter or document he had given in the course of the thirty years which had passed—that Mr. Taylor would most probably have some solid grounds for his claim, and that to risk a costly action under such hazy conditions and after such a lapse of time, was an affair too perilous to be risked.

It seemed a perfect *impasse.* The first volume was nearly ready—its date of publication had been announced. What was to be done ?

My father, of course, was greatly disturbed—De Quincey remained grave and silent.

At this crisis I said to both one day when the trouble was being discussed (I was young and " curly " then), " Will you let me handle this affair ? " Gladly, they responded, half-amused at my eagerness to rush into the fray. Then and there I stipulated for *a free hand* and got De Quincey's authority to act according to my discretion.

My secret feeling was that our worthy family solicitor, although a conveyancer of ability and repute, knew very little about copyright, and was rather frightened at " the authority of two counsel of eminence." Unfortunately I was not acquainted with any legal luminary of the Scottish capital likely to grapple with such an imbroglio satisfactorily.

My *first* step was to examine De Quincey, again and again, very carefully on the whole history of the "Confessions." At the start his mind was cloudy on some important points, but under my repeated, specific questionings, it gradually cleared. After four or five serious interviews he declared to me that he now firmly believed he had never made any assignment of the "Confessions." As to his long acquiescence in the reprint editions he could give no reason whatever. It appeared to be another instance of that inexplicable indifference to money matters of which several striking examples are given throughout the memories here drawn together.

All that had happened, I learned, beyond the original payment as ordinary magazine contributions, was the present of an amount sent by Mr. Taylor in some far back year—after the first reprint of the "Confessions" in volume form. De Quincey had neither authorized nor questioned the various reprints. He had simply lain dormant on the whole affair. The letter containing Mr. Taylor's present of £20 had been acknowledged, with his sanction, by some member of the family.

My *second* step was to read up the whole statute and "case" law bearing on copyright. I thought I saw where the strength and the weakness of our case would lie.

My good friend the late Samuel Halkett, keeper of the Advocates' Library, gave me the run of their shelves, and I busied myself for a week in the dim, silent recesses of the great library—taking a hard spell of legal study. I emerged from my seclusion with very decided views.

Although I foresaw the formidable difficulty created by De Quincey's strange neglect of his interests for the long period of thirty years, I arrived at the opinion, that the courts, even under such extraordinary circumstances, would not intervene to strip an author of his copyright

if he had not parted with it in writing. Mr. Taylor's
reticence, coupled with De Quincey's reviving firmness
of memory on the subject, led me to suppose that no
such cession of copyright had ever been made.

My *third* step was to look out for the most distinguished copyright specialist in the kingdom.

This appeared to be the late Mr. Serjeant Burke,
author of two excellent Manuals of copyright law.   Accordingly I drew a careful " case " and placed it in the
hands of our London agents, Messrs. Groombridge, to be
by them sent to their solicitor Mr. G. F. Shaw (then
editor of *The Bankers' Magazine*), in order that the
opinion of Mr. Serjeant Burke might be taken.   That
learned counsel at once took up the matter with great
zeal.   He sent on some queries for me to answer, and in
a few days thereafter I received an elaborate opinion
which took up every point of the case and discussed
it with scrupulous care ; summing up by an emphatic
support of my own judgment that we ought to win—bar
any unknown document which might be sprung.   Thus
fortified, I instantly took the *fourth* step.

Remembering the ancient friendship of De Quincey
and Messrs. Taylor and Hessey (which rendered the
curtness and singular form of this *caveat* all the more
remarkable) I challenged Mr. Taylor, quietly but firmly,
to an issue.

Frankly stating the nature of the legal opinion which
guided me, I gave him seven days to consider whether
he would withdraw a claim which he had refused to
explain.   If not, I warned him that an action would at
once follow—calling on him for " count and reckoning "
of all the profits accruing from every edition of the
" Confessions " which had been issued by him personally
or under his authority.   [This latter clause bore upon

editions which I found had appeared in "Smith's Standard Library" by Mr. Taylor's license.]

On the fifth day after despatching this *ultimatum* I received Mr. Taylor's brief reply. He remarked that De Quincey and himself were now old men. He had reconsidered the whole matter and withdrew all claim to the " Confessions."

I went straight to De Quincey with this letter. He read it slowly and carefully, then turned it face downwards on the table, and, looking at me with a smile, said :—" I have been watching with extreme interest the lawyer-like ability you have displayed in this complex matter. Pardon me for suggesting that you have mistaken your profession—you ought to have entered the world of the law ! "

So ended, happily, what at one moment seemed an almost insuperable obstacle. Even if litigation had in the course of time removed it, as I have no doubt it would, the great danger was that De Quincey's resolution would have been utterly dissipated by delay and the whole of the arrangements frustrated.

He buckled cheerfully and with fresh vigour to the work, and never again referred to the difficulty. Neither did I.

UNPUBLISHED LETTERS.

FACSIMILE OF LETTER IN DE QUINCEY'S HANDWRITING.

[This was written in 1858. The Title finally adopted for Volume X. of the Collected Works is :—" Classic Records Reviewed or Deciphered."]

The _Cæsars_. But last night the thought sud-
.denly occurred — that by combining with this
paper that upon _Oedipus_ together with that
upon _Ælius Lamia_ in Suetonius, this title

P. at once offers itself

       Classical Records
           Historic in Mythologic

Ancient Records — Legendary and Historic.

      Meantime on attempting to correct _The_
Cæsars, as you will see upon down the vol., I
find the usual bar to operations in the Amer: paper
Could you have had the book interleaved? In that case
I will outrun the Press in correcting. Ever y.

FACSIMILE OF LETTER IN DE QUINCEY'S HANDWRITING.

[This was written in 1859, the year in which De Quincey died. The Title finally adopted for the Eleventh Volume of the Collected Works is :—" Critical Suggestions on Style and Rhetoric."]

Milton : ———
Whately : ———
Coleridge ———
German Tales : } all as Prefatory Notes, or Memoranda

Y all ... within a single page, — the nature of the logic, in the suspended relation, — as practical parts of a whole — that is to ... would appear ... the ... But starting with a long ... of page occupied by 1 solitary element — this is not understood ... if ... & it be better to begin with a couple of short notes.

HUMOROUS LETTER CONCERNING
A PRESS "QUERY."

MY DEAR SIR,—I have just sent down to St. And. Sq. as accurate a reply to your Father's note as your impatient messenger would allow me time for. But for fear of accident through my hurry I send a more cautiously written answer—a sort of duply (tho' not entirely what your Scottish Law means by that term)— and, if need should be, will send a triply.

The name Æthon [Græcè Αἴθων] (as I *now* remember) occurs twice in Homer, once in the ' Iliad,' where it figures as the name of one amongst Hector's four horses. This Quadriga consisted of *Lamprus, Podargus,* our friend ÆTHON, and one beside, whose name has dropped out of my memory. Or possibly the horse might be up the spout, in which case Hector would drive a *Unicorn* (as in my youth people called such an arrangement)—two shaft horses, a *biga* in fact, and one leader. However it might be, I cannot recollect the fourth name. Could it be Δοββιν ?

Out of this Æthon I can make nothing at all relevant. But in the ' Odyssey ' there is another Æthon ; not a horse, but a man ; and by the same token a knave ; viz., the hero of the poem Ulysses ; a descendant of Sisyphus ; and he, like other knaves, being often in want of an *alias,* somewhere pretends that his name is *Æthon* —as, perhaps, it might be amongst his indorsements of bills. This, I conceive, is the man wanted ; and the motto will then be—

Αἴθωνα μεγάθυμον,
Æthon the magnanimous—

in the acc. as governed by some verb understood ; let us hope the verb *knout*, or cowhide.

The other motto should be

Antiquam exquirite matrem.
Searchingly examine your old foster-mother.

Ever yours,

T. DE Q.

Nov. 23.

HUMOROUS LETTER CONCERNING THE SUN'S "GIMLET EYE."

This letter, which has day and month but no year attached, was written in 1857. It came on De Quincey's recovery from an unusually severe attack of dyspepsia and depression. A few days before this date Miss Stark had rushed down from Lothian Street in great alarm to tell me she was sure he was very ill. He would take no food, would scarcely see her, and had ordered that no one should disturb him. I felt puzzled as to whether I should take up our good friend, Dr. Burn, with me at once or—wait. After conferring with my Father we concerted with Miss Stark that the light food which De Quincey liked best should be set down in his room without asking him for any instructions; that his condition should be carefully watched ; and that we should receive a message every morning and evening as to the patient's progress ; or at any moment if he seemed to become worse.

He got round slowly and then I sent some little inclosure about "press" matters, with a note inquiring whether he now felt well enough to see any one. Miss Stark had told me she had not been allowed to touch

P 2

the room for several days ; and I was not at all surprised
when I read the funny report in this letter which came
an hour or two after the delivery of mine.

Friday, March 27.

MY DEAR SIR,—On receiving the little paper containing the note of Wedn. it has occurred to me—since
you had a wish to communicate it to your Father—that
if you would take the trouble to return it to-morrow or
Mond., there can be no objection. I have therefore
inclosed it. I am sorry to give this trouble : but I have
a nervous feeling connected with obscure memoranda
lest some impertinent Layard or Lepsius should paste
them up in Nin. or Thebes and read them into dreadful
symbolic meanings.

N.B.—My demur to the introduction of any friend
into my room under its present chaotic disorder, so fear-
fully and circumstantially lighted up by the solar beams,
applies only to daylight ; for I recall to mind that the
sun in mid-heaven did once start back in horror with his
whole *quadriga* from the cannibal banquet of Thyestes
—doing no doubt "lots" of mischief; and he might
take the same crotchet into his head on peering with
his gimlet eye into my room. But at night gas or
tallow mounts guard, and a mould candle, for example,
has no right to such tragedy airs. So do not interrupt
your *evening* visits whenever circumstances allow you to
make them.

Ever yours,

THOMAS DE QUINCEY.

UNPUBLISHED LETTERS.

"CONFESSIONS" PERIOD.

[From the late Mr. S. J. Davey, the Autograph Collector, of Great Russell Street, through whose hands the original letters passed.]

(No. 33.)   THOMAS DE QUINCEY.

A most interesting series of 6 A. L. S.,* addressed to his friend Hessey, referring to his work on the pleasures and pains of opium. In one of the letters, dated Sep. 1822, De Quincey says : " . . . Here is my case. I am now in my 12th week of a conclusive experiment on the possib. of leaving off opium. 12th, I say, for so I think. At any rate I began on June 24th. Since then my hist. is briefly this. About the 34th day I think I had actually accomplished the end ; for 90 hours [*i.e.* more ½ a week] I had done without a drop ; suffered much ; having demonstrated the possib., I allowed myself a little, then again abstained ; again indulged ; and so on ; letting down (from 50—200 drops my ordinary dose), to about 40 as a maximum for comfort, tho' without losing my station I sometimes ran up the ladder far higher for a day. So far well ; nothing worse than pain. About the 42nd day came on a sudden distention of the stomach ; violent biliousness ; rheumatic pains ; then pains resembling internal rheumatism—and many other evils ; but all trifles compared with the unspeakable, overwhelming, unutterable misery of mind which came on in one couple of days, and has continued almost unabatingly ever since. Tho' suff. pain I was in higher spirits on the 40th day than for many years back ; some sudden revolution in my bodily condit., at which I can hardly guess, has brought me into a state in which I

* Autograph Letters signed.

feel at times the wretchedness of a lunatic. . . ." The other letters in the series, chiefly 4to., contain interesting references to the progress of his Confessions, and also a reference to some drugs he urgently requires, &c. [The extract closes at this point.]

(No. 4045.)   THOMAS DE QUINCEY.

A. L. S. 1 p. 4to. *Complete with address and seal to Hessey.* . . . " I have exerted myself as much as I possibly could, and without any intermission. But on Friday night, from the insufferable heat, increased by a fire which I was under the necessity of keeping in all night, I flung off the bedclothes in my sleep, and rose with a sore throat, which towards evening increased into a fever, and, though I am now again better, yet from the oppression of my spirits I could not work so fast ; and the dose failing, the different parts I had prepared into each other obliged me to many alterations that some parts are still to be written again. . . . The truth is, I am often obliged to compose the whole almost in my mind before I can write a line, . . ." &c.

POOR ANN !

GENERAL HAMLEY'S JEU D'ESPRIT AND DE MUSSET'S FRENCH VERSION.

Two attempts have been made in different ways by writers of very different character in connection with the " Confessions."

Alfred de Musset's rare French translation of the Opium-Eater and his singular interpolation concerning the touching episode of poor Ann of Oxford Street, have been treated with great discrimination and just strictures by Dr. Garnett in the *Parchment Library* edition, and the text of the French original there given.

The other case is the parody entitled "A RECENT CONFESSION OF AN OPIUM-EATER," published in *Blackwood's Magazine* for December 1856 (vol. lxxx., p. 629). It now appears that this was from the pen of the late General E. B. Hamley.

The story opens in a squalid chamber—a garret in the Old Town of Edinburgh, to which a dreamy Opium-Eater has been decoyed by a couple of "body-snatchers," that he might there be "Burked." The two chief characters are "Long-nosed Bill" and "Squabby." They have a faded female confederate called Catherine. Hard drinking begins, pressed on by these worthies—unlimited port wine at first, to which, by and by, a bottle of laudanum is added. The visitor obtains a glimpse of a handy chamber containing a bed and a sack. The bed has mattresses and apparatus for smothering purposes, and the intended victim awakes to the fact that they mean to "hocuss" him, and so procure a subject for their medical employers. Being a seasoned toper, he is on the alert —manages an exchange of glasses and liquids, and so reduces his hosts to insensibility by an opiate drench. In his dazed condition the visitor dreams that he is laid on a bier, and that all the mighty surgeons and physicians whom the world ever saw come to dissect him.

The dream over, he finds his companions still prostrate, and he considers it time to be stirring before they recover. After swallowing the remainder of the laudanum as a parting treat, he stumbles down stairs with the candle. This falls from the bottle in which it had been stuck, and sets fire to some straw. He escapes—the flames crackle joyously until the walls crumble and sink, burying in their ruins the ashes of the body-snatchers.

In spite of some passages which have a spice of humour, the story on the whole will appear to most readers a somewhat coarse and feeble travesty of one of "the world's classics."

Perhaps nothing of its kind, in all literature, is more remarkable for simple pathos and delicate treatment than DE QUINCEY'S record of "his Pariah-Saint, poor Ann of Oxford Street." The ill-judged mockery which underlies the clumsy, jejune passage on "Catherine" in the parody is "worse than a crime, it is a blunder." As Charlotte Brontë said of certain French novels, "it leaves a bad taste in the mouth."

In fact, the whole of this affair is a deplorable mistake—an inconsiderate notion carried out by a writer who had little or no capacity of the kind required to save the rash enterprise from condemnation. The biographer ("Life," by A. Innes Shand, vol. i., p. 105—published in 1895) prints a note in which Hamley writes airily about "*catching the old gent's style.*" This is sufficiently grotesque when we remember the majesty of the Master's style which has to be caught, and examine, by the light of to-day, the wooden performance of this would-be follower. It is like a child trying to catch a rainbow. It may be that, at the time of publication, some people shared the admiration now expressed by General Hamley's biographer or this unfortunate story. But—if they did—it is one of those judgments which get knocked to pieces by the wind and weather of forty years.

—J. H.

A DAUGHTER'S MEMORIES.

[Amongst the various interesting passages contributed by Mrs.
Baird Smith to Dr. Japp's Life the following bears directly on the
purpose of this volume.]

"Excepting now and again from the necessities of
business, he was a man so essentially sociable that he
was never separated from his family, sharing so intimately all their joys and sorrows that I never remember
him absent from any event, whether small or great, and
I cannot point to the time when he was not in constant
habits of association with some good and true friend,
with whom intercourse was both delightful to him and
profitable.

"His work was always an extreme labour and difficulty to him, and could only be carried on under very
special conditions. His best chance of accomplishing
anything was from about nine or ten o'clock in the
evening till about four to six o'clock in the morning.
And his most deadly certainty of failure was the touching of anything in the nature of wine or spirits. There
were wife and children running through much of his life ;
the wife and the oldest son, even in the most depressed
period of the Edinburgh life, sufficient companions even
for a mind such as his, and, as said already, a friend to
drop in of an evening, or to walk with. Even during
the long night-watches, at the period I specially speak
of, my mother was with him much of the time ; and with

many children at hand, there was too often a restless or
fretful child to be the delighted companion of his solitude, had he been in danger of having too much of it.
A certain amount of perfect quiet, though not necessarily
of solitude, was indeed essential to him for the shaping
of his work ; but from the time when I first became
aware of him helping my mother, wearied by a long
journey, to superintend the behaviour of the children at
the dinner-table, examining each little scaramouch to
see that it had not effected an entrance with unwashed
hands, I can vouch that he was a constant presence
among us ; my mother carefully training us to respect
his busy times. After her death, indeed, things went
very ill with him and with us too for a time. But there
was rarely a day I did not spend with him from early
till late, often too late for so young a girl ; and when I
was not by any chance with him, some of my brothers
were. You may smile at the notion of a child being a
companion for such a man, but none the less so it was
then and always.

" But his children were not his only companions. Such
was his exceeding fascination for all sorts and conditions
of men that he invariably attracted a circle around
him, oddly enough composed at times, and this constantly increasing in its demands upon his time and
sympathy, and occasionally becoming such a devouring
pest that he, who could never resist even the most
outrageous claims upon him, had no refuge but in
flight !

" Indeed this too great companionableness, this over-
popularity, was the real occasion of his few changes
rather than any money embarrassments, which, with
growing experience, and the occasional overhauling of
his affairs by skilful friends, we had come to regard with

much equanimity as mainly the figments of his own imagination, and never more than a few days' steady work would clear off.

"Something must also be allowed for his great power of expounding his sufferings, whether mental or bodily ; a power which of itself, it seems to me, removes him from that extreme of loneliness which has no such outlet ; and it is very possible that a matter-of-fact person might mistake a powerful wail over ' a common heritage of woe ' for a complaint of personal isolation, leading to a weird impression of loneliness. Some basis for such an impression might be found in utterances like these, but in my idea they referred more to the inevitable loneliness of the human spirit than to any social failure either in himself or in the loving companionship which ran through much of his life."

RECOLLECTIONS.

BY THE REV. FRANCIS JACOX.

"IT was on the 13th of July, 1852, that I saw Mr. de Quincey for the first time ; but the welcome he gave me at this first meeting was that of an old friend.

"He showed interest in learning from how early a date my interest in him had been cherished. It must have been in the first year of my teens that I became acquainted with his name, as a youthful prodigy in Greek, whose feats of scholarship were commemorated to a class of very different scholars, in Kensington Grammar School, by the head-master, (in my time) the Rev. W. H. Whitworth. For particulars we were referred to the 'Confessions of an English Opium-Eater' ; and that author's consummate mastery of the English language, especially in the range of impassioned prose, was impressed upon us with admiring sympathy. It was not my good fortune to lay hands on the memorable volume until my school career was ending or ended ; but when I did there were mingled with the reading grateful memories of the man who commended its writer, and of the manner of the commendation. Between that time, however, and the period of my summer visit to Mavis Bush, Lasswade, my appetite for the author's *opera omnia* had been constantly growing by what it fed on ; and when, a year or two before my becoming his guest, he had forwarded to me a list of his remembered and recognised contributions to

periodical literature, with a view to collect and reprint
them, or at least a selection from them, requesting me at
the same time to make any additions to the list, if, from
internal evidence, I could,—it was in my power to more
than double the total. Many of the best and most
characteristic of his anonymous essays he had clean forgotten, but there was no mistaking his sign-manual ; and
he was amusedly surprised at the voluminous expanse of
his authorship.

"And now I was seated beside the author himself, a
listener to the dulcet tones of that earnest but softly
subdued voice, often tremulous with emphasis, and most
musical when most melancholy. Gladly and gratefully
would I have compounded for listening only. But Mr.
de Quincey * was himself jealous of his rights as a
listener too, even where, as in my case, those rights might
have been absolutely renounced to our common advantage. Nothing could better manifest the innate courtesy,
the even sensitive considerateness of the man, than his
conduct in this respect. A master of the art of conversation, this he is on all sides known to have been ; but I
do not remember to have seen justice done to his surpassing attainments as a good listener. He was always
for giving way ; scrupulously on the watch for any, the
slightest, token of interruption, objection, comment,
assent, question, or answer, nothing could exceed the
tone of unaffected deference with which he gave heed as
well as ear to whatever his companion might have to say.

* " His name I write with a small *d* in the *de*, as he wrote it
himself. He would not have wished it indexed among the D's,
but the Q's. With all his sincere and pronounced regard for and
admiration of Sara (Mrs. Henry Nelson) Coleridge, he would have
entirely declined to countenance her uniform style of writing and
printing him, all in one word, or at one fell swoop, ' Mr.
Dequincey.' "

Whether his talk was equal to that of Coleridge, or even was superior to it, may be a question that very few survivors now are competent to decide, or so much as to discuss. But if Madame de Staël was right in characterising S. T. C. as 'de monologue,' and so in implying his incapacity to listen patiently, his monopoly of the prerogative and privileges of harangue, then was Mr. de Quincey the flat opposite of that older 'old man eloquent' in this defect or effect, or, as Polonius might word it, effect defective.

" The same inborn and inbred spirit of benignant courtesy was perpetually cropping up in other ways—byways some of them, but leading to the same conclusion. His manner to his three daughters, for instance, was the perfection of chivalric respect as well as affection. Very noticeable was his unfailing habit of turning courteously to them and explaining, in his own choicely finished and graphic diction, any casually employed term from the ' dead languages,' which presumably might lie outside the pale of ladies' lore. When I chanced, at dinner that day, to recall the pronounced preference of his sometime friend and almost neighbour, the self-styled Robert the Rhymer who lived at the Lakes,—' But gooseberry-pie is best,'—at once the father turned to the daughters to remind them that Southey was here pleasantly parodying a line of Pindar's, which might furnish water-drinkers with a plea for all occasions, and Temperance Societies with a motto for all time.

" While sitting with him alone after dinner, he gave me an account of the lets and hindrances which impeded his design of republishing select volumes of his miscellaneous works—a design which was mainly strengthened and justified by the success of the American edition, published by Messrs. Ticknor & Fields, eight volumes of

which he showed me with obvious gratification, qualified
though it might be by his too conscious exclusion from
actual editorial supervision.   Grateful he nevertheless
was to the enterprising Boston firm for collecting what
he had hitherto lacked energy to collect.   ' I must explain
to you,' he said, 'that I have suffered for the last ten
years and more from a most dreadful ailment, to an
extent of which I never heard in any other instance '—a
stagnation of blood in the legs, resulting in an effect upon
the system of 'intense, intolerable torpor,' during which
it was impossible to hold, or at any rate to guide, a pen ;
the torpor being, however, compatible with a 'frightful
recurrence of long-ago imagery and veriest trifles of the
past.' The tendency to sleep was irresistible, but the
waking sensations made up a crisis of torture.   Relief he
found, but slight relief only, in walking from six to seven
miles on an average daily.   But then the weariness of
having to walk so far for a relief so slight ! So many
literary schemes he had in contemplation—an elaborate
history, and a historical novel among the number—some
of which, if not all of which, he would fain finish before
he died.   Yet of these not one was so much as begun.
Could he but begin at once !   Referring to Wordsworth's
happy immunity from distracting anxieties and carking
cares, his lettered ease and tranquil surroundings, Mr. de
Quincey exclaimed, 'Heavens ! had I but ever had his
robust strength, and healthy stomach, and sound nerves,
with the same glorious freedom from all interruptions and
embarrassment ! . . . But, in point of fact, never have I
written but against time, pressed by overbearing anxieties,
and latterly more especially pressed down by physical
suffering.'   For the last six months he had reverted to
the use of opium in small doses ; but any mitigation of
his malady it might afford was avowedly counterbalanced

by the specific suffering that it in turn inflicted. As to the suggested employment of an amanuensis, he replied that he never could dictate, and that his suffering would be increased by the sense of implicating another in the imbroglio of his nervous vacillations.

"Of current literature, and of men of letters past and present, he talked on that day, and on subsequent ones, with freedom and vivacity. With interest he heard that Professor Wilson, ailing as he was, had been driven into Edinburgh expressly to record his vote for Macaulay; and much he had to tell me of Christopher North and his ways, and of their joint association with the Lakes and with *Blackwood*. One grievance, however, against his old comrade-in-arms—for that magazine was politically a militant one—was the trick he had of spoiling a story in the telling. For example, 'when I had lodgings over Waterloo Bridge, near the Surrey Theatre, in 1814, every night towards twelve o'clock a terrific din was caused in and around the playhouse by the explosion scene in a piece that involved the burning of the Kremlin; regularly, to a minute, that explosion awoke a contiguous cock; this cock, in full crow, awoke another; the second cock a third, and the definite three an indefinite chorus, or antiphony, of others; which chorus, again, awoke and provoked a corresponding series of dogs; and so on with other clamorous voices in succession—gradually swelling the aggregate of tumultuous forces. Now, when Professor Wilson, who found my story of the midnight din amusing, retold it in his own vigorous but inaccurate fashion, he spoilt the effect by making the uproar synchronous, instead of gradually successive.' John Galt was another of the *Blackwood* staff discussed, and my host spoke with lively appreciation of the 'Annals of the Parish,' the peculiar interest of which he ascribed to the character of the narrator, as in Goldsmith's ' Vicar of Wakefield,' where we are entertained by Dr. Primrose's shrewd insight into his wife's weak points, while he seems to have no inkling of his own absurdities in the polemics of deuterogamy. Of another contributor, the late R. P. Gillies, he spoke with wistful regret, feelingly deploring the straits and shifts to which that ill-starred scholar had been reduced. This, probably, may have been the friend who wrote from the precincts of Holyrood to Mr. de Quincey, to announce his enforced sojourn in that sanctuary, and to whom the reply came, in a style that savours of Charles Lamb, ' I will be with you on Monday, D.V.; but on Tuesday, D.V. or not.' Of Sir William Hamilton much was said, and the strain then heard was in a higher mood. But his friend and critic deemed him less subtle than Ferrier, though more comprehensive, and took exception to his 'unnecessary display of erudite quotations' all to back up a truism. Dr. Chalmers came in for a word of admiration, on the score of his broad spirit of liberality, and his tolerance of that German theology which, said Mr. de Quincey, 'I studied at my peril thirty or forty years ago.' Admiration was expressed, too, for the 'Christian Year.' Isaac Taylor's works had been read, but without much sense of a remunerative return. 'It is one of the afflictions of life' (said he, with a gentle smile), 'that one must read thousands of books only to discover that one need not have read them.'

"Of Talfourd, Mr. de Quincey spoke with evident regard, but thought his 'Ion' considerably overrated. He was emphatic in praise of Harriet Lee's 'The German's Tale,' as being almost unequalled in narrative skill, so artistic is the arrangement of the story, and so exquisite the delineation of Josephine's character. 'I had believed Miss Lee to have been dead long since, or I should certainly have called upon her in Bath, to offer her my personal respects and to express my gratification at her intellectual prowess.' As, to his own regret, he had assumed Miss Lee to be dead, equally so, in another case, he had assumed Mr. Gillman to be alive when the review of the 'Life of Coleridge' was contributed to *Blackwood*. 'Lockhart wrote to Wilson, "What does De Quincey mean by attacking in that sort of way a man in his grave?" Now this, when told me, was the first intimation I had of Mr. Gillman's death.'

" He owned to a decided disrelish for Miss Edgeworth's novels, assuming, as they seem to do, the existence of no higher virtues than prudence, discretion, and the like sober sisterhood. Both her and Lady Morgan he reckoned inferior in racy Irish portraiture to Maturin (the 'Wild Irish Boy'). Dickens he complained of as repeating himself in 'Bleak House,' then in course of publication ; and a heavier cause of complaint lay in the popular author's dead set against the 'upper classes,' as such, and his glorification at their expense of the idealised working-man. But Dickens he unhesitatingly preferred, because of his genial humanity, to Thackeray, whom I in vain tried to vindicate from the charge of a prevailing 'spirit of caustic cynicism.' Mr. de Quincey appeared to regard as simply a crotchety illusion or a blind partiality my remonstrances in favour of the author of 'Pendennis,' when for him I claimed the merit of supreme tenderness and benignity of heart, as well as sarcasm in its severest and irony in its most subtle forms. It has always been a puzzle to me how such a gracious nature, so delicately responsive to every fine touch, so acutely predisposed to the appeals of genuine pathos,

Q

should have missed the force and beauty of what is tender in Thackeray.

"I have a note of a sauntering to and fro with Mr. de Quincey in his garden on the forenoon of the 22nd, when more than once he was asked for alms by some passing mendicant, and each time with success. There was something at once deprecating and deferential in the tones with which he accosted the applicants severally, whether men or women, as though he were in fear of hurting their feelings by putting them under an obligation. It was the same when, in my walks with him along the country roads, he was similarly beset. In every case he gave at once, and without inquiry or inspection. He had in former years been shocked by the vehemence with which Edward Irving, as they were walking together in London by night, upon one occasion repelled and reproached a street-beggar. He would probably have owned to being equally shocked by Archbishop Whately's sternly systematic repression of any weakness for such casual relief. But with Whately he would have had very little in common.

"During the days that I was his guest I could not but take note of the vicissitudes of temperament and spirits to which he was subject. For some time in the morning of each day he appeared to be grievously depressed and prostrate; the drowsy torpor of which he complained so keenly was then in fullest possession of him, and futile were all endeavours to rouse or to interest him until that tyranny was overpast. Sometimes it extended farther on into the day ; and more than once, when there were visitors at his table, he appeared to be utterly baffled in every effort he made to shake off that oppressive lethargy, as certainly the most persistent and adventurous of those visitors were baffled in their endeavours to cheer him up and to draw him out. In fact, had I seen him, at this period of life, only in company, I should not have seen him at all. It was when alone with him that I learnt to know him. A walk in the fresh air would by degrees revive him ; but nothing seemed to be nearly so effectual to refresh and re-invigorate him, no spell so potent to disperse his languor, as a cup of good coffee. I have seen it act upon him like a charm, bracing. up his energies, clearing up his prospects, accelerating his speech as well as the march of his ideas, and inspiring him with a new fund of that eloquence which held the listener rapt, yet swayed him to and fro at his own sweet will. The eye that had been so heavy, so clouded, so filmy, so all but closed—the eye that had looked so void of life and significance, that had no speculation in it, nothing but a weary look of uttermost lassitude and dejection—now kindled with lambent fire, sparkled with generous animation, twinkled with quiet fun. The attenuated frame seemed to expand, and the face, if still pallid, revealed new capacities of spiritual expression, the most noteworthy a dreamy far-off look, as though holding communion with mysteries beyond our ken, with realities behind the veil.

"In his hours of languishing, when 'drooping woful wan, like one forlorn,' his utterance reminded me of Wordsworth's lines :—

    ' His words came feebly, from a feeble chest,
      But each in solemn order followed each,
      With something of a lofty utterance drest—
      Choice words and measured phrase, above the reach
      Of ordinary men ; a stately speech.'

"Music he spoke of as a 'necessity' to his daily life. If ever again he visited London, it was his hope to frequent the opera, though as to the theatres he felt no kind of attraction in anything *they* could promise him. The idea of seeing 'Lear' on the stage, environed by the surroundings of mere pleasure-seekers and frivolous play-goers, seemed to him profanity outright. He adverted, however, with cordial admiration to the 'Antigone' of Miss Helen Faucit, of whom, and of her distinguished husband (Sir Theodore Martin), he spoke in terms of personal regard. The latter he had recently met, I think he said at Mrs. Crowe's, one of the most intimate, at this time, of his literary friends in Edinburgh. To Mrs. Henry Siddons, too, as a graceful, aerial actress, he referred in terms of lively appreciation. Fond as he was of music, he was not often in the room while the two younger of his daughters played or sang during my stay; but he was a good listener, for all that, in his 'den' downstairs, and would comment on his favourites among their pieces when he rejoined us. Devout was his reference for Beethoven, who alone, I used to think, was capable, among the great composers, of setting his dream fugues to music, or of interpreting their hidden mysteries and complex transitions in strains of some choral symphony. Mendelssohn he had not as yet come really to admire; not even the 'Songs without Words' seemed to speak home to his heart of heart; and alike to 'May-bells' and 'Oh, wert thou in the cauld blast,' warbled by sweet sister voices, he could listen without a thrill. Bellini was so far a favourite with him that he often asked his daughters Florence and Emily to give him the well-worn 'Deh Conte;' nor would he tire of gems from the 'Don Giovanni,' or of 'Questo Semplice,' or of such time-tried strains as 'Time hath not thinned,' 'O lovely peace,' 'In chaste Susanna's praise,' 'Down the dark waters,' 'By limpid streams,' 'And will he not come again,' 'Birds blithely singing,'

&c. He exulted in the fervour of expression and the musician-like touch and facility of execution with which his youngest daughter, still under professional instruction, rendered Beethoven's 'Sonata Pathetica,' Weber's 'Invitation,' and Pergolesi's 'Gloria in Excelsis.' When he had written to invite me to visit him, he had promised me, if I liked such things, music and laughter in abundance, on the part of his three daughters. And well was the promise kept. Yet did he not promise me two things—music *and* laughter? In effect I found it to be all one, for the laughter itself was music.

"His eldest daughter's delicate health was at this period a matter of grave anxiety to him ; and the doctor's report of organic mischief in progress at the lungs overwhelmed him with solicitude and misgivings. She kept house for him, and he expressed to me, with the most charming *naïveté* and innocent candour, his supreme amazement at the economical tact with which, while exercising all the year round a quiet system of modest hospitality, she contrived to make both ends meet. Comfortable as she made his home, and happy as she and her two sisters made himself, he yet lamented piteously the inroads on his time caused by visitors. His only salvation, he said, from this chronic curse of distracting interruptions would entail the loss to his daughters of their only relaxation. He lamented, too, the smallness of his 'den,' overcrowded with books and papers. In this room he had left himself space only to slide along to his table through piles of volumes. His daughters told me this was the first house he had not built them out of, with these ever-accumulating books. Thrice in Westmoreland had such been their fate ; and they laughed at their own imprudence in leaving a bath in this room of his, which he instantly utilised past recovery as a receptacle for literary matter heaped up, pressed down, shaken together, and running over. They laughed, too, over his quaint trick of carrying off every scrap of paper he could lay his hands on, any old envelope or newspaper—not infrequently on the bland pretext of 'burning it for you,' in that fire of his which was never allowed to go out the whole year round, and which, in a little room so densely charged with combustible matter, was to them a source of some natural anxiety.

"It was on July 22nd that I repeated my visit, remaining with him at Mavis Bush until the 27th. Meanwhile, he had been gratified by a visit from Mr. Fields of Boston, U.S.A., who, on leaving, had put into Miss de Quincey's hands a cheque for a part of the profits accruing from the sale of the American edition of his works—to be kept from her father's knowledge till he should have returned home from seeing his American guest to the coach. Miss Martineau had spent the afternoon with him the day before, and he spoke of her with real liking in his words and manner. If her size had impressed him, so had her quietness of demeanour, and, adopting Elia's phrase, he designated her the gentle giantess. She, on her part, had been pleasantly impressed by his voice, and had exclaimed to his eldest daughter apart, alluding to her own deafness, 'Oh, what a voice! so clear, so soft, so sweet ; so delightful a contrast to the way people have of bawling to me.'

"On the 25th he hoped to have taken me to morning service at the Episcopal Chapel on the Duke of Buccleuch's grounds, Dalkeith, but was not well enough at the appointed hour, and I accompanied his three daughters to the chapel, driving through Bonnyrigg and Lowton, and coming within view of Cockpen Tower and

of the Lammermoor Hills by the way. He talked of the
service on our return, and showed how far his sympathies
went with a moderately ornate ritual. Sound Church of
England man as it was his great right and his pride to
call himself, he avowed that his antagonism to Rome
was mainly as a political system. On this Sunday afternoon he avowed the vehement hatred he had always
cherished for the Judaic continuance of a Sabbath in the
Judaic sense. Sabbath he hailed as a sublime word, but
its exclusive beauty and significance were ruined, to
his sense, by the 'base universal usage of it on the
most trivial occasions.' For some Presbyterian ministers,
notably Dr. Hanna, with whom he had agreeable relations in contributing to the *North British Review*, his
regard was unaffectedly cordial. It must be remembered that a Scottish Broad Church party, such as could
better have claimed his sympathies as a party, was hardly
then in existence. The Norman Macleods and the
Tullochs, as a power in the Kirk, were yet to come. He
was curious to know more about Professor Maurice, who
'has been talked of to me as the greatest man in the
Church of England,'—but who thus far had failed to
impress him with a sense of real or definite power. All
seemed so indefinite when looked closely into. What
seemed firm ground gave way beneath your tread. As
to Charles Kingsley and the 'Christian Socialists,' 'I
am puzzled to know what in the world they would be
at.' Mr. Gladstone's splendid powers had a charm for
him : 'But what am I to think (1852) of his sympathies
with a party abroad which at home would be identified
with extreme democracy?' Not that extreme democracy
in politics, any more than abstract atheism as such, was
to Mr. de Quincey otherwise than philosophically interesting. One of the periodicals of the day which he

seemed to read with great zest was *The Leader*, of the
editor of which, Mr. G. H. Lewes, he spoke with inquiring eagerness. During our walk together into Edinburgh
on the day of my finally quitting Mavis Bush, he
expatiated with unprecedented animation on German
theology of the advanced school, and freely recognised
the 'enormity' of the difficulties which rigid orthodoxy
had to confront. Passing on to speak of practical difficulties, he said, 'Frightfully perplexed I am, to this
hour, as to what constitutes the so-called *appropriation*
of the benefits of Christ's death. Never could I get any
one to clear it up to me. Coleridge was utterly vague on
the subject. He talked all about it and about it, but
never talked it out, that I could discover. Often have
I discussed the question with my mother, a clear-headed
and thoughtful woman, devoted to the Evangelical
system, and a devout supporter of *The Record*—which
paper I honour, as, in the other extreme, but for the same
reason, I do *The Leader*, for its candid and obvious
earnestness in enforcing the views it has so sincerely at
heart—but she would utterly fail to comprehend my
difficulties. "My dear child," she would repeat, "you
have simply to trust in the blood of Christ." "Very
well," I would reply, "and I am quite willing; I
reverence Christ; but what does this trusting mean?
How am I to know exactly what to do? Upon what
specifically am I to take hold to support me when flesh
and heart faileth, in the hour of death and at the day
of judgment?" Countless different schemes there are to
expound this doctrine of trust and of appropriation; but
they remind me of the ancilia at Rome, the eleven copies
of the sacred shield or palladium: to prevent the true
one being stolen, the eleven were made exactly like it.
So with the *true* doctrine of the atonement: it is lurking

among the others that look like it, but who is to say
which of them all it is?'

"After taking coffee with me that evening, Mr. de
Quincey surpassed himself in copious eloquence and
vivid variety of discourse, from grave to gay, from lively
to severe. He talked of the history he proposed to
write—a 'philosophical history of England, perhaps up
to the period when Macaulay begins.' The novel he
had in contemplation was to be about two prisoners in
Austria, in the time of Maria Theresa. He said of his
translated novel, 'Walladmor,' that it arose out of a
hasty review of the German original inserted in the
London Magazine. Taylor & Hessey, being struck with
the extracts as he had Englished them, commissioned
him to translate the complete work. The complete work,
he said, turned out to be complete trash; but he did his
best, partly recast the story, and gave more point to the
conversations. It found a few admirers, among whom
it was gratifying to him to reckon Dora Wordsworth
(Mrs. Quillinan).

"As I walked with him along Princes Street to the
Mound on his way home, I noticed the nervous solicitude
with which he refrained from any gesture while passing
a cabstand that might seem to warrant any driver in
concluding himself summoned and engaged. Some unhappy experience of a mistake of this kind may have
been the secret of his disquiet, for evidently he entertained a dread of the 'overbearing brutality of these
men.' He spoke of his short-sightedness, which at
Oxford had been so marked, that he was rumoured to
be a bit of a Jacobin because he failed to 'cap' the
Master of his college (Worcester) when he met him,
only from sheer inability to recognise him by sight.
We paused to look at the display of French and German

books in Seton's window, and he would willingly have
lingered there till sunset, glancing from author to
author, with a word for (or against) each. Seeing in
Bell & Bradfute's window a copy of Hawthorne's ' Mosses,'
about which I had been speaking to his daughters, I
went in to buy it, he readily undertaking the light
porterage ; and it led him to talk of Hawthorne's genius,
and to mention a recent visit of Emerson's,—to neither
of whom could he accord quite the degree of admiration
claimed for them by the more thoroughgoing of their
respective admirers.* Our way lay through George
Square to the Meadows, and at the end of 'Lovers'
Walk' he insisted on my not incurring the fatigue of
accompanying him farther. It was between eight and
nine on that lovely July evening that I took leave—my
last leave—of the man to whom I owed so much. At
the very moment of parting, all seemed to me like a
dream : that we had ever met, that we were now parting.
Could it all be but the baseless fabric of a vision, and
was this the break-up, to leave not a rack behind ?

> ' The old man still stood talking by my side ;
> But now his voice to me was like a stream
> Scarce heard ; nor word for word could I divide ;
> And the whole body of the man did seem
> Like one whom I had met with in a dream.'

"The parting was over, and he went on his way.
Lingering, I watched that receding figure, as it dimmed
in the distance. The last I saw of him, he had opened
Hawthorne's book, and went along reading as he walked.
In that attitude I lost sight of him. He went on his
way, and I saw him no more.

"FRANCIS JACOX."

* Later than this, Mr. de Quincey read the " Scarlet Letter "
and other works of Hawthorne with great access of admiration.
—ED.

JAMES PAYN'S REMINISCENCES.

(From "Literary Recollections.")

IN the ensuing summer (1853), after the publication
of another volume of poems, I visited Edinburgh and
called upon De Quincey, to whom I had a letter
of introduction from Miss Mitford. He was at that
time residing at Lasswade, a few miles from the town,
and I went thither by coach. He lived a secluded
life, and even at that date had become to the world
a name rather than a real personage; but it was a
great name. Considerable alarm agitated my youthful
heart as I drew near the house: I felt like Burns on the
occasion when he was first about "to dinner wi' a lord";
it was a great honour, but something rather to be talked
about afterwards than to be enjoyed in itself. There
were passages in De Quincey's writings which showed
that the English Opium-Eater was not always in a
dreamy state, but could be severe and satirical. My
apprehensions, however, proved to be utterly groundless, for a more gracious and genial personage I never
met. Picture to yourself a very diminutive man, carelessly—very carelessly—dressed; a face lined, careworn,
and so expressionless that it reminded one of that "chill,
changeless brow, where cold obstruction's apathy appals
the gazing mourner's heart"—a face like death in life.
The instant he began to speak, however, it lit up as
though by electric light; this came from his marvellous

eyes, brighter and more intelligent (though by fits) than I have ever seen in any other mortal. They seemed to me to glow with eloquence. He spoke of my introducer, of Cambridge, of the Lake Country, and of English poets. Each theme was interesting to me, but made infinitely more so by some apt personal reminiscence. As for the last-named subject, it was like talking of the Olympian gods to one not only cradled in their creed but who had mingled with them, himself half an immortal.

The announcement of luncheon was perhaps for the first time in my young life, unwelcome to me. Miss De Quincey did the honours with gracious hospitality, pleased, I think, to find that her father had so rapt a listener. I was asked what wine I would take, and not caring which it was, I was about to pour myself out a glass from the decanter that stood next to me. "You must not take that," whispered my hostess, "it is not port wine, as you think." It was in fact laudanum, to which De Quincey presently helped himself with the greatest *sang-froid*. I regarded him aghast, with much the same feelings as those with which he himself had watched the Malay at Grasmere eat the cake of opium, and with the same harmless result. The liquor seemed to stimulate rather than dull his eloquence. As I took my leave, after a most enjoyable interview, to meet the coach, I asked him whether he ever came by it into Edinburgh.

" What ! " he answered, in a tone of extreme surprise ; "by coach? Certainly not."

I was not aware of his peculiarities ; but the succession of commonplace people and their pointless observations were in fact intolerable to him. They did not bore him in the ordinary sense, but seemed, as it were, to outrage

his mind.   To me, to whom the study of human nature
in any form had become even then attractive, this was
unintelligible, and I suppose I showed it in my face, for
he proceeded to explain matters.   "Some years ago,"
he said, "I was standing on the pier at Tarbet, on Loch
Lomond, waiting for the steamer.   A stout old lady
joined me; I felt that she would presently address me ;
and she did.   Pointing to the smoke of the steamer,
which was making itself seen above the next headland,
'There she comes,' she said ; 'La, sir ! if you and I had
seen that fifty years ago, how wonderful we should have
thought it !'   Now the same thing," added my host, with
a shiver, "might happen to me any day, and that is why
I always avoid a public conveyance."

My interview with De Quincey I was not likely to
forget, but I never flattered myself that he would have
any remembrance of his youthful visitor.   A few years
afterwards, however, I received from him an entire
edition of his works, with a most gracious allusion (in
the "Autobiographical Sketches") to my poems.   "The
'Story of the Student of St. Bees,'" he says, "has been
made the subject of a separate poem by my friend, Mr.
James Payn, of Trinity College.   The volume contains
thoughts of great beauty, too likely to escape the vapid
and irreflective reader."   This good-natured eulogy rang
in my ears for many a day, nor did my college friends
forget, at all events, one portion of it ; with a monstrous
misapplication of terms, they henceforth dubbed me
"the vapid and irreflective reader."   I remember my
mother showing, with pardonable pride, this criticism of
De Quincey to a dean of the English Church, who was
then at the head of the High Church party at Oxford.
"Very flattering to your son, madam, no doubt," he
said ; "but who is this Mr. de Quincey ?"

Such ignorance was, of course, unpardonable in my
eyes, but it is quite amazing how ignorant so-called
scholars often are of matters connected with the literature of their own country ; in many cases they even fail
to understand its beauties when they are pointed out to
them, while, on the other hand, anything written in a
dead language, however dull and poor, they value at a
fancy price.   I was at the time undergoing the infliction
of "The Seven against Thebes " in the Trinity lecture-
room ; the play was introduced to us under the most
favourable circumstances, for W. G. Clark was our
lecturer, who had the art of illustrating everything he
had to discourse upon in the happiest manner.   I questioned him in private as to what he really thought of it.
"Do pray, be honest with me," I said ; "the play is
by Æschylus, I know, but is it not rubbish ? "   " It is
certainly not his masterpiece," was all I could get out of
him, accompanied, however, with a drop of the eye that
spoke volumes.   It was hardly to be expected that an
augur should have been more frank, save to another
augur.

SOUVENIRS AND ANECDOTES.

By VARIOUS FRIENDS AND ASSOCIATES.

THERE is a speculation in the eyes, a curl of the lip, and a general character in the outline that reminds one of some portraits of Voltaire. . . . He looks, thinks, writes, talks, and walks, eats and drinks and no doubt sleeps philosophically, *i.e.* deliberately. There is nothing abrupt about his motions ; he goes and comes calmly and quietly ; like the phantom in *Hamlet,* he is here—he is there—he is gone ! So it is with his discourse. He speaks slowly, clearly, and with very marked emphasis ; the tide of talk flows like Denham's river, "strong without rage, without o'erflowing full."—THOMAS HOOD (*Literary Reminiscences*).

When it was my frequent and agreeable duty to call on Mr. de Quincey . . . . and I have found him at home, quite at home, in the midst of a German Ocean of Literature in a storm, flooding all the floor, the tables, billows of books tossing, tumbling, surging open, on such occasions I have willingly listened by the hour whilst the philosopher, standing with his eyes fixed on one side of the room, seemed to be less speaking than reading from a " handwriting on the wall." Now and then he would diverge, for a Scotch mile or two, to the right or left, till I was tempted to inquire with

"Peregrine" in *John Bull*, "Do you never deviate?"
but he always came safely back to the point where he
had left, not lost the scent, and thence hunted his topic
to the end.   But look! we are in the small hours, and a
change comes o'er the spirit of that "old familiar face."
A faint hectic tint leaves the cheek, the eyes are a degree
dimmer, and each is surrounded by a growing shadow;
signs of the waning influence of that potent drug whose
stupendous pleasures and enormous pains have been so
eloquently described by the English Opium-Eater.—
THOMAS HOOD (*Literary Reminiscences*).

. . .

WHEN he sate, you would have taken him, by candle-
light, for the beautifulest little child ; blue-eyed, sparkling face, had there not been a something, too, which
said "*Eccovi*—this child has been in hell."—THOMAS
CARLYLE (*Reminiscences*).

DURING the winter of 1815–16 (or the next) Mr. de
Quincey accompanied his friend, the author of the "Isle
of Palms," from Westmoreland to Edinburgh. I had then
an opportunity of observing the literary character in an
entirely new phasis, for up to that time, De Quincey,
though he had spent long years in assiduous study, and
by his friends was regarded as a powerful author, had
not, so far as I know, published a single line.   He
seemed, indeed, to live for the sake of the labour alone,
and to fling overboard all considerations of the *palma*
or *pecunia*.   His various literary compositions, written
in his exemplary hand (the best I ever saw, except
Southey's) on little scraps of paper, must have reached
to a great extent, but in his own estimation they were

by no means "ready for the press;" like an over-cautious
general he withheld his fire, and remained *multa et
pulchra minans.* Not only for this reason, but in other
respects Mr. de Quincey seemed to me to bring out the
literary character in a new light. Very decisively he
realized my plan of moving in a separate world (having,
no doubt, realities of its own); moreover, he neither
spoke nor acted in the every-day world like any one
else, for which, of course, I greatly honoured him. He
was then in the habit of taking opium daily as an article
of food, and the drug, though used for years, had scarcely
begun to tell on his constitution, by those effects which,
sooner or later, overtake every one of its persevering
votaries; and which, when they once appear, make
quick work in demolishing together the man physical
and the man intellectual; the latter being reduced to
the pitiable plight of a musician who essays to play by
means of a harp unstrung and broken. But in his case,
it had not worked any such evils as yet, and in after
years, though not without a long and tough battle, Mr.
de Quincey succeeded in vanquishing the narcotic devil.

His voice was extraordinary; it came as if from
dreamland; but it was the most musical and impressive
of voices. In convivial life, what then seemed to me the
most remarkable trait of De Quincey's character, was
the power he possessed of easily changing the tone of
ordinary thought and conversation into that of his own
dreamland, till his auditors, with wonder, found themselves moving pleasantly along with him in a sphere of
which they might have heard and read, perhaps, but
which had ever appeared to them inaccessible, and far,
far away! Seeing that he was always good-natured and
social, he would take part, at commencement, in any
sort of tattle or twaddle. The talk might be of "beeves,"

R

and he could grapple with them if expected to do so, but his musical cadences were not in keeping with such work, and in a few minutes (not without some strictly logical sequence) he could escape at will from beeves to butterflies, and thence to the soul's immortality, to Plato, and Kant, and Schelling, and Fichte, to Milton's early years and Shakespeare's sonnets, to Wordsworth and Coleridge, to Homer and Æschylus, to St. Thomas of Aquin, St. Basil, and St. Chrysostom. But he by no means excluded themes from real life, according to his view of that life, but would recount profound mysteries from his own experinces—visions that had come over him in his loneliest walks among the mountains, and passages within his own personal knowledge, illustrating, if not proving, the doctrines of dreams, of warnings, of second sight, and mesmerism. And whatever the subject might be, every one of his sentences (or of his chapters I might say) was woven into the most perfect logical texture, and uttered in a tone of sustained melody.

Such powers and acquirements could not fail to excite wonder at Edinburgh. He had, indeed, studied "all such books as are never read" in that enlightened capital, and was the first friend I had ever met who could profess to have a command over the German language, and who consequently was able (*ex cathedra*) to corroborate my notions of the great stores that were contained therein. I flatter myself that he found our house not altogether uncongenial, as he was kind enough to visit there more frequently than in any other.—R. P. GILLIES (*Memoirs of a Literary Veteran*).

"OH for one hour of Dundee!" One hour of De Quincey —better three hours, from nine till midnight—for a rapt

listener to be "under the wand of a magician," spellbound by his wonderful affluence of talk such as that of
the fairy whose lips dropped rubies and diamonds.
Many a night have I, with my wife by my side, sat
listening to the equable flow of his discourse, both of us
utterly forgetting the usual regularity of our habits, and
hearing the drowsy watchman's "past one o'clock" (for
the old watchman then walked his round) before we
parted.   There was another newly acquired intimate of
that time—Barry St. Leger—who also had contributed
to the *Quarterly Magazine.*   Our friendship was of the
warmest nature during the remainder of his short life.
The wit-combats between him and De Quincey were
most amusing.   Never were two men greater contrasts
in their intellectual characters.   The one passionately
rhetorical, the other calmly logical ; the one making a
fierce onslaught upon his apparently unwatchful oppo-
nent, the other with a slight turn of his wrist striking
the sword out of his adversary's hand, leaving him
defenceless.   In the ordinary intercourse of society, St.
Leger was self-possessed, perfectly at his ease, ready for
every emergency, a man of the world, yet with a heart
for friendship as warm as that of a schoolboy.   De
Quincey, vast as were his acquirements, intuitive as was
his appreciation of character and the motives of human
actions, unembarrassed as was his demeanour, pleasant
and even mirthful his table-talk, was as helpless in every
position of responsibility as when he nightly paced
"stony-hearted Oxford Street" looking for the lost one.
He was constantly beset by idle fears and vain imaginings.   His sensitiveness was so extreme, in combination
with the almost ultra-courtesy of a gentleman, that he
hesitated to trouble a servant with any personal requests
without a long prefatory apology.   My family were in

the country in the summer of 1825 when he was staying at my house in Pall Mall East. A friend or two had met him at dinner, and I had walked part of the way home with one of them. When I returned I tapped at his chamber door to bid him good-night. He was sitting at the open window, habited as a prize-fighter when he enters the ring. "You will take cold," I exclaimed. "Where is your shirt?" "I have not a shirt—my shirts are unwashed." "But why not tell the servant to send them to the laundress?" "Ah! how could I presume to do that in Mrs. Knight's absence?"

One more illustration of the eccentricity of De Quincey. I had been to Windsor. On my return I was told that Mr. de Quincey had taken his box away, leaving word that he was gone home. I knew that he was waiting for a remittance from his mother, which would satisfy some clamorous creditors and enable him to rejoin his family at Grasmere. Two or three days after I heard that he was still in town. I obtained a clue to his hiding-place, and found him in a miserable lodging on the Surrey side of Waterloo Bridge. He had received a large draft on a London banker at twenty-one days' sight. He summoned courage to go to Lombard Street, and was astonished to learn that he could not obtain the amount till the draft became due. A man of less sensitive feeling would have returned to Pall Mall East and have there waited securely and comfortably till I came. How to frame his apology to our trusty domestic was the difficulty that sent him into the den where I found him. He produced the draft to me from out of his Bible, which he thought was the best hiding-place. "Come to me to-morrow morning, and I will give you the cash." "What? How? Can such a thing be possible? Can the amount be got before the draft is due?" "Never

fear—come you—and then get home as fast as you can."
—CHARLES KNIGHT (*Passages of a Working Life*).

HIS tastes were very simple, though a little troublesome, at least to the servant who prepared his repast. Coffee, boiled rice, and milk, and a piece of mutton from the loin were the materials that invariably formed his diet. The cook, who had an audience with him daily, received her instructions in silent awe, quite overpowered by his manner ; for, had he been addressing a duchess, he could scarcely have spoken with more deference. He would couch his request in such terms as these :—" Owing to dyspepsia, afflicting my system, and the possbility of any additional derangement of the stomach taking place, consequences incalculably distressing would arise, so much so, indeed, as to increase nervous irritation, and prevent me from attending to matters of overwhelming importance, if you do not remember to cut the mutton in a diagonal rather than in a longitudinal form."—Mrs. GORDON (*Memoir of Wilson*).

I REMEMBER his coming to Gloucester Place* one stormy night. He remained hour after hour in the vain expectation that the waters would assuage and the hurly-burly cease. There was nothing for it but that our visitor should remain all night. The professor ordered a room to be prepared for him, and they found each other such good company that this accidental detention was prolonged, without further difficulty for the greater part of a year. During this visit some of his eccentricities

* The residence of Professor Wilson.

did not escape observation. For example, he rarely appeared at the family meals, preferring to dine in his own room at his own hour, not unfrequently turning night into day.

The time when he was most brilliant was generally towards the early morning hours; and then, more than once, my father arranged his supper-parties so that, sitting till three or four in the morning, he brought Mr. de Quincey to that point at which in charm and power of conversation he was so truly wonderful.—Mrs. GORDON (*Memoir of Wilson*).

WHEN I had made a few visits to him, Mr. de Quincey was so kind as to take some particular notice of me; and afterwards when he wrote his Grasmere article about "George and Sarah Green" (1839), he spoke to me of the subject, and read me a passage from the proof before it appeared in *Tait*. Mr. de Quincey occasionally made his appearance at the warehouse of Mr. Tait, where he would sometimes be asked to dinner, for which some special light dishes had to be provided for him, as he was unable to partake of ordinary fare. On these rare occasions, when Mr. Tait could prevail on Mr. de Quincey to be entertained, I was sent to the master's residence to inform the housekeeper, so that she might make some special preparations; but on one inconvenient occasion Mr. de Quincey invited himself. Mr. Tait had invited a friend, well known for his love of the good things of this life, to dine with him, and before leaving in the morning told his housekeeper, who also officiated as his cook, to be sure and have something nice for them. About one o'clock, however, Mr. de Quincey arrived at Walker Street, and told the housekeeper, who was a new hand, and did not know him, that he would stay to dinner. Thinking he was the expected guest, she said, " Oh yes, sir, I know, and I am just going to send out for a gigot of black-faced mutton and a moor-fowl ; dinner is to be at five o'clock." " Pardon me, madam," said the ever-courteous Opium-Eater, " the state of my stomach, which I may tell you is a perpetual source of woe to me, will prevent my eating flesh-meats of the kind you mention. If, therefore, you could procure a portion of tripe, and stew it for me, as also a pudding of the batter or custard kind, I should indeed be grateful to you." The housekeeper, knowing that her master would be perfectly satisfied with the cold roast beef stored in her larder, acted at once on Mr. de Quincey's suggestion, and procured the wished-for dish of tripe instead of the mutton and game, wondering much at the exceeding politeness of the gentleman, whom she had never seen before. Mr. Tait and his guest duly arrived ; he was not a little surprised at finding Mr. de Quincey comfortably seated in his drawing-room, reading a proof and laughed heartily when the housekeeper mentioned what had occurred. The Opium-Eater gave an elaborate explanation ; but the guest who expected to " dine " was not appeased until he found that the talk of De Quincey made ample amends for the loss of his dinner.

Mr. de Quincey was wont to frequent a small hotel called the " Guildford Arms," in Register Street (situated near the renowned tavern which was the scene of the " Noctes Ambrosianæ," in Gabriel's Road) in search of his favourite tripe ; and it was one of the places in which Mr. de Quincey was occasionally pleased to hide himself.

One of the numerous " warehouse stories " about the English Opium-Eater may be worth repeating, although

the circumstance occurred before my day. It was told
me by my fellow-apprentice, who, one morning, upon his
arrival at the shop to open it found a " noddy " (a one-
horse hackney carriage) standing before the door with
the blinds down. After a few minutes had elapsed the
occupant contrived to attract the attention of George,
and blandly addressed him somewhat in this fashion :—

"I am Mr. de Quincey, and I presume that you are
one of the young gentlemen who assist Mr. Tait in
conducting his business. I am at this moment much
embarrassed for want of a sum of money ; the difficulty
will not, however, I can assure you, be permanent, but it
is in the meantime most urgent, and I fancied that even
at this early hour I should be able to obtain the required
amount by coming here." George thought he might be
wanting a five-pound note at least, so he said to him
anxiously : " How much do you require, Mr. de
Quincey ? " " You see, young sir, in arriving at my
journey's end I shall require to pay the coachman his
fare, including a small gratuity to himself, not less than
three shillings in all, and having but half-a-crown in my
pocket, I am anxious to be accommodated with the loan
of sixpence." Not less astonished than relieved, George
handed the coin to him at once, and after thanking his
benefactor profusely for his great politeness, Mr. de
Quincey drove off.

I now take leave of the English Opium-Eater, the
chief features of his life being well known. Owing to
his kindness our acquaintance ripened, and in after days,
both during the period of his contrubutions to *Tait*, and
also while his papers were appearing in *Hogg's Instructor*,
to which periodical I was, myself, a contributor, we had
many conversations. Often in Princes Street, of an
evening, if the street was not thronged, he would take a

turn or two with me, speaking his beautiful English, and talking to me in his engaging voice (as if I had been in all respects his equal) upon literary subjects, his information seeming to be boundless. I shall never forget one of those evenings he allowed me to walk with him, an evening when he spoke of Joan of Arc, a favourite theme on which he contributed a paper to *Tait's Magazine.* No feature of Mr. de Quincey's character was more marked, perhaps, than his evident desire to put his inferiors on a footway of perfect equality. He did all the talking, but he talked in such a way as to inform, but never to make you feel your ignorance. Such, at all events, was my experience of this remarkable man.— J. G. BERTRAM (*Some Memoirs of Books, Authors, and Events*).

"THOMAS PAPAVERIUS."

(From *THE BOOK HUNTER*.)

By JOHN HILL BURTON, LL.D.

THE next slide of the lantern is to represent a quite
peculiar and abnormal case. It introduces a strangely
fragile, unsubstantial and puerile figure, wherein, however, resided one of the most potent and original spirits
that ever frequented a tenement of clay. He shall be
called, on account of associations that may or may not
be found out, Thomas Papaverius. But how to make
palpable to the ordinary human being one so signally
divested of all the material and common characteristics
of his race, yet so nobly endowed with its rarer and
loftier attributes, almost paralyses the pen at the very
beginning.

In what mood and shape shall he be brought forward?
Shall it be as first we met at the table of Lucullus,
whereto he was seduced by the false pretence that he
would there meet with one who entertained novel and
anarchical opinions regarding the Golden Ass of Apu-
leius? No one speaks of waiting dinner for him. He
will come and depart of his own sweet will, neither
burdened with punctualities, nor burdening others by
exacting them. The festivities of the afternoon are far

on when a commotion is heard in the hall as if some dog
or other stray animal had forced its way in. The instinct
of a friendly guest tells him of the arrival—he opens the
door and fetches in the little stranger. What can it be?
a street boy of some sort? His costume, in fact, is a boy's
duffle great-coat, very threadbare, with a hole in it and
buttoned tight to the chin, where it meets the fragments of
a parti-coloured belcher handkerchief; on his feet are
list-shoes covered with snow, for it is a stormy winter
night; and the trousers—some one suggests that they are
inner linen garments blackened with writing-ink, but that
Papaverius never would have been at the trouble so to
disguise them. What can be the theory of such a
costume? The simplest thing in the world—it consisted
of the fragments of apparel nearest at hand. Had
chance thrown to him a court single-breasted coat, with
a bishop's apron, a kilt and top-boots, in these he would
have made his entry.

The first impression that a boy has appeared vanishes
instantly. Though in one of the sweetest and most
genial of his essays he shows how every man retains in
him so much of the child he orginally was—and he
himself retained a great deal of that primitive simplicity
—it was buried within the depths of his heart—not
visible externally. On the contrary, on one occasion
when he corrected an erroneous reference to an event
as being a century old, by saying he recollected its
occurrence, one felt almost a surprise at the necessary
limitation in his age, so old did he appear, with his
arched brow loaded with thought, and the countless
little wrinkles which engrained his skin, gathering
thickly round the curiously expressive and subtle lips.
These lips are speedily opened by some casual remark,
and presently the flood of talk passes forth from

them, free, clear and continuous—never rising into declamation—never losing a certain mellow earnestness, and all consisting of sentences as exquisitely jointed together as if they were destined to challenge the criticism of the remotest posterity.   Still the hours stride over each other, and still flows on the stream of gentle rhetoric, as if it were *labitur et labetur in omne volubilis ævum.*   It is now far into the night, and slight hints and suggestions are propagated about separation and home-going.   The topic starts new ideas on the progress of civilisation, the effect of habit on man in all ages, and the power of the domestic affections.   Descending from generals to the special, he could testify to the inconvenience of late hours ; for, was it not the other night that, coming to what was, or what he believed to be, his own door, he knocked and knocked, but the old woman within either couldn't or wouldn't hear him, so he scrambled over a wall, and having taken his repose in a furrow, was able to testify to the extreme unpleasantness of such a couch.   The predial groove might indeed nourish kindly the infant seeds and shoots of the peculiar vegetable to which it was appropriated, but was not a comfortable place of repose for adult man.

Shall I try another sketch of him, when, travel-stained and footsore, he glided in on us one night like a shadow, the child by the fire gazing on him with round eyes of astonishment, and suggesting that he should get a penny and go home—a proposal which he subjected to some philosophical criticism very far wide of its practical tenor.   How far he had wandered since he had last refreshed himself, or even whether he had eaten food that day, were matters on which there was no getting articulate utterance from him.   Though his costume was muddy however, and his communications about the material wants of life very hazy, the ideas which he had stored up during his wandering poured themselves forth as clear and sparkling, both in logic and language, as the purest fountain that springs from a highland rock.

How that wearied, worn, little body was to be refreshed was a difficult problem ; soft food disagreed with him—the hard he could not eat. Suggestions pointed at length to the solution of that vegetable unguent to which he had given a sort of lustre, and it might be supposed that there were some fifty cases of acute toothache to be treated in the house that night. How many drops? Drops! nonsense, if the wineglasses of the establishment were not beyond the ordinary normal size, there was no risk—and so the weary is at rest for a time.

At early morn a triumphant cry of *Eureka!* calls me to his place of rest. With his unfailing instinct he has got at the books, and lugged a considerable heap of them around him. That one which specially claims his attention—my best bound quarto—is spread upon a piece of bedroom furniture, readily at hand, and of sufficient height to let him pore over it, as he lies recumbent on the floor, with only one article of attire to separate him from the condition in which Archimedes, according to the popular story, shouted the same triumphant cry. He had discovered a very remarkable anachronism in the commonly received histories of a very important period. As he expounded it, turning up his unearthly face from the book with an almost painful expression of grave interest, it occurred to me that I had seen something like the scene in Dutch paintings of the temptation of St. Anthony.

Suppose the scene changed to a pleasant country
house, where the enlivening talk has made a guest
forget

> "The lang Scots miles,
> The mosses, waters, slaps, and stiles"

that lie between him and his place of rest. He must be
instructed in his course, but the instruction reveals more
difficulties than it removes, and there is much doubt
and discussion, which Papaverius at once clears up as
effectually as he had ever dispersed a cloud of logical
sophisms; and this time the feat is performed by a
stroke of the thoroughly practical, which looks like
inspiration—he will accompany the forlorn traveller, and
lead him through the difficulties of the way—for have
not midnight wanderings and musings made him
familiar with all its intricacies? Roofed by a huge
wideawake, which makes his tiny figure look like the
stalk of some great fungus, with a lantern of more than
common dimensions in his hand, away he goes down the
wooded path, up the steep bank, along the brawling
stream, and across the waterfall—and ever as he goes
there comes from him a continued stream of talk, concerning the philosophy of Immanuel Kant, and other
kindred matters. Surely if we two were seen by any
human eyes, it must have been supposed that some
gnome, or troll, or kelpie, was luring the listener to his
doom. The worst of such affairs as this, was the consciousness that, when left, the old man would continue
walking on until, weariness overcoming him, he would
take his rest, wherever that happened, like some poor
mendicant. He used to denounce, with his most fervid
eloquence, that barbarous and brutal provision of the
law of England, which rendered sleeping in the open

air an act of vagrancy, and so punishable, if the sleeper
could not give a satisfactory account of himself—a thing
which Papaverius never could give under any circumstances. After all, I fear this is an attempt to describe
the indescribable. It was the commonest of sayings
when any of his friends were mentioning to each other,
"his last," and creating mutual shrugs of astonishment,
that, were one to attempt to tell all about him, no man
would believe it, so separate would the whole be from
all the normal conditions of human nature.

The difficulty becomes more inextricable in passing
from specific little incidents to an estimation of the
general nature of the man. The logicians lucidly
describe definition as being *per genus et differentiam.*
You have the characteristics in which all of the *genus*
partake as common ground, and then you individualise
your object by showing in what it differs from the others
of the genus. But we are denied this standard for
Papaverius, so entirely did he stand apart, divested of
the ordinary characteristics of social man—of those
characteristics without which the human race as a body
could not get on or exist. For instance, those who
knew him a little might call him a loose man in money
matters; those who knew him closer laughed at the idea
of coupling any notion of pecuniary or other like
responsibility with his nature. You might as well
attack the character of the nightingale, which may have
nipped up your five-pound note and torn it into shreds
to serve as nest-building material. Only immediate
craving necessities could ever extract from him an
acknowledgment of the common vulgar agencies by
which men subsist in civilised society; and only while
the necessity lasted did the acknowledgment exist.
Take just one example, which will render this clearer

than any generalities. He arrives very late at a friend's
door, and on gaining admission—a process in which he
often endured impediments—he represents with his
usual silver voice and measured rhetoric the absolute
necessity of his being then and there invested with a
sum of money in the current coin of the realm, the
amount limited, from the nature of his necessities, which
he very freely states, to seven shillings and sixpence.
Discovering, or fancying he discovers, signs that his
eloquence is likely to be unproductive, he is fortunately
reminded that, should there be any difficulty in connection with security for the repayment of the loan, he is at
that moment in possession of a document, which he is prepared to deposit with the lender—a document calculated,
he cannot doubt, to remove a feeling of anxiety which the
most prudent person could experience in the circumstances. After a rummage in his pockets, which
develops miscellaneous and varied, but as yet by no
means valuable possessions, he at last comes to the
object of his search, a crumpled bit of paper, and spreads
it out—a fifty-pound bank-note I   The friend, who knew
him well, was of opinion that, had he, on delivering over
the seven shillings and sixpence, received the bank-note
he would never have heard anything more of the transaction from the other party.   It was also his opinion
that, before coming to a personal friend, the owner of the
note had made several efforts to raise money on it among
persons who might take a purely business view of such
transactions ; but the lateness of the hour, and something in the appearance of the thing altogether, had
induced these mercenaries to forget their cunning, and
decline the transaction.

He stretched till it broke the proverb that to give
quickly is as good as to give twice. His giving was

quick enough on the rare occasions when he had where-
withal to give, but then the act was final, and could not
be repeated.   If he suffered in his own person from this
peculiarity, he suffered still more in his sympathies, for
he was full of them to all breathing creatures, and, like
poor Goldy, it was agony to him to hear the beggar's cry
of distress, and to hear it without the means of assuaging
it, though in a departed fifty pounds there were doubtless
the elements for appeasing many a street wail.   All
sums of money are measured by him through the
common standard of immediate use ; and with more
solemn pomp of diction than he applied to the bank-
note, might he inform you that, with the gentleman
opposite, to whom he had hitherto been entirely a
stranger, but who happened to be nearest to him when
the exigency occurred to him, he had just succeeded in
negotiating a loan of " twopence."   He was and is a
great authority in political economy.   I have known great
anatomists and physiologists as careless of their health
as he was of his purse, whence I have inferred that something more than a knowledge of the abstract of political
economy is necessary to keep some men from pecuniary
imprudence, and that something more than a knowledge
of the received principles of physiology is necessary to
bring others into a course of perfect sobriety and general
obedience to the laws of health.   Further, Papaverius
had an extraordinary insight into practical human life ;
not merely in the abstract, but in the concrete ; not
merely as a philosopher of human nature, but as one who
saw into those who passed him in the walk of life with
the kind of intuition attributed to expert detectives—a
faculty that is known to have belonged to more than one
dreamer, and is one of the mysteries in the nature of
J. J. Rousseau ; and, by the way, like Rousseau's, his hand-

S

writing was clear, angular, and unimpassioned, and not
less uniform and legible than printing—as if the medium
of conveying so noble a thing as thought ought to be
carefully, symmetrically, and decorously constructed, let
all other material things be as neglectfully and scornfully
dealt with as may be.

This is a long proemium to the description of his
characteristics as a book-hunter ; but these can be briefly
told. Not for him were the common enjoyments and
excitements of the pursuit. He cared not to add volume
unto volume, and heap up the relics of the printing-press.
All the external niceties about pet editions, peculiarities
of binding or of printing, rarity itself, were no more to
him than to the Arab or the Hottentot. His pursuit
indeed was like that of the savage who seeks but to
appease the hunger of the moment. If he catch a prey
just sufficient for his desires it is well ; yet he will not
hesitate to bring down the elk or the buffalo, and sati-
ating himself with the choicer delicacies, abandon the
bulk of the carcase to the wolves or the vultures. So
of Papaverius. If his intellectual appetite were craving
after some passage in the Œdipus, or in the Medeia, or
in Plato's Republic, he would be quite contented with
the most tattered and valueless fragment of the volume, if
it contained what he wanted ; but, on the other hand, he
would not hesitate to seize upon your tall copy in russia
gilt and tooled. Nor would the exemption of an *editio
princeps* from everyday sordid work restrain his sacri-
legious hands. If it should contain the thing he desires
to see, what is to hinder him from wrenching out the
twentieth volume of your *Encyclopédie Méthodique*, or
Ersch and Gruber, leaving a vacancy like an extracted
front tooth, and carrying it off to his den of Cacus? If
you should mention the matter to any vulgar-mannered

acquaintance given to the unhallowed practice of jeering, he would probably touch his nose with his extended palm and say, "Don't you wish you may get it?" True, the world at large has gained a brilliant essay on Euripides or Plato; but what is that to the rightful owner of the lost sheep?

The learned world may very fairly be divided into those who return the books borrowed by them, and those who do not. Papaverius belonged decidedly to the latter order. A friend addicted to the marvellous boasts that, under the pressure of a call by a public library to replace a mutilated book with a new copy, which would have cost £30, he recovered a volume from Papaverius, through the agency of a person specially bribed and authorised to take any measures, insolence and violence excepted; but the power of extraction that must have been employed in the process excites very painful reflections. Some legend, too, there is of a book-creditor having forced his way into the Cacus den, and there seen a sort of rubble-work inner wall of volumes, with their edges outwards, while others, bound and unbound, the plebeian sheepskin and the aristocratic russian, were squeezed into certain tubs drawn from the washing establishment of a confiding landlady. In other instances the book has been recognised at large, greatly enhanced in value by a profuse edging of manuscript notes from a gifted pen—a phenomenon calculated to bring into practical use the speculations of the civilians about pictures painted on other people's panels.* What became

* "Si quis in aliena tabula pinxerit, quidam putant, tabulam pictura cedere: aliis videtur picturam (qualiscunque sit) tabulæ cedere: sed nobis videtur melius esse tabulam picturæ cedere. Ridiculum est enim picturam Apellis vel Parrhasii in accessionem vilissimæ tabulæ cedere."—*Just.* ii. 1, 34.

CARLYLE AND DE QUINCEY.

I INTRODUCE this memorable record of an early friend-ship with a few words touching briefly on later days.

Doubtless, De Quincey's adverse review of "Wilhelm Meister" was keenly felt by Carlyle and for many a day resented. Perhaps we have there the key to various acrimonious observations which came to light in the "Reminiscences."

But, referring again to that touching interview with Carlyle (which I have detailed in "Days and Nights"), when I delivered De Quincey's "message from the grave," I can testify that with both "*it was light at eventide.*"

"Craigenputtoch,
"December 11, 1828.

"MY DEAR SIR,—Having the opportunity of a frank, I cannot resist the temptation to send you a few lines, were it only to signify that two well-wishers of yours are still alive in these remote moors, and often thinking of you with the old friendly feelings. My wife encourages me in this innocent purpose; she has learned lately that you were inquiring for her of some female friend; nay, even promising to visit us here—a fact of the most interesting sort to both of us. I am to say, therefore, that your presence at this fireside will diffuse

no ordinary gladness over all members of the household ; that our warmest welcome, and such solacements
as even the desert does not refuse, are at any time
and at all times in store for one we love so well.
Neither is this expedition so impracticable. We lie but
a short way out of your direct route to Westmoreland ;
communicate by gravelled roads with Dumfries and
other places in the habitable globe. Were you to
warn us of your approach, it might all be made easy
enough. And then such a treat it would be to hear
the sound of philosophy and literature in the hitherto
quite savage wolds, where since the creation of the
world no such music, scarcely even articulate speech
had been uttered or dreamed of! Come, therefore,
come and see us ; for we often long after you. Nay, I
can promise, too, that we are almost a unique sight in
the British Empire ; such a quantity of German periodicals and mystic speculations embosomed in plain
Scottish peat-moor being nowhere else that I know of
to be met with. In idle hours we sometimes project
founding a sort of colony here, to be called the
' Misanthropic Society ; ' the settlers all to be men of a
certain philosophic depth, and intensely sensible of the
present state of literature : each to have his own cottage,
encircled with roses or thistles as he might prefer ; a
library and pantry within and huge stack of turf-fuel
without ; fenced off from his neighbours by fir-woods,
and, when he pleased, by cast-metal railings, so that
each might feel himself strictly an individual, and free as a
son of the wilderness ; but the whole settlement to meet
weekly over coffee, and there unite in their *Miserere*, or
what were better, hurl forth their defiance, pity, expostu-
lation, over the whole universe, civil, literary, and religious. I reckon this place a much fitter site for such an

establishment than your lake country—a region abounding in natural beauty—but blown on by coach-horns,
betrodden by picturesque tourists, and otherwise exceedingly desecrated by too frequent resort : whereas here,
though still in communication with the manufacturing
world we have a solitude altogether Druidical, grim hills
tenanted chiefly by the wild grouse, tarns and brooks
which have soaked and slumbered unmolested since the
deluge of Noah, and nothing to disturb you with speech,
except Arcturus and Orion, and the Spirit of Nature, in
the heaven and in the earth, as it manifests itself in
anger or love, and utters its inexplicable tidings, unheard
by the mortal ear. But the misery is the almost total
want of colonists! Would you come hither and be
king over us ? then, indeed we had made a fair beginning, and the ' Bog School ' might snap its fingers at the
' Lake School ' itself, and hope to be one day recognised
of all men. But enough of this fooling. Better were it
to tell you in plain prose what little can be said of my
own welfare, and inquire in the same dialect after yours.
It will gratify you to learn that here, in the desert as in
the crowded city, I am moderately active and well ; better
in health, not worse ; and though active only on the
small scale, yet in my own opinion honestly, and to as
much result as has been usual with me at any time.
We have horses to ride on, gardens to cultivate, tight
walls and strong fires to defend us against winter ; books
to read, paper to scribble on ; and no man or thing, at
least in this visible earth, to make us afraid : for I reckon
that so securely sequestered are we, not only would no
Catholic rebellion, but even no new Hengist and Horsa
invasion, in any wise disturb our tranquillity. True, we
have no society ; but who has in the strict sense of that
word ? I have never had any worth speaking much

about since I came into this world ; in the next, it may
be, they will order matters better. Meanwhile, if we
have not the wheat in great quantity, we are nearly
altogether free from the chaff, which often in this matter
is highly annoying to weak nerves. My wife and I are
busy learning Spanish ; far advanced in Don Quixote
already. I purpose writing *Mystical Reviews* for somewhat more than a twelvemonth to come ; have Greek to
read, and the whole universe to study (for I understand
less and less of it); so that here as well as elsewhere I
find a man may ' dree his wierd ' (serve out his earthly
apprenticeship) with reasonable composure, and wait
what the flight of years may bring him, little disappointed (unless he is a fool) if it bring him mere nothing
save what he has already—a body and a soul—more
cunning and costly treasures, than all Golconda and
Potosi could purchase for him. What would the vain
worm, man, be at ? Has he not a head to speak of
nothing else—a head (be it with a hat or without one)
full of far richer things than Windsor Palace, or the
Brighton Teapot added to it ? What are all Dresden
picture-galleries and *magasins des arts et des métiers* to
the strange painting and thrice precious workmanship
that goes on under the cranium of a beggar ? What
can be added to him or taken from him by the hatred
or love of all men ? The grey paper or the white silk
paper in which the gold ingot is wrapped ; the gold
is inalienable ; he is the gold. But truce also to this
moralizing. I had a thousand things to ask concerning
you : your employments, purposes, sufferings and
pleasures. Will you not write to me ? Will you not
come to me and tell ? Believe it you are well loved
here, and none feels better than I what a spirit it is at
present eclipsed in clouds. For the present it can only

be : time and chance are for all men; that troublous season will end ; and one day with more joyful, not deeper or truer regard I shall see you 'yourself again.' Meanwhile pardon me this intrusion ; and write if you have a vacant hour which you would fill with a good action. Mr. Jeffrey is still anxious to know you ; has he ever succeeded? We are not to be in Edinburgh, I believe, till spring ; but I will send him a letter to you (with your permission) by the first conveyance. Remember me with best regards to Professor Wilson and Sir W. Hamilton, neither of whom must forget me : not omitting the honest Gordon, who I know will not. The bearer of this letter is Henry Inglis, a young gentleman of no ordinary talent and worth, in whom, as I believe, *es steckt gar viel.* Should he call himself pray let this be an introduction, for he reverences all spiritual worth, and you also will learn to love him. With all friendly sentiments,

"I am ever,

"My dear Sir,

"Most faithfully yours,

"T. CARLYLE."

"DE QUINCEY'S REVENGE."

A BALLAD IN THREE FITTES.

BY DELTA (DR. D. M. MOIR).

THIS interesting Ballad appeared in *Blackwood's Magazine* in 1840, and is specially referred to by De Quincey in a long and elaborate note on his family name. This was appended to the revised edition of the " Confessions."

It is there stated that the De Quincey family which split into three national divisions—English, French, and American—was originally Norwegian. " They assumed a territorial denomination from the district or village of Quincey, in the province now called Normandy, transplanted themselves to England ; where, and subsequently by marriage in Scotland, they ascended to the highest rank in both kingdoms, and held the highest offices open to a subject."

In the copious notes attached to this Ballad, Dr. Moir " took the trouble of tracing their aspiring movements in Scotland, through a period when Normans transferred themselves from England to Scotland in considerable numbers, and with great advantages." It was the first collection of facts concerning the career of the family in Scotland.

" Meanwhile in England they continued to flourish through nine or ten generations ; took a distinguished

part in one, at least, of the Crusades ; and a still more
perilous share in the Barons' wars under Henry III. No
family drank more deeply or more frequently from the
cup of treason, which in those days was not always a
very grave offence in people who having much territorial
influence, had also much money. But happening to
drink once too often, or taking too long a ' pull ' at the
cup, the Earls of Winchester suddenly came to grief."
So it came to pass, as related by Dr. Moir, that on the
accession of Bruce to the throne, the estates of the De
Quinceys, being declared forfeited, were conferred on
the Setons.

De Quincey humorously observes : " The omission of
the *De*, as an addition looking better at a tournament
than as an indorsement on a bill of exchange, began as
to many hundreds of English names, full three hundred
years ago. Many English families have disused this
affix from sheer indolence. As to the terminal variations
cy, *cie*, *cey*, those belong, as natural and inevitable ex-
ponents of a transitional condition, to the unsettled
spelling that characterised the early stages of literature
in all countries alike."

DE QUINCEY'S REVENGE.

A BALLAD IN THREE FITTES.

By Delta.

I.

De Quincey, lord of Travement,
  Has from the Syrian wars return'd ;
As near'd his train to his own demesne,
  His heart within him burn'd.

Yet heavy was that heart, I ween ;
  A cloud had o'er him pass'd ;
And all of life, that once was green,
  Had wither'd in the blast.
Say, had he sheath'd his trusty brand,
  Intent no more to roam,
Only to find the Scottish strand
  For him no fitting home ? *

II.

Who stands at hush of eventide
  Before Newbottle's sacred walls,
While eastward far, in arch and aisle,
  Its mighty shadow falls?
That steel-clad knight stood at the porch,
  And loud he knock'd, and long,
Till out from the chancel came a Frere,
  For it was even-song.
To an alder stump his steed was tied,
  And the live wind from the west
Stirr'd the blue scarf on his corslet side,
  And the raven plumes of his crest.

III.

" Why knock'st thou here ? No hostel this,
  And we have mass to say ;
Know'st thou, that rises our vesper hymn
  Duly at close of day?

* Robert de Quincey, a Northamptonshire baron, acquired the
manor of Travernent (*vulgo*, Tranent), which, in the reign of David
the First, had been held by Swan, the son of Thor, soon after the
accession of William the Lion ; and he served for some time as
justiciary to that monarch. At the end of the twelfth century he
was succeeded in his immense estates by his son, Seyer de Quincey,
the hero of the following ballad, who set out for Palestine in 1218.
where he died in the year following.

And in the chantry, even now,
   The choristers are met;
For lo! o'er Pentland's summits blue,
   The western sun hath set?
But if thou return'st at morning tide,
   Whatever be thy behest—"
"Nay," said the stranger hastily,
   "Delay not my request.

IV.

"For I have come from foreign lands,
   And seen the sun of June
Set over the holy Jerusalem,
   And its towers beneath the moon;
And I have stood by the sepulchre
   Wherein the Lord was laid,
And drunk of Siloa's brook, that flows
   In the cool of its own palm shade.
Yea! I have battled for the Cross,
   'Tis the symbol on my mail—
But why, with idle words should I
   Prolong a bootless tale?

V.

"The Lady Elena—woe to me
   Brought the words that tale which told!—
Was yesternight, by the red torchlight,
   Left alone in your vaults so cold.
'Tis said, last night by the red torchlight
   That a burial here hath been;
Now show me, prithee, her tomb, who stood
   My heart and heaven between.
Alas! alas! that a cold damp vault
   Her resting-place should be,
Who, singing, sate among the flowers
   When I went o'er the sea."

VI.

"'Tis nay, Sir Knight," the Frere replied,
  "If thou turn'st thy steed again,
And hither return'st at matin prime,
  Thou shalt not knock in vain."
Then ire flash'd o'er that warrior's brow,
  Like storm-clouds o'er the sky,
And, stamping, he struck his gauntlet glove
  On the falchion by his thigh.
" Now, by our Lady's holy name,
  And by the good St. John,
I must gaze on the features of the dead,
  Though I hew my path through stone !"

VII.

The Frere hath lighted his waxen torch,
  And turn'd the grating key,
Down winding steps, through gloomy aisles,
  The damp, dull way show'd he ;
And ever he stood and cross'd himself,
  As the night-wind smote his ear,
For the very carven imageries
  Spake nought but of death and fear—
And sable 'scutcheons flapp'd on high,
  Mid that grim and ghastly shade ;
And coffins were ranged on tressels round,
  And banners lowly laid.

VIII.

From aisle to aisle they pass'd the while,
  In silence both—the one in dread—
So solemn a thing it was to be
  With darkness and the dead !

At length the innermost vault they gain'd,
  Last home of a house of fame,
And the Knight, looking up with earnest eye,
  Read the legend round the name—
" *Unsullied aye our honours beam,*"
  'Neath fleur-de-lis and crescent shone ;
And, o'er the Dragon spouting fire,
  The battle-word " Set on ! " *

IX.

" Yes ! here, good Frere—now, haste thee—ope ! "—
  The holy man turn'd the key ;
And ere ever he had an " Ave " said,
  The Knight was on his knee.
He lifted the lawn from her waxen face,
  And put back the satin soft ;
Fled from her cheek was the glowing grace
  That had thrill'd his heart so oft !
The past came o'er him like a spell,
  For earth could now no bliss afford,
And thus, within that cheerless cell,
  His bitter plaint he pour'd.

---

* " *Intaminatis fulget honoribus,*" was the proud motto of the Seton family.

The original Seton arms were three crescents with a double tressure, flowered and counterflowered with fleurs-de-lis. A sword supporting a royal crown was afterwards given by Robert the Bruce, for the bravery and loyalty of the family during the succession wars. At a later period, three garbs azure were quartered with the Seton arms, by George the second lord of that name.

" This lord George," saith old Sir Thomas Maitland, " tuk the armes of Buchan, quhilk ar thrè cumming schevis, quarterlie wyth his awin armes, allegeand himself to be air of the said erldome, be ressoun of his gudedame."—*Chronical of the Hous of Seytoun*, p. 37.

The crest was a green dragon spouting fire surmounting a ducal coronet, with the words over it, " *Set on.*" The supporters were two foxes collared and chains.

X.

"Oh ! Elena, I little dreamt,
 When I sailed o'er the sea,
That, coming back, our meeting next
 In a charnel-vault should be !
I left thee in thy virgin pride,
 A living flower of beauty rare,
And now I see thee at my side
 What words may not declare !
Oh ! I have met thee on the waves,
 On the field have braved thee, Death,
But ne'er before so sank my heart
 Thy withering scowl beneath !

XI.

" How different was the time, alas !
 When, in the sunny noon of love,
I trysted with thee in the stag coppice,
 In the centre of the grove !
How different was the time, alas !
 When, from the tower of high Falsyde,*
We mark'd along the Bay of Forth
 The streamer'd galleys glide !
How different was the time, alas !
 When the gay gold ring I gave,
And thou didst say, when far away,
 I will bear it to my grave !"

---

* Sir Robert Sibbald, in his History of Fife, quotes a charter by
the Earl of Winchester to Adame de Seton, 1246, " *De Maritagio
hærædis Alani de Fawside*," from which, as well as from some in-
cidental passages in Maitland's " History of the Hous of Seytoun,"
it is evident that Falside Castle was a heritage of the younger
branches of the Seton family. It was first acquired by them from
intermarriage with the De Quinceys.
 The date of Falsyde Castle is uncertain. It was burned by the

T

XII.

The Knight turn'd back the satin fold
    Where her hand lay by her side,
And there, on her slender finger cold,
    He the token ring espied !
"Now know I thou wert true to me,
    Ah ! false thou couldst not prove ;
Vain was the hate that strove to mate
    Thy heart with a stranger love."
And then he kiss'd her clay-cold cheek,
    And then he kiss'd his sword.
-"By this," he said, "sweet injured maid,
    Thy doom shall be deplored !

XIII.

"Yes ! darkly some shall make remead,
    And dearly some shall pay
For griefs that broke thy faithful heart,
    When I was far away !"

English under the Duke of Somerset, 1547, the day following the
fatal battle of Pinkie. The strength of the mason-work, however—
the tower being arched at the top of the building, as well as at the
first story—prevented its entire demolition. Paton, in his Diary,
gives a very cool description of the burning to death of its little
garrison, and calls it "a sorry-looking castle." In 1618, the family
of Fawside of that Ilk appear to have removed to a more modern
mansion in the immediate vicinity, which has the initials J. F., J. L.,
above one of its windows. The dovecot of the ancient fortalice still
remains ; and within it is a curious place of concealment, secured by
an antique grated door. There is a similar hole of secrecy in the
staircase of the oldest part of the castle.

It is now the property of Sir George Grant Suttie of Prestongrange
and Balgone, having descended to him through his maternal
ancestors the Setons, Earls of Hyndford.

In peaceful pride, by Esk's green side,
　The shy deer stray'd through Roslin glen;
And the hill-fox to the Roman Camp *
　Stole up from Hawthornden.†

II.

Where hurries so fast the henchman?
　His steed seems froth'd with spray;
To Newbottle's shrine, 'mid the dawning lone,
　He speeds his onward way.
From grey Caerbarrin's walls he came, ‡
　By Smeaton Shaw, through Golden Wood,
And up thy royal way, Derstrette, §
　His path he hath pursued—

* The parish of Newbottle rises from its extremities—Fordel
House and Newbyres Tower—till it terminates in a ridge of
considerable extent, termed the Roman Camp, the elevation of which
is 680 feet. The neighbourhood abounding in hares, the Roman
Camp is a favourite meeting-place of the Mid-Lothian Coursing
Club. From antlers found in the neighbourhood, and even at
Inveresk, no doubt can exist, that, at the era of our ballad, the hart
and hind were visitants of at least the Morth-thwaite hills.

† The building of Roslin Castle is anterior to the dawn of
authentic record. " Its origin," says Chalmers (" Caledonia,"
vol. ii. p. 571), is laid in fable." According to Adam de Cardonnel
(" Picturesque Antiquities "), William de Sancto Claro, son of
Waldernus Compte de St Clare, who came to England with William
the Conqueror, obtained from King Malcom Canmore a grant of
the lands and barony of Roslin. Hawthornden and Roslin are
associated with many bright names in literature—Drummond, Ben
Jonson, Ramsay, Macneil, Scott, Wilson, and Wordsworth.

‡ Chalmers traces back the name "*Caerbairin*" to the time of the
ancient Britons, and instances the modern one, "*Carberry*," to show
how English adjuncts have been engrafted on British roots.
Every reader of Scottish history will remember that it was on the
rising ground above the fortalice of Carberry, that Mary and
Bothwell awaited the approach of the confederate lords ; and that
there they were parted, never to meet again.

§ During the Scoto-Saxon period, the king's highways are often

Until, upon its flowery lawn,
  By murmuring Esk's enamour'd side,
The Abbey's grand and massive walls
  Were 'mid its groves espied.*

---

mentioned in chartularies, as local boundaries. In that of Newbottle we find reference made to a *regia via*, leading from the
village of Ford to the Abbey, in a charter of Hugh Riddel, in the
time of Alexander III. (chart. 22.) The king's highway from the
same Abbey to Edinburgh in 1252, is also there mentioned (16) ;
and Gervaise, the abbot, in his charter (*Ib.* 163), alludes to a certain
road called *Derstrette*, near Colden, in the district of Inveresk.
Near the same locality there is now a place called *D'Arcy*, which I
have little doubt is a corruption of the ancient appellation.

* Newbottle Abbey was beautifully situated on the banks of the
South Esk, nearly on the same site as the modern mansion of the
Marquis of Lothian, who is a descendant of the last abbot. It was
founded by that " sore saint for the crown," King David I., in the
year 1140. "The monks," says Bishop Keith, " were brought from
Melrose, together with their abbot, Radulphus. Patrick Madort,
a learned divine, who is mentioned from the year 1462 until 1470,
recovered a great number of original writs and charters belonging
to this place, which were transcribed into a chartulary, which is now
in the Advocates' Library."—*Religious Houses*, p. 417. Ed. 1824.

The only relics of antiquity now about the place, are the remains
of the stone inclosure which surrounded the Abbey, still called
Monkland Wall—a striking and venerable gateway, surmounted by
its time-worn lions ; a solemn line of yew-trees ; and a doorway,
amid the lawn to the east, said to be the entrance of a subterranean
passage to the old Abbey.

Many of the trees in the park are beautiful and majestic,
especially some of the planes and elms ; and a beech, in the
neighbourhood of the house, measures twenty-two feet in circum-
ference, at a yard from the ground. It contains nine hundred cubic
feet of wood, and its branches cover a circle of thirty-three feet
diameter.

The remains of monastic architecture now seen at Newbottle are
said to have been brought by the late Marquis from the ruins at
Mount Teviot. They are beautiful and interesting.

We should also state, in referring to the antiquities of the place,

III.

"Awake!" he cries, as loudly he knocks.
    "Ho! arise, and haste with me;
For soon, alas, Caerbarrin's lord
    Among the dead must be!"
Then forth outspake the abbot grey
    From his couch, as he arose—
"Alack! thou bring'st us evil news,
    For thy lord he was of those
Who dower'd our church with goodly lands,
    And his sword hath ever been,
For Scotland's glory and for ours,
    At the call, unsheath'd and keen.

IV.

"But the best are aye the first to die,
    This sinful earth is not their place;
Sure is the passage of the good—
    Mary Mother yield them grace!
Then rest thee in our porter's keep,
    While our brother Francis will repair
To the house of woe, and soothe the soul
    Of the dying man with prayer!"

---

that a little below the Abbey there is a venerable bridge over the Esk, rudely built, and overspread with ivy, which has long survived all accounts of its age and founder.

The present parish of Newbottle consists of the ancient parish of Maisterton, and the Abbey parish. During the Scoto-Saxon period, the patronage of Maisterton was possessed by the lord of the manor. Near the end of the thirteenth century this belonged to Robert de Rossine, knight, whose daughters, Mariot and Ada, resigned it to the Monks of Newbottle, with two-thirds of their estates.

The henchman sate him down to rest,
    And wiped the toil-drops from his brow ;
While in hurry and haste, on shrieving quest,
    The Frere was boune to ride and go.

V.

Through the green woodlands spurr'd the monk—
    The morning sun was shining bright,
Upon his bosom lay the Book,*
    Under his cloak of white ;
Before him, in the pleasant prime,
    The willow'd stream meandering flow'd—
From wildflowers by the pathway side
    The gallant heathcock crow'd ;
Glisten'd the dew on the harebells blue—
    And, as the west wind murmur'd by,
From yellow broom stole forth perfume,
    As from gardens of Araby.

VI.

Now lay his road by beechen groves—
    Now by daisied pastures green,
And now, from the vista'd mountain road,
    The shores of Fife were seen ;—

*
        "Much he marvell'd a knight of pride
        Like a book-bosom'd priest should ride."

So says Sir Walter Scott (Lay, canto iii. stanza 8), and, in
annotation, quotes from a MS. Account of Parish of Ewes, apud
Macfarlane's MSS. :—"At Unthank, two miles north-east from the
church (of Ewes), there are the ruins of a chapel for Divine service
in time of Popery. There is a tradition that friars were wont to
come from Melrose or Jedburgh, to baptize and marry in this
parish ; and, from being in use to carry the mass-book in their
bosoms, they were called by the inhabitants " *Book a bosomes.*"

And now Dalcaeth behind him lay; *
And now its castle, whence the Græme
Sent forth his clump of Border spears,
    The vaunting Gael to tame;
Now by coppice and corn he urged his steed,
    Now by dingle wild and by dell,
Where down by Cousland's limestone rocks
    The living waters well.

VII.

Then he came to a clump of oak-trees hoar,
    Half over the steep road hung,
When up at once to his bridle rein
    The arm of a warrior sprung;

---

  * *Dalcaeth*, in the Celtic, means the narrow dale. (*Vide* Richard and Owen's Dictionary, *in voce* Caeth.) Dalkeith, as a parish, does not appear in the ancient *Taxatio*. Indeed, as such, it did not then exist; but as the manor of Dalkeith, as well as that of Abercorn, was granted by David I. to William de Grahame, it is easily to be supposed, that, being an opulent family, they had a chapel to their court. "No memorial remains of the Grahames, unless the fading traditions of the place, and two curious but wasted tombstones, which lie within the circuit of the old church. They represent knights in chain armour, lying cross-legged upon their monuments, like those ancient and curious figures on the tombs in the Temple Church, London."—*Provincial Antiquities of Scotland.* From Robertson's "Index," 40—44; and from the "Douglas Peerage," 489, we find, that in the reign of David II., John de Grahame of Dalkeith resigned the manor, with its pertinents, to William Douglas, the heir of Sir James Douglas of Lothian, in marriage with his daughter Margaret. Dalcaeth is first written Dalkeith in a charter of Robert the Bruce. It is proper to mention, however, that Froissart, who himself visited the Earl of Douglas at his castle of Dalkeith, has the following passage, in mentioning the single combat between the Earl and Sir Henry Percy, at the barriers of Newcastle. The former having, by force of arms, won the banner of the latter, is thus made to say:—"I shall bear this token of your prowess into

With sudden jerk, the startled steed
  Swerved aside with bristling mane :
"Now halt thee, Frere, and rest thee here,
  Till I hither return again.
I know thine errand—dismount, dismount—
  That errand for thee I'll do ;
But, if thou stirrest till I return,
  Such rashness thou shalt rue !

VIII.

"Then doff to me thy mantle white,
  And eke thy hood of black ; *
And crouch thee amid these brackens green,
  To the left, till I come back."
"Oh! bethink thee, Knight," the good Frere said,
  "I should kneel by his couch and pray ;
How awful it is for the soul of man
  Unanneal'd to pass away !

Scotland, and shall set it high on my castle of Dalkeith. (D'Alquest)
that it may be seen far off."—*Froissart*, Berners' reprint, 1812.
Vol. ii. p. 393.

* The monks of Newbottle were of the Cistertian order. " They
were called *Monachi Albi*," says Cardonnel, " to distinguish them
from the *Benedictines*, whose habit was entirely black ; whereas the
Cistertians wore a black cowl and scapular, and all their other
clothes were white. They had the name of *Cistertians*, from their
chief house and monasteries, Cistertium, in Burgundy ; and
Bernardines, from St. Bernard, who, with a number of his followers,
retired to the monastery, and was afterwards called Abbot of
Clairvaux."—*Picturesque Antiquities*, Part. I., pp. 12, 13 ; and
Keith's *Scottish Bishops*, p. 415.

There were thirteen monasteries of the Cistertian order in Scotland, among which were Melrose, Dundrennan, Culross, Sweetheart,
and Glenluce.

How awful it is, with sins unshrived,
To pass from the bed of pain!
Caerbarrin's chief may a dead man be,
Ere thou comest hither again!"

IX.

He must needs obey, he durst not say nay,
That monk to the warrior stern;
His corslet unlaced, and his helm unbraced,
Down rattled among the fern;
And he hath mounted the Frere's good steed,
Clad in mantle and cowl he rode,
Till 'neath him, on its own green knoll,
Caerbarrin's turrets glow'd.*

* The ancient history of the lands of Carberry is lost in obscurity. The lower rooms of the square tower are strongly arched, and evidently of great age. At the time of the Duke of Somerset's expedition it was the property of Mr. Hugh Rigg, the king's advocate, who is more than once mentioned in the histories of Knox and Pitscottie. We observe also, from the *Inquisitiones Speciales*, that the property was conveyed to several subsequent generations of the same family—from whom it passed to the Dicksons—of whom we find that, during the Rebellion of 1745, Sir Robert was chief bailie of Musselburgh.

The assumption of the lords of this wealthy district having been donators to the Abbey of Newbottle, however unwarranted by record, is far from unlikely, the practice having been a common one with the wealthy for very weighty reasons.

In 1184, as we learn from the Chartulary of Newbottle (71), Robert de Quincey, the father of our hero, granted to the monks of the Abbey the lands of Preston, where they formed an agricultural establishment—hence called Preston Grange—with common of pasture for ten sheep, and a sufficiency of oxen to cultivate their grange. Seyer de Quincey confirmed to the monks all these privileges gifted by his father, by which confirmation we learn that their lands of Preston were bounded on the west by the rivulet of Pinkie, in his manor of Travernent.

A curious fact is also ascertained by these charters of the De

Caerbarrin ! famed by History's pen
  In Scotland's later day,
When Bothwell fled, and Mary was led
  In weeping beauty away.

Quinceys, which is the date at which coals were first worked in Scotland ; and, in contradiction to the pretensions of Fifeshire, this appears to have taken place on this spot. The charter of Robert grants to the monks the right of *digging peats* and of *cutting wood* for fuel ; whereas, in that of his son Seyer, we find the addition of *carbonarium et quarrarium,*" with free access to, and recess from the same by the sea.

"This charter" (that of Seyer), says Chalmers in his erudite "Caledonia," vol. ii. p. 486, "must necessarily have been granted between the years 1202 and 1218, as it is witnessed by William, who became Bishop of St. Andrew's in 1202, and was granted by Seyer de Quincey, who set out for the Holy Land in 1218, where he died in the subsequent year."

From Keith's "Scottish Bishops," p. 15, we learn that William Malvoisine was translated from the see of Glasgow to that of St. Andrew's in 1202. It is also added, on the authority of the "Chart. of Dunfermline," that he was "contemporary with Pope Honorius and Sayerus de Quincey."

In connection with the same family, we also find from the Chartulary of Newbottle, that Elena, the youngest daughter of Roger de Quincey, the Constable of Scotland, married Alan la Zouche, an English baron, and that in the division of his great estates among his three daughters, the barony of Heriot fell to her share ; and that, in her great liberality, she granted to the monks of Newbottle the church of " Heryeth," with the tithes and other rights. (Chart. 270.)

The lands themselves of Heryeth were afterwards acquired by the monks ; but whether from the liberality of Elena, or from her son La Zouche, who lost his estates in the succession wars, does not appear.

Such transfers of property to religious houses were of common occurrence. We have already alluded to the cession of Maisterton, by the daughters of Sir Robert de Rossine—Mariot, who married Neil de Carrick, and Ada, the wife of Gilbert de Ayton—in 1320 ; and from the Chartulary of Newbottle we learn, that the monks had

X.

The warder hail'd him from the keep,
  As through the forest of oak he hied,
Now down the path, by the winding strath,
  That leads from Chalkyside.
"Speed, speed thee!" cried the porter old,
  As the portals wide he threw;
"Speed—speed thee!" cried the sentinel,
  The court as he pass'd through;
And "Speed thee!" echo'd the seneschal,
  As he show'd the way before,—
"For much I fear, most holy Frere,
  That the struggle shall soon be o'er."

FITTE THIRD.

I.

Bright on Caerbarrin shines the sun,
  But all within is woe and gloom;
For there Sir Malcolm bends in death—
  Before him yawns the tomb!
Unfolded were the chamber doors,
  Where moan'd he, stretch'd in prone decay;
And his rattling breath spake of coming death,
  As life's sands ebb'd away;

---

various lands in Clydesdale, in order to have easy access to which they obtained, from various proprietors in Mid and West Lothian, special grants of free passage to these distant granges. (Chart. 218 to 227, and 240.)

In conclusion we may add, as showing the extensive possessions at this early period of the De Quincey family, that Roger de Quincey, Earl of Winton, gave also to the canons of Dryburgh a toft "*in villa de Hadintune.*" (Chart. Dryb. 1c6.)

But, when the mantled Monk he saw,
  On his arm he strove to rise,
And the light, that erst was waning fast,
  Flash'd back to his sunken eyes.

II.

"Welcome! holy Father," he said,
  In accents fond, but low and weak—
"I would pour my sins in thy pitying ear,
  And absolution seek;
For I have been a sinful man,
  And repent me of my sin;
Yet, as pass the hopes of life away,
  The terrors of death begin;
But chiefly would I tell to thee
  My crime of the blackest dye,
Which a sea of tears might scarce wash out,
  Though I could weep it dry!

III.

"A gentle ladye my kinsman loved,
  And before he cross'd the sea,
To combat afar with the Saracen,
  He trust reposed in me;
But a demon held my soul in thrall,
  And evil thoughts within me brew'd;
So, instead of nursing her love for him,
  Her hand for myself I woo'd.
I threw forth doubts, that only were
  The coinage of my brain;
I praised her high fidelity,
  Yet mourn'd that her love was vain!"

IV.

Upstarted the Frere ;—"Ah, holy man,
  Yet the worst I have not told ;
In me—though sprung from noblest blood`!—
  A perjured wretch behold—
For my love that ladye no love return'd,
  Although, with hellish sleight,
We forged a cartel, whose purport show'd
  That De Quincey had fallen in fight.
Yes ! my suit that lofty ladye scorn'd—
  More distant she look'd and cold,
And for my love no love return'd—
  Though I woo'd her with gifts and gold !"

V.

Uprose the Frere ;—"Nay, sit thee down ;
  Not mine was the guilt alone :
Father Francis was the clerke thereof,
  And his Abbey is your own !
To fair Elena's hand that scroll he bore,
  Then she folded her palms and sighed ;
And she said, 'Since true he has died to me,
  I will be no other's bride !'
Still woo'd I her in her mourning weeds,
  Till she show'd a poinard bare,
And wildly vow'd—if again I vex'd,
  Her heart—to plunge it there !

VI.

" Day after day, ray after ray,
  She waned like an autumn sun,
When droop the flowers, 'mid yellow bowers,
  And the waters wailing run ;—

Day after day, like a broken rosebud,
  She wither'd and she waned,
Till, of her beauty and wonted bloom,
  But feeble trace remain'd :—
Then seem'd she, like some saintly form,
  Too pure for the gazer's eye,
Melting away, from our earthly day,
  To her element—the sky!

VII.

"She died—and then I felt remorse—
  But how could I atone?
And I shook, when, by her breathless corse,
  In silence I stood alone :—
Yes! when I saw my victim lie,
  Untimely, in her swathing shroud,
The weight of my burden'd conscience hung
  Upon me like a cloud!
There was no light—and all was night,
  And storm, and darkness drear;
By day 'twas joyless, and my sleep
  Was haunted by forms of fear!

VIII.

"Lonely I stray'd, until, dismay'd,
  I sought the feast, where mirth was none,
Only to find that man is mind
  And form and features dust alone.
Yes—of my kinsman oft I dreamt—
  Of his woe, and his vengeance dire,
Till yesternight he cross'd
  Like a demon in his i

I had not heard of his home return—
  Like a spectre there he stood—
Appall'd I sank, and his falchion drank
  Deeply my forfeit blood.

IX.

"Oh ! grant remission of my sins,
  A contrite, humbled man I die !"
Ere yet the words were out, the monk
  Beheld his glazing eye;
And rising away from the couch, he said—
  "May Heaven forgive my vow !"
With horror thrill'd his yielding frame,
  And he smote his bursting brow:
Then pass'd he from the chamber forth,
  And in silence from the gate,
And off to the south, through the steep hill pass,
  On his steed he journey'd straight.

X.

A weight of woe is at his heart,
  Despair's grey cloud is on his brow,
For hope and fear both disappear
  In that absorbing *now !*
The world is one vast wilderness,
  Vain all its pomp, its honours vain;
De Quincey sigh'd, and onwards pass'd
  Slowly with slacken'd rein;
Thus wound he down through Cousland glen,
  O'erhung with willows grey,
Until he came to the brackens green
  Wherein Father Francis lay.

U

XI.

"Ho! Frere, arise! Thy cloak and cowl
  Have done their office meet."
Father Francis sprang from his lurking-place,
  And stood at the warrior's feet.
"Now tell me," cried De Quincey, fierce,
  "For thou art learn'd in lore,
What the meaning of this riddle is
  That a bird unto me bore—
A lady in her chamber mourn'd,
  Her true knight he was abroad,
Fighting afar with the Saracen,
  Under the Cross of God!

XII.

"A false Friend, and a falser Frere,
  Combined to shake her faith;
They forged—ah, wherefore dost thou fear?
  Base caitiff, take thy death!"
The knight he struck him to the heart;
  Through the branches with a crash
Down reel'd the corse, and in the swamp
  Sank with a sullen dash.*

* Cousland-dean, a ravine of considerable depth, which commences where the highway from Dalkeith branches off towards Pathhead on the right, and towards Inveresk on the left, although now partially drained, shows every indication of having been in the olden time a wide and extensive morass; and, at its narrowest points, is still spanned by two bridges, one of considerable antiquity. Indeed, the traces of the water-course are still evident from behind Chalkyside, on the west, running eastwards along the hollow, mid-way between Elphinstone Tower and Cousland Park, where it assumes the form of a rivulet.

"Thus perish all, who would enthrall
  The guileless and the true;
Yet on head of mine no more shall shine
  The sun from his path of blue.

XIII.

"No more on me shall pleasure smile—
  A heartless, hopeless man;
The tempest's clouds of misery
  Have darken'd for aye my span.
Farewell—farewell! my native land,
  Hill, valley, stream, and strath;
And thou, who held my heart's command,
  And ye who cross'd my path.
Blow, blow, ye winds! in fury blow,
  And waft us from this baleful shore;
Rise, rise, ye billows, and bear us along,
  Who hither return no more!"*

* In the grants made by Seyer de Quincey to the Abbey of Newbottle, mention is made of "his baronies of Preston and Tranent,
bounded on the west by the rivulet of Pinkie." We find also, that
Falsyde and Ephingston were in his possession; and he is elsewhere
styled Earl of Wyntoun ("Caledonia," vol. ii. 486, note 6), a proof that
the barony of that name formed also a part of his immense possessions. It is not a little curious, therefore, that a charter of King
William, the brother of Malcolm, surnamed the Maiden, should be
still extant, wherein, in the thirteenth year of that monarch's reign,
he makes *confirmation* to Philip de Seytune of the lands of Seytouner ·
Wintoun, and Winchelburgh (*nunc* Winchburgh), "quhilk," as Sir
Richard Maitland observes ("Historie," p. 17), "was auld heretage
of befor, as the said charter testifies."

"Willielmus, Dei gra. rex Scotorum, &c. Sciatis presentis et
futuri, me concessisse, et hac carta mea confirmasse, Phillipo de
Seytune, terram *quæ fuit patris sui;* scilicet, Seytune, et Wintune,
et Winchilburgh, tenendam sibi et hæredibus suis de me et
hæredibus meis, in fædo et hæreditate," &c.

Philip de Seytune was succeeded, on his death, by his son

U 2

Alexander ; and, by another singular preservation, we have, in the forty-sixth year of the same king, another royal charter of infeftment of the same lands. It is nearly in the same words ; and, strange to say, two of the witnesses to it are Robert de Quincey and Henry de Quincey. Both of these charters are printed in Dr. M'Kenzie's "Lives of Scottish Writers." They have also been transcribed by the author, or rather compiler of the "Diplomata Scotiæ," which transcripts are still preserved, being now, or lately, in the possession of Mr. Dillon, a member of the Maitland Club.

In the succession wars, the De Quincey family took side with Baliol, and the Setons with Bruce. Sir Christopher, or Chrystal Seton saved the life of that great man at the disastrous battle of Methven ; and afterwards married his sister. On the accession of Bruce to the throne, the estates of the De Quinceys, being declared forfeited, were conferred on the Setons ; and in Sir Richard Maitland's Chronicle we find, that "the said King Robert gave to the said Alexander (Seton) the barony of Tranent, with the tenendury thairof for the tyme, viz. Falsyde mylis and Elphinstoune, as the charteris testifiis, geven thairupoun." The "landis of Dundas and Cragye" were also bestowed upon him "for service, done by his father and himself, with the landes and barony of Barnis, aboue Hadingtoun, with dyuers uther landis, quhilk I emit for schortnes." (Glasgow reprint, 1829, p. 21.)

For centuries the name of De Quincey hath perished from out of the rich and extensive district which owned its sway ; and, in contemplating the destinies of this once great family, how apposite is the exclamation of Claudian—

> " Tolluntur in altum
> Ut lapsu graviore ruant ! "

DE QUINCEY

ON

THE DOCTRINE OF FUTURE PUNISHMENT.

THE origin and history of this profoundly interesting essay, which does not appear in any British edition of the author's "collected works," will be explained by an extract from the Prefatory Note attached to a volume * which I published in 1890, to which this essay was prefixed :—

"Forty-three years ago, while engaged in the editorship of the new series of *The Instructor*—my father's weekly magazine—I had frequent conversations with Thomas de Quincey, on questions relating to the future state.

"He reviewed, amidst other problems, of the soul, our dim knowledge of that momentous question—the duration of future punishment, to which the yearning human spirit ever turns with awe. He dwelt on the great mysteries surrounding us, which the children of men must be content now to 'see through a glass, darkly ; '

* THE WIDER HOPE : Essays and Strictures on the Doctrine and Literature of Future Punishment, by Numerous Writers, Lay and Clerical ; including Archdeacon Farrar, the late Dean Plumptre, the late Principal Tulloch, the late Dr. Allon, the late Rev. J. Baldwin Brown, Rev. William Arthur, Rev. James H. Rigg, D.D., &c. 1890.

and the lights and shadows of belief, which, age by age, perplex and agitate anxious, storm-tossed minds—in their honest endeavour to arrive at the true teaching of Scripture.

"Again and again, during the discussion of these solemn and moving subjects, he recurred to the interpretation of the expression for *eternity*, until at length, one day in the autumn of 1852, he said to me, '*If I write this, dare you print it ?*' With a full sense of the far-reaching responsibility, I replied, 'I *dare.*' Accordingly the essay was written, and soon afterwards published, viz.— in the number of *The Instructor* for the first week of 1853.

"It attracted much attention through the English-speaking world, and provoked criticism of a very mixed nature, privately, and in the press. Forty-three years ago, it will be remembered, the rigour of theological opinion, particularly in the Modern Athens, operated with a severity differing greatly from what now prevails. I will only remark, that I have always felt satisfied at having done what lay in my power, to promote a clear understanding of the Greek words in question, by enabling the distinguished author to offer to thoughtful men a contribution so deserving of their attentive consideration.

"This remarkable essay—a legacy of De Quincey's keen intellect and scholarly power—has been in some respects more fully appreciated in the recent literature of Eschatology, than on its first appearance. I refer especially to its influence on the American mind, it having been for a long time widely disseminated throughout the United States."

I cannot better indicate the tone of those conversations with De Quincey, which led to the production of the following essay, than by the suggestive words of John Foster, which I printed as "foreword" to "The Wider Hope."

"There is one question which combines with the interest of speculation and curiosity an interest incomparably greater, nearer more affecting, more solemn. It is the simple question—'What shall we be?' How soon it is spoken ; but who shall reply? Think how profoundly this question, this mystery concerns us ; and, in comparison with this, what are to us all questions of all sciences? What to us all researches into the constitution and laws of material nature? What—all investigations into the history of past ages? What to us the future career of events in] the progress of states and empires? What to us—what shall become of the globe itself, or all the mundane system? What we shall be, we ourselves, is the matter of surpassing interest."

ON THE SUPPOSED
SCRIPTURAL EXPRESSION FOR ETERNITY.

By THOMAS DE QUINCEY.

FORTY years ago (or, in all probability, a good deal more, for we have already completed thirty-seven years from Waterloo, and my remembrances upon this subject go back to a period lying much behind that great era), I used to be annoyed and irritated by the false interpretation given to the Greek word *aiōn*, and given necessarily, therefore, to the adjective *aionios* as its immediate derivative. It was not so much the falsehood of this interpretation, as the narrowness of that falsehood, which disturbed me. There was a glimmer of truth in it ; and precisely that glimmer it was which led the way to a general and obstinate misconception of the meaning. The word is remarkably situated. It is a Scriptural word, and it is also a Greek word ; from which the inevitable inference is, that we must look for it only in the *New* Testament. Upon any question arising of deep, aboriginal, doctrinal truth, we have nothing to do with translations. Those are but secondary questions, archæological and critical, upon which we have a right to consult the Greek translation of the Hebrew Scriptures known by the name of the Septuagint.

Suffer me to pause at this point for the sake of premising an explanation needful to the unlearned reader. As the reading public and the thinking public, is every year outgrowing more and more notoriously, the mere *learned* public, it becomes every year more and more the right of the former public to give the law preferably to the latter public, upon all points which concern its own separate interests. In past generations, no pains were taken to make explanations that were not called for by the *learned* public. All other readers were ignored. They formed a mob, for whom no provision was made. And that many difficulties should be left entirely unexplained for *them*, was superciliously assumed to be no fault at all. And yet any sensible man, let him be as supercilious as he may, must on consideration allow that amongst the crowd of unlearned or half-learned readers, who have had neither time nor opportunities for what is called "erudition" or learned studies, there must always lurk a proportion of men that, by constitution of mind, and by the bounty of nature, are much better fitted for thinking, originally more philosophic, and are more capaciously endowed, than those who are, by accident of position, more learned. Such a natural superiority certainly takes precedency of a merely artificial superiority ; and, therefore, it entitles those who possess it to a special consideration. Let there be an audience gathered to any book of 10,100 readers ; it might be fair in these days to assume that 10,000 would be in a partial sense illiterate, and the remaining 100 what would be rigorously classed as "learned." Now, on such as distribution of the readers, it would be a matter of certainty that the most powerful intellects would lie amongst the illiterate 10,000, counting, probably, to 15 to 1 as against those in the learned minority. The inference, therefore, would be, that, in all equity, the interest of the unlearned section claimed a priority of attention, not merely as the more numerous section, but also as, by a high probability, the more philosophic. And in proportion as this unlearned section widens and expands, which every year it does, in that proportion the obligation and cogency of this equity strengthens. An attention to the unlearned part of an audience, which 15 years ago might have rested upon pure courtesy, now rests upon a basis of absolute justice. I make this preliminary explanation, in order to take away the appearance of caprice from such occasional pauses as I may make for the purpose of clearing up obscurities or difficulties. Formerly in a case of that nature, the learned reader would have told me that I was not entitled to delay *him* by elucidations that in *his* case must be supposed to be superfluous ; and in such a remonstrance there would once have been some equity. The illiterate section of the readers might then be fairly assumed as present only by accident ; as no abiding part

of the audience ; but, like the general public in the
gallery of the House of Commons, as present only by
sufferance ; and officially in any records of the house
whatever, utterly ignored as existences. At present,
half-way on our pilgrimage through the nineneenth
century, I reply to such a learned remonstrant—that it
gives me pain to annoy him by superfluous explanations,
but that, unhappily, this infliction of tedium upon *him* is
inseparable from what has now become a duty to others.
This being said, I now go on to inform the illiterate
reader, that the earliest translation of the Hebrew
Scriptures ever made was into Greek. It was undertaken on the encouragement of a learned prince, Ptolemy
Philadelphus, by an association of Jewish emigrants in
Alexandria. It was, as the event has shown in very
many instances, an advantage of a rank rising to providential, that such a cosmopolitan version of the Hebrew
sacred writings should have been made at a moment
when a rare concurrence of circumstances happened to
make it possible ; such as, for example, a king both
learned in his tastes and liberal in his principles of
religious toleration ; a language, viz., the Greek, which
had already become, what for many centuries it continued to be, a common language of communication for
the learned of the whole οἰκουμένη (*i.e.*, in effect of the
civilised world, viz., Greece, the shores of the Euxine,
the whole of Asia Minor, Syria, Egypt, Carthage, and
all the dependencies of Carthage, finally, and above
all, Rome, then beginning to loom upon the western
horizon), together with all the dependencies of Rome,
and, briefly, every state and city that adorned the
imperial islands of the Mediterranean, or that glittered
like gems in that vast belt of land, roundly speaking,
1000 miles in average breadth, and in circuit running up

to 5000 miles. 1000 multiplied into 5 times 1000, or, otherwise expressed, a thousand thousand 5 times repeated, or, otherwise, a million 5 times repeated, briefly, a territory measuring 5,000,000 of square miles, or 45 times the surface of our two British islands, such was the boundless domain which this extraordinary act of Ptolemy suddenly threw open to the literature and spiritual revelation of a little obscure race, nestling in a little angle of Asia, scarcely visible as a fraction of Syria, buried in the broad shadows thrown out on one side by the great and ancient settlements on the Nile, and on the other by the vast empire, that for thousands of years occupied the Tigris and the Euphrates. In the twinkling of an eye, at a sudden summons, as it were from the sounding of a trumpet, or the Oriental call by a clapping of hands, gates are thrown open, which have an effect corresponding in grandeur to the effect that would arise from the opening of a ship canal across the Isthmus of Darien, viz., the introduction to each other—face to face—of two separate infinities. Such a canal would suddenly lay open to each other the two great oceans of our planet, the Atlantic and the Pacific; whilst the act of translating *into* Greek and *from* Hebrew, that is, transferring out of a mysterious cipher as little accessible as Sanscrit, and which never *would* be more accessible through any worldly attractions of alliance with power and civic grandeur, or commerce, *out* of this darkness *into* the golden light of a language the most beautiful, the most honoured amongst men, and the most widely diffused through a thousand years to come, had the immeasurable effect of throwing into the great crucible of human speculation, even the beginning to ferment, to boil, to overflow—that mightiest of all elements for exalting the chemistry of philosophy—grand and, for the first time, adequate conceptions of the Deity. For, although it is true that, until Elias should come—that is, until Christianity should have applied its final revelation to the completion of this great idea—we could not possess it in its total effulgence, it is, however, certain that an immense advance was made, a prodigious usurpation across the realms of chaos, by the grand illumination of the Hebrew discoveries. Too terrifically austere we must presume the Hebrew idea to have been ; too undeniably it had not withdrawn the veil entirely which still rested upon the Divine countenance ; so much is involved in the subsequent revelations of Christianity. But still the advance made in reading aright the Divine lineaments had been enormous. God was now a holy Spirit that could not tolerate impurity. He was a fountain of justice, and no longer disfigured by any mode of sympathy with human caprice or infirmity. And, if a frown too awful still rested upon His face, making the approach to Him too fearful for harmonising with that perfect freedom and that childlike love which God seeks in His worshippers, it was yet made evident that no step for conciliating His favour did or could lie through any but *moral* graces.

Three centuries after this great epoch of the *publication* (for such it was), secured so providentially to the Hebrew theology, two learned Jews—viz., Josephus and Philo Judæus—had occasion to seek a cosmopolitan utterance for that burden of truth (or what they regarded as truth), which oppressed the spirit within them. Once again they found a deliverance from the very same freezing imprisonment in an unknown language, through the very same magical key, viz., the all-pervading language of Greece, which carried their communications to the four winds of heaven, and carried them precisely amongst the class of men, viz.—the enlightened and educated class—which pre-eminently, if not exclusively, their wish was to reach. About one generation *after* Christ it was, when the utter prostration, and, politically speaking, the destruction of Jerusalem and the Jewish nation, threw these two learned Jews upon this recourse to the Greek language, as their final resource, in a condition otherwise of absolute hopelessness. Pretty nearly three centuries *before* Christ it was (284 years, according to common reckoning), when the first act of communication took place between the sealed-up literature of Palestine and the Greek Catholic interpretation. Altogether, we may say that 320 years, or somewhere about ten generations of men, divided these two memorable acts of intercommunication. Such a space of time allows a large range of influence and of silent unconscious operation to the vast and potent ideas that brooded over this awful Hebrew literature. Too little weight has been allowed to the probable contagiousness, and to the preternatural shock, of such a new and strange philosophy, acting upon the jaded and exhausted intellect of the Grecian race. We must remember, that precisely this particular range of time was that in which the Greek system of philosophy, having thoroughly completed their evolution, had suffered something of a collapse ; and, having exhausted their creative energies, began to gratify the cravings for novelty by remodellings of old forms. It is remarkable, indeed, that this very city of Alexandria founded and matured this new principle of remodelling applied to poetry not less than to philosophy and criticism. And, considering the activity of this great commercial city and port, which was meant to act, and *did* act, as a centre of communication between the East and the West, it is probable

that a far greater effect was produced by the Greek
translation of the Jewish Scriptures, in the way of
preparing the mind of nations for the apprehension of
Christianity, than has ever been distinctly recognised.
The silent destruction of books in those centuries has
robbed us of all means for tracing innumerable revolutions, that nevertheless, by the evidence of results, must
have existed. Taken, however, with or without this
additional result, the translation of the Hebrew Scriptures
in their most important portions must be ranked
amongst what are called "providential" events. Such
a king—a king whose father had been a personal friend
of Alexander, the mighty civilising conqueror, and had
shared in the liberalisation connected with his vast
revolutionary projects for extending a higher civilisation
over the globe, such a king, conversing with such a
language, having advantages so absolutely unrivalled,
and again this king and this language concurring with
a treasure so supernatural of spiritual wisdom as the
subject of their ministrations, and all three concurring
with political events so auspicious—the founding of a
new and mighty metropolis in Egypt, and the silent
advance to supreme power amongst men of a new
empire, martial beyond all precedent as regarded *means*,
but not as regarded *ends*—working in all things towards
the unity of civilisation and the unity of law, so that
any new impulse, as, for instance, impulse of a new
religion, was destined to find new facilities for its own
propagation, resembling electric conductors, under the
unity of government and of law—concurrences like these
so many and so strange, justly impress upon this translation, the most memorable, because the most influential
of all that have ever been accomplished, a character of
grandeur that place it on the same level of interest

as the building of the first or second temple at Jerusalem.

There is a Greek legend which openly ascribes to this translation all the characters of a miracle. But, as usually happens, this vulgarising form of the miraculous is far less impressive than the plain history itself, unfolding its stages with the most unpretending historical fidelity. Even the Greek language, on which, as the natural language of the new Greek dynasty in Egypt, the duty of the translation devolved, enjoyed a double advantage ; 1st, as being the only language then spoken upon earth that could diffuse a book over *every* part of the civilised earth ; 2ndly, as being a language of unparalleled power and compass for expressing and reproducing effectually all ideas, however alien and novel. Even the city, again, in which this translation was accomplished, had a double dowry of advantages towards such a labour, not only as enjoying a large literary society, and, in particular, a large Jewish society, together with unusual provision in the shape of libraries, on a scale probably at that time unprecedented, but also as having the most extensive machinery then known to human experience for *publishing*, that is, for transmitting to foreign capitals, all books in the readiest and the cheapest fashion, by means of its prodigious shipping.

Having thus indicated to the *unlearned* reader the particular nature of that interest which invests this earliest translation of the Hebrew Scriptures, viz., that in fact this translation was the earliest publication to the human race of a revelation which had previously been locked up in a language destined, as surely as the Welsh language or the Gaelic, to eternal obscurity amongst men, I go on to mention that the learned Jews selected for this weighty labour happened to be in

number seventy-two ; but, as the Jews systematically
reject fractions in such cases (whence it is that always,
in order to express the period of six weeks, they say
forty days, and not, as strictly they should, forty-two
days), popularly, the translators were called " the
seventy," for which the Latin word is *septuaginta.* And
thus in after ages the translators were usually indicated
as " The LXX," or, if the work and not the workmen
should be noticed, it was cited as *The Septuagint.* In
fact this earliest of Scriptural versions, viz., into Greek
is by much the most famous ; or, if any other approaches
it in notoriety, it is the Latin translation by St. Jerome,
which, in this one point, enjoys even a superior importance, that in the church of Rome it is the authorised
translation.   Evidently, in every church, it must be a
matter of primary importance to assign the particular
version to which that Church appeals, and by which, in
any controversy arising, that Church consents to be
governed.   Now, the Jerome version fulfils this function
for the Romish Church ; and accordingly, in the sense
of being published (*vulgata*), or publicly authorised by
that Church, it is commonly called *The Vulgate.*

But, in a large polemic question, unless, like the
Romish Church, we uphold a secondary inspiration as
having secured a special privileged translation from the
possibility of error, we cannot refuse an appeal to the
Hebrew text for the Old Testament, or to the Greek
text for the New.   The word *aeonios* (αιωνιος), as purely
Grecian, could not connect itself with the Old Testament
unless it were through the Septuagint translation into
Greek.   Now, with that version, in any case of controversy, none of us, Protestants alike or Roman Catholics
have anything whatever to do.   Controversially, we *can*
be concerned only with the original language of the

Scriptures, with its actual verbal expressions textually produced. To be liable, therefore, to such a textual citation, any Greek word must belong to the *New* Testament. Because, though the word might happen to occur in the Septuagint, yet, since *that* is merely a translation, for any of us who occupy a controversial place, that is, who are bound by the responsibilities, or who claim the strict privileges of controversy, the Septuagint has no virtual existence. We should not be at liberty to allege the Septuagint as any authority, if it happened to countenance our own views : and, consequently, we could not be called on to recognise the Septuagint in any case where it should happen to be against us. I make this preliminary *caveat*, as not caring whether the word *aeonios* does or does not occur in the Septuagint. Either way, the reader understands that I disown the authority of that version as in any degree affecting myself. The word which, forty years ago, moved my disgust by its servile misinterpretation, was a word proper to the *New* Testament ; and any sense which it may have received from an Alexandrian Jew in the third century before Christ, is no more relevant to any criticism that I am now going to suggest, than is the classical use of the word *aeon* (αιων) familiar to the learned in Sophocles or Euripides.

The reason which gives to this word *aeonian* what I do not scruple to call a *dreadful* importance, is the same reason, and no other, which prompted the dishonesty concerned in the ordinary interpretation of this word. The word happened to connect itself—but *that* was no practical concern of mine : me it had not biassed in the one direction, nor should it have biassed any just critic in the counter direction—happened, I say, to connect itself with the ancient dispute upon the *duration* of future

X

punishments. What was meant by the *aeonian* punishments in the next world? Was the proper sense of the
word *eternal*, or was it not? I, for my part, meddled
not, nor upon any consideration could have been tempted
to meddle, with a speculation repellent alike by the horror
and by the hopeless mystery which invest it. Secrets of
the prison-house, so afflicting to contemplate steadily, and
so hopeless of solution, there could be no proper motive
for investigating, unless the investigation promised a great
deal more than it could ever accomplish : and my own
feeling as to all such problems is, that they vulgarise
what, left to itself, would take its natural station amongst
the freezing horrors that Shakespeare dismisses with so
potent an expression of awe, in a well-known scene of
Measure for Measure. I reiterate my protest against
being in any way decoyed into the controversy. Perhaps
I may have a strong opinion upon the subject. But, anti-
cipating the coarse discussions into which the slightest
entertainment of such a question would be every moment
approaching. once for all, out of reverential regard for
the dignity of human nature, I beg permission to decline
the controversy altogether.

But does this declinature involve any countenance to
a certain argument which I began by rejecting as abomi-
nable? Most certainly not. That argument runs thus
—that the ordinary construction of the term *aeonian*, as
equivalent to *everlasting*, could not possibly be given up
when associated with penal misery, because in that case,
and by the very same act, the idea of eternity must be
abandoned as applicable to the   ` of Paradise.
Torment and blessedness, it   punishme
and beatification. stood upon
word it was. the word
duration of either ; and, if eter

acceptation fell away from the one idea, it must equally fall away from the other. Well ; be it so. But that would not settle the question. It might be very painful to renounce a long-cherished anticipation ; but the necessity of doing so could not be received as a sufficient reason for adhering to the old unconditional use of the word *aeonian*. The argument is—that we must retain the old sense of *eternal*, because else we lose upon one scale what we had gained upon the other. But what then ? would be the reasonable man's retort. We are not to accept or to reject a new construction (if otherwise the more colourable) of the word *aeonian*, simply because the consequences might seem such as upon the whole to displease us. We may gain nothing ; for by the new interpretation our loss may balance our gain ; and we may prefer the old arrangement. But how monstrous is all this ! We are not summoned as to a choice of two different arrangements that may suit different tastes, but to a grave question as to what *is* the sense and operation of the word *aeonian*. Let the limitation of the word disturb our previous estimate of Paradise, grant that it so disturbs that estimate, not the less all such consequences leave the dispute exactly where it was ; and if a balance of reason can be found for limiting the extent of the word *aeonian*, it will not be the less true because it may happen to disturb a crotchet of our own.

Meantime, all this speculation, first and last, is pure nonsense. *Aeonian* does not mean *eternal;* neither does it mean of limited duration ; nor would the unsettling of *aeonian* in its old use, as applied to punishment, to torment, to misery, etc., carry with it any necessary unsettling of the idea in its application to the beatitudes of Paradise. Pause, reader ; and thou, my favoured and ʼʼileged reader, that boastest thyself to be unlearned,

X 2

pause doubly whilst I communicate my views as to this remarkable word.   :   .

What is an *aeon?*   In the use and acceptation of the Apocalypse, it is evidently this, viz., the duration or cycle of existence which belongs to any object, not individually for itself, but universally in right of its genus.   Kant, for instance, in a little paper which I once translated, proposed and debated the question as to the age of our planet the Earth.   What did he mean?   Was he to be understood as asking whether the earth were half a million, two millions, or three millions of years old?   Not at all.   The probabilities certainly lean, one and all, to the assignment of an antiquity greater by many thousands of times than that which we have most idly supposed ourselves to extract from Scripture, which assuredly never meant to approach a question so profoundly irrelevant to the great purposes of Scripture as any geological speculation whatsoever.   But this was not within the field of Kant's inquiry.   What he wished to know was simply the exact stage in the whole course of her development which the Earth at present occupies. Is she still in her infancy, for example, or in a stage corresponding to middle age, or in a stage approaching to superannuation?   The idea of Kant presupposed a certain average duration as belonging to a planet of our particular system ; and supposing this known, or discoverable, and that a certain assignable development belonged to a planet so circumstanced as ours, then in what particular stage of that development may we, the tenants of this respectable little planet *Tellus*, reasonably be conceived to stand?

Man, again, has a certain *aeonian* life ; possibly ranging somewhere about the period of 70 years assigned in the Psalms.   That is, in a state as highly improved as human infirmity and the errors of the earth herself together with the diseases incident to our atmosphere, etc., could be supposed to allow, possibly the human race might average 70 years for each individual. This period would in that case represent the "*aeon*" of the *individual* Tellurian ; but the "*aeon*" of the Tellurian RACE would probably amount to many millions of our earthly years ; and it would remain an unfathomable mystery, deriving no light at all from the septuagenarian "aeon" of the individual ; though between the two aeons I have no doubt that some secret link of connection does and must subsist, however undiscoverable by human sagacity.

The crow, the deer, the eagle, &c., are all supposed to be long-lived. Some people have fancied that in their normal state they tended to a period of two* centuries. I myself know nothing certain for or against this belief ; but, supposing the case to be as it is represented, then this would be the *aeonian* period of these animals, considered as individuals. Among trees, in like manner, the oak, the cedar, the yew, are notoriously of very slow growth, and their aeonian period is unusually long as regards the individual. What may be the *aeon* of the whole species is utterly unknown. Amongst birds, one

---

* I have heard the same normal duration ascribed to the tortoise, and one case became imperfectly known to myself personally. Somewhere I may have mentioned the case in print. These, at any rate, are the facts of the case : A lady (by birth a Cowper, of the Whig family, and cousin to the poet Cowper, and equally with him related to Dr. Madan, Bishop of Peterborough) in the early part of this century mentioned to me that, in the palace at Peterborough, she had for years known as a pet of the household a venerable tortoise, who bore some inscription on his shell indicating that from 1638 to 1643 he had belonged to Archbishop Laud, who, if I am not mistaken, held the bishopric of Peterborough before he was translated to London, and finally to Canterbury.

species at least has become extinct in our own generation :
its *aeon* was accomplished. So of all the fossil species
in zoology, which Palæontology has revealed. Nothing,
in short, throughout universal nature, can for a moment
be conceived to have been resigned to accident for its
normal *aeon*. All periods and dates of this order belong
to the certainties of nature, but also, at the same time, to
the mysteries of Providence. Throughout the Prophets,
we are uniformly taught that nothing is more below the
grandeur of Heaven than to assign earthly dates in
fixing either the revolutions or the duration of great
events such as prophecy would condescend to notice.
A day has a prophetic meaning, but what sort of day ?
A mysterious expression for a time which has no resemblance to a natural day—sometimes comprehending
long successions of centuries, and altering its meaning
according to the object concerned. "A time," and
"times," or "half a time"—"an aeon," or "aeons of
aeons"—and other variations of this prophetic language
(so full of dreadful meaning, but also of doubt and perplexity), are all significant. The peculiar grandeur of
such expressions lies partly in the dimness of the
approximation to any attempt at settling their limits,
and still more in this, that the conventional character,
and consequent meanness of ordinary human dates, are
abandoned in the celestial chronologies.   Hours and
days, or lunations and months, have no true or philosophic relation to the origin, or duration, or periods of
return belonging to great events, or revolutionary
agencies, or vast national crimes ; but the normal period
and duration of all acts whatever, the time of their
emergence, of their agency, or their reagency, fall into
harmony with the secret proportions of a heavenly scale,
when they belong by mere necessity of their own internal

constitution to the vital though hidden motions that are at work in their own life and manifestation. Under the old and ordinary view of the apocalyptic *aeon*, which supposed it always to mean the same period of time— mysterious, indeed, and uncertain, as regards *our* knowledge, but fixed and rigorously certain in the secret counsels of God—it was presumed that this period, if it lost its character of infinity when applied to evil, to criminality, or to punishment, must lose it by a corresponding necessity equally when applied to happiness and the golden aspects of hope. But, on the contrary, every object whatsoever, every mode of existence, has its own separate and independent *aeon*. The most thoughtless person must be satisfied, on reflection, even apart from the express commentary upon this idea furnished by the Apocalypse, that every life and mode of being must have hidden within itself the secret *why* of its duration. . It is impossible to believe of *any* duration whatever that it is determined capriciously. Always it rests upon some ground, ancient as light and darkness, though undiscoverable by man. This only is discoverable, as a general tendency, that the *aeon*, or generic period of evil, is constantly towards a fugitive duration. The *aeon*, it is alleged, must always express the same idea, whatever *that* may be ; if it is less than eternity for the evil cases, then it must be less for the good ones. Doubtless the idea of an *aeon* is in one sense always uniform, always the same, viz., as a tenth or a twelfth is always the same. Arithmetic could not exist if any caprice or variation affected these ideas—a tenth is always more than an eleventh, always less than a ninth. But this uniformity of ratio and proportion does not hinder but that a tenth may now represent a guinea, and next moment represent a thousand guineas. The exact amount of the duration expressed by an *aeon* depends altogether upon the particular subject which yields the *aeon*. It is, as I have said, a radix ; and, like an algebraic square-root or cube-root, though governed by the most rigorous laws of limitation, it must vary in obedience to the nature of the particular subject whose radix it forms.

Reader, I take my leave. I have been too loitering. I know it, and will make such efforts in future to cultivate the sternest brevity as nervous distress will allow. Meantime, as the upshot of my speculation, accept these three propositions :—

(A.) That man (which is in effect *every* man hitherto), who allows himself to infer the eternity of evil from the counter eternity of good, builds upon the mistake of assigning a stationary and mechanic value to the idea of an *aeon* ; whereas the very purpose of Scripture in using this word was to evade such a value. The word is always varying, for the very purpose of keeping it faithful to a spiritual identity. The period or duration of every object *would* be an essentially variable quantity, were it not mysteriously commensurate to the inner nature of that object as laid open to the eyes of God. And thus it happens, that everything in this world, possibly without a solitary exception, has its own separate *aeon* : how many entities, so many *aeons*.

(B.) But if it be an excess of blindness which can overlook the aeonian differences amongst even neutral entities, much deeper is that blindness which overlooks the separate tendencies of things evil and things good. Naturally, all evil is fugitive and allied to death.

(C.) I separately, speaking for myself only, profoundly believe that the Scriptures ascribe absolute and metaphysical eternity to one sole Being, viz, to God ; and derivatively to all others according to the interest which they can plead in God's favour. Having anchorage in God, innumerable entities may possibly be admitted to a participation in divine *aeon*. But what interest in the favour of God can belong to falsehood, to malignity, to impurity? To invest *them* with aeonian privileges, is in effect, and by its results, to distrust and to insult the Deity. Evil would *not* be evil, if it had that power of self-subsistence which is imputed to it in supposing its aeonian life to be co-eternal with that which crowns and glorifies the good.

ON THE GENIUS OF DE QUINCEY.

By SHADWORTH H. HODGSON, LL.D.

EIGHTEEN years had passed since De Quincey's death, when the summer of 1877 brought the day so much to be dreaded for some, so much to be desired by others, when concerning him also the truth was at last to be told to the world. The admirable Life then published by Mr. Page * gives as full and adequate an account of him, in all essential particulars, as in all probability ever will or can be given ; and from that account De Quincey can be only a gainer. It is now obvious that the various events related by himself in his " Confessions," " Autobiographic Sketches," and other papers, which might have seemed to wear the colouring of romance, partly from the discontinuity of the narrative, but more, perhaps, from the embellishing style of the narrator are not themselves romance but strict and sober fact. At least they so *fit* in with the rest of his surroundings, and with other events of his life now made known to us, as to obtain an additional guarantee of authenticity.

* Thomas de Quincey. His Life and Writings. With unpublished Correspondence. By H. A. Page. 2 vols. John Hogg, 1877. [The first edition appeared under the pseudonym " H. A. Page." In the second the real name of the Author was given— " Alexander H. Japp, LL.D."]

This, however, is a small matter. What will justly be of far greater importance to the general reader is, that here at last De Quincey stands before us in the light of common day, is at last rendered intelligible, a human and not a mythical being, rescued from the atmosphere of legend, which had not only hidden but grievously distorted his image, by making him a mark for thoughtless exaggeration, unsubstantial and sometimes even apocryphal anecdote. Thus it is now made clear, that to describe him as " dreaming always," " his existence a series of dreams," " large in promises, helpless in failure of performance," to speak of him as " for once exerting himself to write," and to say that " the human mind " was the " one thing he knew anything about," is to give a picture which is the very reverse of the truth.

These things may to some seem trifles. Still, how they could ever have been said, in the face of the fourteen published volumes, revised by himself before his death, since increased to sixteen, and even then not including his " Logic of Political Economy," surpasses my comprehension. Again, the imputation that the " credit of being *up* in German Metaphysicians, Latin Schoolmen, Thaumaturgic Platonists, Religious Mystics, &c.," was a motive with De Quincey, or in the least degree led him to speak with a pretension of knowledge where he possessed none, becomes incredible from the true delineation of De Quincey's character now given by Mr. Page, and supported by the facts of his life.

My present purpose is solely with De Quincey as a writer ; what the leading traits of his intellectual character are, what his rank, what his functions and achievements in literature ; in one word with his genius. But for this purpose how great, I would almost say how indispensable, is a true picture of the man. It would not be so in every case, or at least not to the same extent; some men's writings are of plain and easy interpretation; but in De Quincey's case we have already seen how a mistaken appreciation of the writings may flow from a false imagination of the person. Mr. Stirling's theory of the cause of De Quincey's error concerning Kant (*Fortnightly Review*, Oct. 1867), for from this it was that my last quotation came, will not hold water in presence of the true account of De Quincey's character now at last made public; some other explanation of that error (if error it be) must be sought; and I shall return to this point in its proper place, seeing that it touches an important feature in De Quincey's literary reputation.

For my own part I may say, that I needed not to wait for Mr. Page's book to form a truer estimate of De Quincey's character than the current legends afforded. Not only as a relative of the family was I acquainted with the outlines of his life, but it was my privilege in the summer of 1853 to pass several days as a guest under his roof. His writings, those that I was then acquainted with, had been to me a source of the most valuable instruction; not of delight only, but of instruction and insight into regions which would else have remained closed to me. No one touches and lays bare the inmost heart of a subject like De Quincey. You are not kept at the surface or delayed with commonplaces, nor are you told the "thing to say" about it, as from a well-informed tutor getting up his pupils for the examination room. But you are taken by the hand and led into the centre of the subject by a direct though flowery path, the path probably by which the teacher himself had entered; and while you are thinking only of the flowers that strew, and the music that accompanies your route, suddenly the region is illuminated, and a pamoramic view disclosed of its branching recesses.

The independence, the originality, the *proprio marte* (to use a phrase often used by himself) of his exposition, is in every case the most remarkable feature of it. You have the subject treated at first hand. What struck me most when I saw him was the precise resemblance of his uttered to his written speech. The sentences flowed forth on the air, in manner and form just the same as they flowed along the printed page. They came spontaneously forth, embodying the associative act of thought as that action itself proceeded, and adapted, like that act itself, to the remarks of the interlocutors, in the ordinary course of give and take conversation. It was thought made visible ; the verification and exemplification of the dictum—*the style is the man.*

He was, besides, the very soul of courtesy in conversation, studious not only to listen but respond to every remark, and make it bear its full fruit. I remember particularly his jubilant applause when an afternoon visitor reported a supposed epitaph on a great talker, beginning *Hic tacet——*. His fancy was captivated by the effect which the change of a single letter produced, the sudden heightening of the garrulousness which nothing but death could check, making it leap, as it were, to infinity, and at the same moment contrasting it with an infinite silence.

But, after all, his own quiet flow of talk was the greatest charm. *Philomelus* was the name which afterwards in my own mind I gave him. For no description that I have read of him seems to me to surpass in truth and vividness the lines in which Thomson describes the

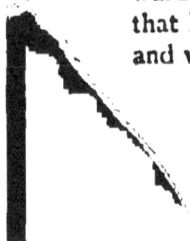

bard Philomelus in the second canto of the "Castle of Indolence":

> "a little druid wight,
> Of withered aspect ; but his eye was keen,
> With sweetness mixed. In russet brown bedight,
>   *   *   *   *   *
> He crept along, unpromising of mien.
> Gross he who judges so. His soul was fair,
> Bright as the children of yon azure sheen ! "

There you have De Quincey ; at least in his later days. And few as are the touches, the portrait which they compose is that of a living and breathing mortal.

The key to the comprehension of De Quincey's place in literature may be given in few words. Two circumstances combined. First, he was by natural constitution of an intellectual turn, interested in " the things of the mind " genuinely and for their own sake ; " intellectual in the highest sense my pursuits and pleasures have been, even from my schoolboy days," he tells us in the Preface to the first edition of the " Confessions " (1822) ; and this claim is fully borne out by the picture now presented in the Life. He sat down as it were in a theatre, to study and enjoy the spectacle of existence, past as well as present, with keen and eager curiosity, needing no alien stimulus derived either from the wish for applause or from the necessity of bread-getting ; and resolved to see it with his own and not with others' eyes. His love for learning was self-originated, his judgment self-guided, his mind self-educated, at least if by self-education is meant, not an impossible independence of instructors, but the active use and choice of instruction by whomsoever offered, as contrasted with passive submission to a teacher's guidance.

But, secondly, this aptitude and the knowledge which

it had led him to acquire, he was afterwards compelled by circumstances, not led by choice, to turn to account in the way of bread-getting for himself and his family. He had to make the best of his acquirements, whatever they were, in that direction. He had therefore to write what would bring in immediate returns. He was a private student suddenly called upon to become a professional writer. The outward shape and form which his activity should take was thus determined for him ; its peculiar independence and originality remaining what they were, and would have been, had he never published a single magazine article.

What then was the value, what was the character, of that mental independence and originality ? To answer this, we must see what that epoch was at which his career commenced. Now he was just fifteen at the commencement of the present century. The nineteenth century was dawning when his intellect was approaching its early maturity. Two great tendencies seem to divide between them the history of human mental development, though their ultimate causes are still a mystery ; periods of criticism and demolition alternate with periods of creation and reconstruction. The nineteenth century has been a period of the latter class. Speaking only of England,—for to discuss the connection of English with Continental thought, or the causes of development which are special to the latter, would carry us too far afield,— speaking only of England, the nineteenth century was created, was made what it was, so far as the two vast fields of Literature and Philosophy are concerned, by a constellation of poets. *They* are the fathers of that reaction, that reconstruction, that revival of the *heart* as the unifying principle against the dispersing, criticising, *understanding,* as the end or τέλος of all action and of all thought,—which we call the nineteenth century. A constellation of six stars, of primary magnitude though variously coloured light,—Wordsworth, Scott, Coleridge ; Byrcn, Shelley, Keats.

Of these, two at least, and those the two of keenest radiance, shed their light over the total surface of human interest, and are philosophers as well and as much as they are poets,—Wordsworth and Coleridge. Of these it may be truly said, that the Englishman who has not entered through them into the nineteenth century has not fully and thoroughly entered therein. They are the Door of the century. For just as there are two great tendencies which give rise to alternating epochs of dissolution and reconstruction in the mental history of mankind, so also, and perhaps as a condition of its being so, are there two orders of individual minds ; minds genial, flexible, and imaginative, on the other side, minds ungenial, inflexible, ratiocinative, on the other ; minds that seem to be Nature's offspring and inherit her spontaneity, and minds that seem to be her handiwork and perform her tasks.

Foremost among the purely intellectual characteristics which distinguish these two orders of minds, are those of intellectual subtilty and intellectual acuteness. Subtilty is a perfection of the perceptive powers, acuteness of the ratiocinative. A subtil mind is one that perceives minute differences and similarities, and minute shades of total character, in objects which it pictures ; an acute mind perceives the remote logical consequences of given facts, whether traced backwards to causes or forwards to effects. The genial order of mind, when powerful, is subtil ; t
powerful, is acute. And ac
of either order of minds, t

they belong; or rather, since the bulk of mankind consists always and everywhere of minds of the latter order, the greatest *talent* being but the highest grade of ordinary common sense, and there being always fifty minds that are acute for one that is subtil,—whenever minds of imaginative genius and subtility appear in conjunction, their epoch is marked, and their influence is manifested by the occurrence of a period of reconstruction. The eighteenth century was, intellectually, the reign of acuteness; the nineteenth the reaction of subtility.

Through the door of Wordsworth and Coleridge, De Quincey entered, and then became one of the main channels by which their influence was diffused and made operative in moulding the thoughts of other men after the image of theirs. There is nothing more remarkable than the way in which De Quincey himself recurs to this, as one of his chief titles to consideration, thus voluntarily and joyfully making it his pride to claim a secondary place, and shine by a reflected light. The first publication of the Lyrical Ballads (1798), including, as he expressly mentions, Coleridge's "Ancient Mariner," he calls "the greatest event in the unfolding of my own mind." (Works, vol. ii. p. 142, Hogg's edition.) And in the revised and enlarged "Confessions," in 1856, we read: "Was I then, in July, 1802, really quoting from Wordsworth? Yes, reader; and I only in all Europe." ("Confessions," Hogg's edition, p. 98.)

But there are ranks in the order of genius, as there are ranks in that of talent. De Quincey, by virtue of his combining great emotional sensibility with great intellectual subtilty, belongs to the order of genius; but he does not belong to the first rank in it. He has genius, but it is not creative; originality and independ-

Y

ence, but they are employed in analysing, interpreting,
and expounding.   There is such a thing as an original
and independent *expositor*.   The insight which such an one
brings is drawn from his own sympathetic intelligence,
and is proportioned to its keenness and closeness ; it is
the insight of subtilty, not of acuteness.   That is the
shape De Quincey's genius takes ; not creative, but
illuminative ; widely different in method and results
from that of merely talented expounders, however
conscientious and well-informed, who are acute without
being subtil.   He precedes you with a torch.   And
presently, or perhaps even at the first sentence, the
subject glows and the reader kindles ; as for instance in
the " Joan of Arc " :

"What is to be thought of *her ?*   What is to be thought of the
poor shepherd girl from the hills and forests of Lorraine, that—
like the Hebrew shepherd boy from the hills and forests of Judæa
—rose suddenly out of the quiet, out of the safety, out of the
religious inspiration, rooted in deep pastoral solitudes, to a station
in the van of armies, and to the more perilous station at the right
hand of kings ? "

De Quincey had a theory of his own about genius,
which, if good things will bear repeating, well deserves
to recur, as it does, more than once in his works :

" Genius is intellectual power impregnated with the *moral* nature,
and expresses a synthesis of the active in man with his original
organic capacity of pleasure and pain.   Hence the very word
genius, because the *genial* nature in its whole organisation is
expressed and involved in it.   Hence, also, arises the reason that
genius is always peculiar and individual ; one man's genius never
exactly repeats another man's.   But talent is the same in all men ;
and that which is effected by talent, can never serve to identify or
indicate its author.   Hence, too, that, although talent is the object
of respect, it never conciliates love ; you love a man of talent
perhaps *in concreto*, but not talent, whereas genius, even for itself,
is idolized."

Mrs. Browning's fine saying about Napoleon in
" Crowned and Buried " irresistibly occurs to one. The
man, she says, was flawed :

> —" but since he had
> *The genius to be loved*, why let him have
> The justice to be honoured in his grave."

De Quincey's analysis, in my opinion, exactly hits the
mark, and I am not aware that it can be claimed by any
one before him.

His own genius, as we have seen, takes the shape of
insight, employed in exposition. A clear, subtil, and
penetrating intelligence is employed, not without
humour, in exhibiting and unfolding the essential
characters of whatever subject he takes in hand. He
has enjoyed and comprehended the spectacle himself,
and he is resolved that you also shall enjoy and comprehend it. His own consciousness of this is the cause
of that didactic tone which is often noticeable, as well as
of that digressiveness and introduction of anecdote,
which some critics seem to have found somewhat weari-
some. If you want, as so many do want, a brief
handbook of any subject, De Quincey's are not the
pages to go to. If, again, you want pure amusement
and entertainment, without effort of your own, without
any previous interest in the subject-matter, this, too, is
not to be expected of De Quincey. He is neither a
schoolmaster nor a showman. But if you want any of
those subjects which he has treated shown to you as in
a magician's glass, its core laid bare, its relations to
kindred subjects, and its bearing on human interest
unfolded, and that in a manner which kindles and sus-
tains the interest, while it calls out your own energies
of mind to make the subject your own,—if this is what
you want, and if, at the same time, you will not grudge

a little time and some slight effort of attention,—then
take up a volume of De Quincey, say for example one
of those containing the articles on Parr or Bentley, Pope
or Goldsmith, or the Last Days of Kant, or in history
the Cæsars, Cicero, Herodotus, Secret Societies, Homer
and the Homeridæ, the Casuistry of Roman Meals, or
—last not least—the genial and penetrative sketch of
Shakespeare, and I venture to promise that you will
rise from the reading of it charmed, invigorated, and
instructed.   Often, indeed, you will stumble on some
saying or *aperçu*, or on some piece of information, which
has since become common property, or been followed
up by others.   Chance will have led you to its original
quarrying and purveyorship, to the first candle of which
your own knowledge is possibly a distant reverberation.

Nor is it a meagre list of subjects to which De
Quincey can introduce you.   His sixteen volumes are
filled with essays in every direction of history, biography,
scholarship, criticism, literature.   They are a perfect
mine of instruction for any one who is willing, not to
take his information and his opinions ready made from
his author, but to have subjects opened up for him,
questions concerning them broached, foundations for
future reading laid.   In this way it is that De Quincey,
more truly than perhaps any author that can be named,
is a *popular* writer ; he writes to and for the people ;
and for the people it is that his writings are most
valuable.   To quote from a little essay of his, " On
the Scriptural Expression for Eternity," written so
late as 1852, " As the *reading* public and the *thinking*
public is every year outgrowing more and more
notoriously the mere *learned* public, it becomes every
year more and more the right of the former public to
give the law preferably to the latter public, upon all

points which concern its own separate interests ;" which is as fine a democratic sentiment as need be expected from a high professing Tory. He aims at interesting a wide and universal, not merely a select literary, audience, notwithstanding the solidity of the information he has to convey. And this very aim it is, or rather the style adopted in consequence of it, which sets the seal of permanence upon his writings, promising them more than that ephemeral existence which is the inevitable fate of most magazine articles, even when they are more fully abreast of the latest information.

And here, at the risk of possibly seeming tedious, I must interpose a remark which, as will shortly appear, is most important for a true appreciation of our author. It is that he belongs not to science but to literature. He is an original expositor and interpreter, but, except in one single case, he is a literary and not a scientific expositor. His subjects for the most part are recognised as literary subjects, and he does not attempt to transcend that mode of treatment. He has no scientific theory of History, or of Politics, to propound ; no science of criticism ; no system of metaphysic, or of ethic. Not that he was unacquainted, indeed very much the reverse, with the best of what had been written on these subjects ; but he comes forward with no speculations of a systematic kind of his own. *Every* subject is open to a literary, as well as to a scientific, treatment, and a literary treatment is that which it receives at De Quincey's hand. The sole exception is Political Economy, to which he devotes a separate work, the " Logic of Political Economy," published in 1844, in which he appears as the expositor of Ricardo. The English edition of his works excludes this admirable book, though admitting the " Templars' Dialogues " on the same subject, probably on

account of its more literary form.   I shall recur to this
book presently.*

It is, then, as a literary writer that De Quincey must
in the first instance be judged.   And here we are again
met by a distinction which is his property ; again we
have to judge him as it were out of his own mouth,
simply because he it is who has laid down the funda-
mental distinctions of the matter.   Do his works take
rank under the *Literature of Power*, or merely under
the *Literature of Knowledge ?*   Do they aim at moving
the heart as well as teaching the understanding, or are
they confined to the latter function alone ?   The distinction will be found in the essay on Pope (vol. ix. p. 5,
Hogg's edition).   The passage is far too long for
transcription in its entirety ; a word or two from it must
suffice :

" Were it not that human sensibilities are ventilated and continually called out into exercise by the great phenomena of infancy,
or of real life as it moves through chance and change, or of literature as it recombines these elements in the mimicries of poetry,
romance, etc., it is certain that, like any animal power or muscular
energy falling into disuse, all such sensibilities would gradually
droop and dwindle.   It is in relation to these great *moral* capacities
of man that the literature of power, as contra-distinguished from
that of knowledge, lives and has its field of action.   It is concerned
with what is highest in man ; for the Scriptures themselves never
condescended to deal by suggestion or co-operation with the mere
discursive understanding : when speaking of man in his intellectual
capacity, the Scriptures speak not of the understanding, but of
' *the understanding heart*,'—making the heart, *i.e.* the great *intuitive*

* Since the above was written, which was in 1877, just after the
appearance of the Life, this omission has been happily rectified,
and the " Logic of Political Economy " included in a supplementary
volume, paged so as to be continuous with vol. xiii. of Messrs.
Black's edition of the Works.   The   plementary volume was
published in 1878.

(or non-discursive) organ, to be the interchangeable formula for man in his highest state of capacity for the infinite."

There is a certain class of works, then, which by their aim alone proclaim themselves as belonging to the Literature of Power. They may be good bad, or indifferent, in that class ; they may hit or they may miss their aim ; but the class to which they belong is marked out by their aim and scope alone. Their scope proclaims their class, be their success in attaining it what it may. The poem, the drama, the romance, the novel, the sermon, for instance, for all belong clearly and inevitably to the *power* literature ; history, biography, travels, criticism, philosophy, belong *primâ facie* at least to the *knowledge* literature. Their avowed and obvious aim is to *instruct* by communicating or interpreting facts. And it is under one or other of these latter heads that most of De Quincey's writings fall, except the "Political Economy," which is scientific.

But observe the limitation. I said their *avowed* and *obvious* aim would mark them as belonging to the knowledge literature. Is there, then, any other consideration which can entitle them to a place in the literature of power ? There certainly is. The two classes are not *finally* distinguished by the avowed and obvious aim, or even by the title of the works which are to be ranged under them. Wherever the subject, being capable of an imaginative and emotional treatment, is so handled as to be made the vehicle of moving the sympathies as well as instructing the understanding, then the work rises, in virtue of this handling alone, into the power literature, and that without any formal claim being put forward in the preface. But then see what follows ; so far from the scope, irrespective of the success, determining its class, the reverse becomes the law, and the *success* of the work in rousing and enlisting our sympathies ensures our ranking it as a work of *power*, irrespective of the avowed and obvious scope indicated by its title.

Even subjects which already belong to science, much more those which belong to literature, may be so treated as to raise the work that treats them into a work of power. The great didactic poems of Virgil and Lucretius, and (in prose) Edgar Poe's "Eureka," are instances. Criticism, especially art-criticism, is closely allied to the power literature. Mr. Ruskin's greater works for instance,—who can mistake their claim to this rank? And Mr. Carlyle's "French Revolution" is an instance of the same thing in the domain of history. There are such things, then, as works which belong to the Literature of Power, by virtue of the way in which the subjects are handled, the mode and manner of their treatment, the key in which they are composed, the style in which they are embodied. The manner and the style create in them a soul under the ribs of death.

To this class of writings the Works of De Quincey belong. They are *militant* for a place in the Literature of Power. Not militant in the sense in which he himself applies that term to the knowledge literature, but in the sense that only success in moving our sympathies, the recognition of which lies in opinion not in proof, makes good the rank and dignity of the work. If they rank with power literature, they do so not by reason of the subjects treated of, but by virtue of the method and manner of treatment, in one comprehensive word, by their *Style*.

Of what, then, do De Quincey's works consist? His own "rude general classification" of them in the Preface to the first volume of the collected English edition revised by himself, and written therefore when the revision was only just begun, is as follows. He makes three classes, (1) papers which propose primarily to amuse the reader, but which may happen occasionally to reach a higher station, at which the amusement passes into an impassioned interest ;—instance, the "Autobiographic Sketches"; (2) what he calls simply " Essays," which address themselves purely to the understanding ; *e.g.* the Essenes, the Cæsars, and Cicero ; (3) "a far higher class of compositions, the 'Confessions of an Opium-Eater,' and also (but more emphatically) the 'Suspiria de Profundis.'" This classification dates back to the beginning of the English revised edition, that is, to 1853, at which time also the American edition, referred to in the Preface, numbered not more than seven volumes, if even so many. At present, with the sixteen volumes of the English edition before us, a somewhat more detailed classification may be of service.

The English edition, even though for the most part revised by the author, is, in some important respects, a chaos. It does not, as a rule, inform us either of the date at which the papers were written, or of the magazine or periodical in which they appeared. Its omissions are not unimportant, excluding, for instance, both the tale of " Klosterheim " and the " Logic of Political Economy." The latter is a serious defect, bearing, as the edition now does, the ambitious title of Works. The original title adopted by De Quincey was " Selections, Grave and Gay, from Writings published and unpublished "; a title admirably expressing the nature and purpose of the contents. I suppose it was thought that Works would be more generally attractive, as promising more ; while at the same time the public would not care to be bored with so unpromising a subject as political economy, let alone its *Logic*, or drouth upon drouth.*

Be it as it may, let us take stock of the most important items of its contents. And suppose we classify as follows. First let us place those works which are more predominantly creative, and belong the most clearly to the literature of power ; in the second group, those in which this is less markedly the case, owing to the claims of the matter predominating, in them, over those of the manner. I say less markedly, for in almost all there is some touch, and in many the touches are frequent and brilliant, of the creative spirit of genius and the spontaneous eloquence which embodies it.

I. (*Literature of Power.*) The Confessions and Suspiria. The English Mail Coach ; with its adjuncts, The Glory of Motion, The Vision of Sudden Death, The Dream Fugue. The Autobiographic Sketches in vol. i. and ii. to the end of Early Memorials of Grasmere. The two papers on Murder. Joan of Arc.

These are the writings which, in my opinion, are the chief pillars of De Quincey's fame, his surest title to a lasting place, secure from chance and change, among the immortals of his epoch. An original genius, individual and therefore inimitable, has invested these works with a perennial charm, disparate but not inferior to that which breathes from the choicest among the " Essays of Elia," or the " Imaginary Conversations " of Landor.

---

* I let this passage stand as it was written in 1877 ; and why ? Because the publication of the supplement ⬛⬛⬛⬛⬛⬛⬛ining the " Logic of Political Economy " ha⬛⬛⬛⬛⬛⬛⬛ expresses into a deserved complimen⬛

II. (*Literature of Knowledge.*) This, which is the most numerous class, I would roughly subdivide as follows :

1. *Historical and Political.* The Cæsars. Cicero. The Essenes. Judas Iscariot. The Philosophy of Herodotus. Plato's Republic. The Revolution of Greece. Greece under the Romans. Modern Greece. Charlemagne. On War. Secret Societies. A Tory's Account of Toryism. Political Parties of Modern England. Falsification of English History. The Revolt of the Tartars. Ceylon. Memorial Chronology. &c. &c.

2. *Social and Ethical.* The Templars' Dialogues on Political Economy. The Casuistry of Roman Meals. French and English Manners. National Temperance Movements. Modern Superstition. Protestantism. Casuistry. The Pagan Oracles. The Theban Sphinx. Miracles as Subjects of Testimony. Christianity as an Organ of Political Movement. System of the Heavens as revealed by Lord Rosse's Telescope. Glance at the Works of Mackintosh. Presence of Mind. The Spanish Military Nun (which in form is a tale). &c. &c.

3. *General Literature.* Homer and Homeridæ. Theory of Greek Tragedy. The Antigone of Sophocles. The Knocking at the Gate in "Macbeth." Schlosser's Literary History of the 18th Century. Milton. Alexander Pope. On Wordsworth's Poetry. Language. Rhetoric. Style. Milton *versus* Southey and Landor. Letters to a Young Man, &c. Orthographic Mutineers. Conversation. Ælius Lamia. &c. &c.

4. *Personal Criticism and Biography.* Life of Shake-

speare. The Sketches of Coleridge, Wordsworth, and Southey. The Last Days of Kant. Whiggism in its relations to Literature (Dr. Parr). Oliver Goldsmith. Richard Bentley. Shelley. Keats. Charles Lamb. Notes on Walter Savage Landor. Lord Carlisle on Pope. Life of Pope. Life of Milton. Sortilege and Astrology, Numerous minor biographical notices, criticisms and translations, among them of Lessing's Laocoon, of Kant's idea of an Universal History; &c. &c.

It would take me far beyond the limits of a single paper, as it would be also far beyond my own powers, to follow De Quincey through this varied list, endeavouring to appraise the value of the several essays, as contributions to the knowledge of the subjects treated. Notwithstanding, it would be requisite in this place to make some remarks on the only important work not included in it, the "Logic of Political Economy," did it not appear a better plan to give that subject a separate treatment. For this is the only work in which De Quincey appears as a distinctly scientific expositor, and therefore is of peculiar importance in estimating his mental powers. It has also been the subject of a disparaging remark by John Stuart Mill, who is justly considered a high authority on economical questions. It is necessary, therefore, on De Quincey's behalf that this matter should be exami
considered a sound reasoner o
be vindicated. This it will b
the following essay.

To keep, then, to literary grou
is long and miscellaneous.
Quincey exerted himself to write

that often happened. The reader will find traces, too,
of knowledge, power, and skill in treating other subjects
besides that of "the human mind." The basis of
whatever power he showed as an essayist was laid in a
large range of philosophic reading, and a habit of deep
and genuine philosophic thought. It is in vain for any
man to rely on *mere* acquaintance with the subject which
he treats, even when combined with great readiness and
skill in writing, if the result is to be in any measure an
acquisition to futurity. The subtil links that connect
it with the general fears and hopes and efforts of mankind will be inevitably wanting. The relations which
bind it to the other parts of human history, not being
perceived by the writer, will not be suggested by tacit
pervadure or explicit announcement to the reader.
There will be a charm wanting which alone can preserve
it in perennial freshness. Writings to live must be
impregnated with philosophy.

De Quincey's reputation among his contemporaries
both for depth of range and philosophic knowledge
stood very high. It was just the kind of reputation we
should expect from the character of the man ; the reputation not of a professor of any of the different branches
of philosophy, but of one who had studied at first hand
from love of the subject, and with a view to satisfy the
obstinate questionings of his own mind. His philosophic
reading has left indeed but little *direct* trace in his essays ;
and some of what there is he has not cared to include
among his republished works. But of his genuine delight
in philosophical literature there can be no doubt. It is
a mere straw, but it shows the way of the wind, to
mention that I have seen his copy of Giordano Bruno's
*De Monade Numero et Figura. Item de Innumerabilibus
Libri Octo*, 12mo, 1591 : and on the fly-leaf at the end,

there is written in De Quincey's clear hand, "Bought this day, Wednesday, May 31st, 1809 ;—brought home this evening between 8 and 9 o'clock." And I am told by one who knew him well that, in later years, this same little volume was his frequent companion, that he would pace up and down the room with it in his hand, repeating from it and referring to it. His copy of Spinoza's Ethic also, the *Opera Posthuma* of 1677, bears on its fly-leaf, in the same hand, " Paid Mr. Webber 25*s.* for this book,—this morning, Thursday, July 26th, 1810." Possibly the very same volume spoken of in an amusing note to the essay on Bentley. These things bear witness to something more than a mere book-hunter's enthusiasm.

In ethical matters too De Quincey was a master. Years ago I remember extracting from one of the earlier published volumes of the American edition (" Life and Manners," vol. i. p. 309, 1851) a passage in which Paley is criticised. The passage is not reproduced in the English edition, but may be found in *Tait's Edinburgh Magazine* for August 1835 (vol. ii. New Series, p. 549). I hold it to have been the best piece of instruction in Ethic I ever received ; it led me right into the heart of the theory, and became a foundation for future thought to build on. The scope of the passage was to distinguish two great questions in Ethic, one concerning the *ratio cognoscendi*, the other the *ratio essendi*, of virtue, and then to point out how the two are by Paley confused with each other, and his answer to the latter (and that according to De Quincey a wrong answer, namely, *Utility*) offered as if it were an answer to the former, which is the real question which Ethic has to answer.

De Quincey thus takes strong anti-utilitarian ground in Ethics. He is disposed also by natural temperament to take anti-determinist views in the question of free-will; but in this case, such is his logical clearness that, in stating this question for decision, he shows himself a necessarian (as it was then generally called) in *fact*, though contesting the propriety of the *name*. De Quincey was thus what we should now call a Free-will Determinist. I have found a note in his well-known hand on the cover of a copy of Crombie on "Philosophical Necessity," 1793, which from its clearness and brevity is well worth transcribing.

"Any reason, which has reference to action, we call a motive. To act without a motive—*i.e.* without a reason—is (otherwise expressed) to act irrationally. Now all action in obedience to a motive the Necessarians call *necessity :* and to establish liberty, as against *them*, it would be required of us to establish a case of action without (or against) motives. The true liberty however—the true self-determination—lies in this, that we by our own internal acts *create* our own motives : those considerations, which to you or me are motives, to another are not so: and why? Because my reflexions upon the tendency of particular acts, or because my feelings connected with them, have given to certain considerations a weight which raises them into the strength and power of motives. Here lies our liberty. And to an obedience to motives thus created it is an easy artifice to give the name of necessity : but that creates no real necessity. The autonomy of Man is still secure.

"The answer to the Necessarians therefore—is to grant all they urge,—but to deny their consequence or rather the propriety of their denomination."

Yes, the automony, the self-determination, of the conscious agent is the fact which once appeared imperilled by the doctrine of necessity; and De Quincey's words depict the state of mind of one who, being in the first place fully alive to the truth and value of the automony, is then awakened to the fact that it is not endangered by a truth which is its complement, this namely, that, "nothing is that swerves from law;"

liberty itself being obedience to law, but to law imposed
from within, not from without ; or in other words, that
liberty is one of the modes of necessity, and the
human will, in all its freedom, one of the works of
nature.

The foundations of De Quincey's success as critic and
essayist were thus laid in wide philosophic reading, deep
and accurate philosophic thinking. But these foundations were for the most part kept out of sight. He
wrote but little on philosophy, and even that little he
did not see fit to include in the revision of his works.
Indeed, it seems as if, in later years, having achieved
nothing in philosophy, he would obliterate whatever
claims he may once have had to rank as a philosopher,
and bury in oblivion the hopes which as a young man
he had cherished in that direction. "My proper
vocation, as I well knew, was the exercise of the
analytic understanding. Now, for the most part,
analytic studies are continuous, and not to be pursued
by fits and starts, or fragmentary efforts,"—he writes
in the first edition of the "Confessions" (1822), p. 148.
But these words are omitted from the second edition
of 1856.

Still it remains true, that his real vocation *was* what
he says, and the power and faculty of mind remained
the same, although one part of the career was missed,
which might have been opened by it. He *did* exercise
the analytic understanding, but it was upon non-philo-
sophical subjects. It is a rare combination of faculties
that distinguishes him ; the triple combination of
analytic subtilty and grasp of thought with (1) memory
for and interest in all kinds of details relating however
remotely to life and manners, and (2) a profound power
of appreciating and enjoy the most imaginative

poetry.   And two of these are rare in combination ; how much rarer the three.

One result of this suppression of what he had thought or written on philosophy, seeing that it was not and could not be *complete*, has been unfortunate.   It has caused him to be judged by the fragmentary utterances which remain, and by these read in connection with the high admiration for his philosophic powers entertained by his contemporaries.   I have a special instance of this in view, Mr. J. H. Stirling's demolition of a passage of De Quincey on Kant (*Fortnightly Review*, Oct. 1867). I say *demolition* because I think that in the main Mr. Stirling's criticism of that passage is correct.   It is so because the point of view from which it is pronounced is more commanding and comprehensive.   What De Quincey's point of view was I will presently show ; but first I must say that it strikes me as somewhat ungenerous, to use no stronger term, when one of a generation far better versed in German philosophical literature, than was De Quincey's, is extreme to tax the shortcomings of a writer who not only lacked the advantages which we enjoy, but who was himself among the foremost of those to whom our own generation mainly owes its enjoyment of them.   The deadness of those times to those matters was far greater than the deadness of the present time, great as that is ; and in England at least I do not know of any one who did more than De Quincey to kindle a genuine interest in them.

Passing over points of secondary importance, the main drift of the passage in question is briefly this, that De Quincey represents Kant's mind as essentially a destructive one, whereas Mr. Stirling says it was constructive essentially, and construction his great ruling purpose.

Z

And Mr. Stirling's view is, in my opinion at least, clearly right; De Quincey's clearly wrong. But I would urge that it is only fair to take De Quincey's point of view into account. The passage in question occurs in connection with the subject of Christianity and Coleridge's Unitarianism. It is in fact a waif and stray from a larger body ; and if read in connection with the rest, the point of view occupied by De Quincey in regard to Kant will become manifest ; and his expressions from that point of view, if not justified, will at any rate be shown to demand an explanation very different from the charlatanism which (to sum it up in a word of my own) is Mr. Stirling's hypothesis.

It is one thing to read philosophy with a view to make a systematic study of the subject for its own sake ; it is another to read it for the purpose of throwing light on questions and views with which the reader's mind is already pre-occupied ; and it is yet another to read it for the sake of being able to display one's reading afterwards. Mr. Stirling supposes that, because De Quincey was not in the first case, therefore he was in the third. The second case, which is the real one, escaped him.

De Quincey approached Kant with the pre-occupation of theology ; the philosophy, or rather what did duty for one, with which he started was that of a thoughtful disciple of the Church of England ; the question with him was, what light was thrown by the originator of the Transcendental Theory upon *this* world of thought and belief. From that point of view it was that Kant appeared to him, as he did to many others, utterly destructive, leaving no basis which was at once positive and speculative, for a theological creed at all. Kant's theory sweeps wholly away the old speculative foundations of theology, replaces them by proving that we can neither affirm nor yet deny any speculative doctrine in their place, and then relies, not on the speculative but on the practical reason, for supplying a positive foundation for religion. This could not but appear utterly unsatisfactory to one in De Quincey's position, who was not studying the philosophy for its own sake, but for the sake of its bearing on the questions suggested by his creed.

Whoever will take the trouble to look into a paper of De Quincey's contributed to *Tait's Edinburgh Magazine* for June 1836 (vol. iii. New Series, p. 350), will find there not only a very good, though brief, sketch of the main points in the "Critic of Pure Reason," but also ample confirmation of what I have said about De Quincey's point of view. "Let a man," he says, "meditate but a little on this" [the transcendental theory of the idea of Cause] "or other aspects of this transcen-dental philosophy, and he will find the steadfast earth rocking as it were beneath his feet ; a world about him, which is in some sense a world of deception ; and a world before him, which seems to promise a world of confusion, or a '*world not realised*'" (p. 357). And again : "As often as I looked into his works, I exclaimed in my heart, with the widowed queen of Carthage, using her words in an altered application—
'Quæsivit lucem—*ingemuitque repertâ*.' "

For from the same paper we find that, in spite of its apparent unprofitableness and negation, the Transcendental theory had in the main commanded his assent. "These are the two primary merits of the transcendental theory—1st, Its harmony with mathematics, and the fact of having first, by its doctrine of space, applied philosophy to the nature of geometrical evidence ; 2ndly, That it has filled up, by means of its doctrine of the categories, the great *hiatus* in all schemes of the human understanding from Plato downwards. All the rest, with a reserve as to the part which concerns the *practical* reason (or will), is of more questionable value, and leads to manifold disputes. But I contend that, had transcendentalism done no other service than that of laying a foundation, sought but not found for ages, to the human understanding—namely, by showing an intelligible genesis to certain large and indispensable ideas—it would have claimed the gratitude of all profound inquirers " (p. 359).

De Quincey's position, then, is that of a man forced to give an unwilling assent to the main conceptions of a system which he regards with dismay, as destroying, or at least endangering, the best hopes and aspirations of humanity. Observe, however, his expressly excepting the doctrine of the practical reason from what is doubt-ful, and placing it with what is sound and valuable, in Kant's system. The exception is significant, especially when read in the light of some words on the same subject, written nearly four years later. I refer to one of the most interesting of all the personal sketches which ever came from De Quincey's pen, that on the highly gifted Charles Lloyd, a sketch which I suppose there were valid reasons for omitting from his republished writings. At the end of this touching memoir there is a passage of singular beauty on the voices of nature which speak to us of hopes of immortality beyond the grave ; a passage which concludes as follows :

" But on that theme—Beware, reader ! Listen to no *intellectual* argument. One argument there is, one only there is, of philosophic value : an argument drawn from the *moral* nature of man : an argument of Immanuel Kant's. The rest are dust and ashes."

Now there is no law, I suppose, either human or

divine, against any man's reading Kant, and even letting the world know what he for his part finds there, if any one is interested in hearing it. Nor is it, I believe, necessary, first to produce a certificate from a college of authors, stating that you are enamoured of Metaphysic for her own sake, and intend to lecture on her sublime perfections. De Quincey made no such announcement; but there were hundreds who were glad to hear his report of Kant, having themselves much the same questions to put to that oracle as De Quincey had. It is beside the mark to contrast, as Mr. Stirling does, the sound and genuine work which Kant did in philosophy with the hollow and windy work which is all that De Quincey gets credit for. Kant was a man of science, De Quincey a man of letters. True, we might possibly have had a man of science in De Quincey; but then we should hardly have had the man of letters also. It is unjust to represent his powers as wasted and thrown away, merely because they were not turned into scientific channels.

More might be said in reply to Mr. Stirling's strictures on De Quincey; for instance, as to his criticism of Kant's style, and as to the " limited circle " within which "none durst tread but he," which clearly refers to the little group of conceptions which are the core of the Transcendental theory. But to go into detail on minor points would require a separate paper. Judgment once amended on the main point, the rest must be left to rule themselves as best they may, in accordance therewith. ne word, however, before parting with Mr. Stirling, on urely *literary* matter. Possibly he may be pleased next edition) to alter his remark, twice re-that *tumultuosissimento* is a word used by De I remember on one occasion, he uses the word

tumultuosissimamente.   But the former word I find
neither in De Quincey nor yet in the dictionary.

After all, then, it is very questionable whether any
part of De Quincey's vocation was really missed, whether
in declining studies of a scientific character he was
yielding to a stress of circumstances which another
might have eluded, whether he was not really obeying
the instincts of character with which nature had endowed
him.   His real turn of mind, subtil and acute as it was,
inclined strongly to the concrete and the personal, to
the pomps and glories of the world and the interests of
living human beings.   He loved imaginations more than
thoughts, and thoughts for the sake of imaginations.
Had he given himself to philosophy, it is easy to predict
his affinities ; his name would have been one of that
numerous list, in which those of Plato and Giordano
Bruno are the most illustrious.

This is clear from many passages ; for instance, one
in which, speaking of the Lucretian—*Primus in orbe
deos fecit timor,* he says, No, not *timor,* say rather *sensus
infiniti* (" Modern Superstition," vol. iii. p. 290).   In this
he puts his finger on the characterising *differentia* of
religion.   It is not fear, no, nor yet love, which by
themselves are the source of religion ; these by themselves are terrestrial ; It is the *mystery* that accompanies
them that makes them celestial, by giving them a
celestial object, and giving man a sense of belonging,
through them, to the infinite and unseen world.   The
remark here made by De Quincey has yet a gr
to play, a part too often unsuspected, in
the origin of religions and early s
But this, of course, by no me
theory must be true, which prof
that idea.——Or again, takin

of the Dream Vision, in the "System of the Heavens," embodying an image which he tells us is taken from Jean Paul Richter :

"Then the angel threw up his glorious hands to the heaven of heavens, saying, ' End there is none to the universe of God? Lo! also THERE IS NO BEGINNING.'"

There is a winged as well as a wingless genius in philosophy ; and those that are endowed with it belong irrevocably to literature, whether they pursue philosophy or not as their employment in chief.

Humour and pathos,—these *in literature* are the wings of genius, being two chief modes of imagination. Whatever ministers occasion for mirth becomes humorous when it is illumined by imagination, and whatever ministers to sorrow, under the same magic touch, becomes pathetic. As wit is the fun of talent, so is humour the fun of genius. Now both with humour and with pathos De Quincey abounds. They spring up spontaneously under his pen. And much of the beauty of his style consists, when the burden is pathetic, in its quietness and simplicity, in what it withholds rather than in what it expresses, so that, owing to this unexpressed background, we are made to feel the special case as part and parcel of the universal lot.

Many are the passages of exquisite and tender beauty scattered up and down his writings, free from ambitious ornament and turgid phrase, passages in which we are swiftly but gently lifted into a serener region, or in which sometimes "the tender grace of a day that is dead" is brought home to the heart, as by the placid spectacle of a clear autumn sunset. Take, for instance, the following :

" At present, and for many a year, I am myself the sole relic from that household sanctuary—sweet, solemn, profound—that concealed, as in some ark floating on solitary seas, eight persons, since called away, all except myself, one after one, to that rest which only could be deeper than ours was then."—*Confessions*, p. 30, Hogg's edition.

Or this from the essay on Goldsmith :

" Their names ascend in songs of thankful commemoration, but seldom until the ears are deaf that would have thrilled to the music."

Or this in another key, a crime being in question, the massacre of prisoners at Jaffa in 1799 :

" The fugitives did so ; they came back—some trusting, some doubting. But strictly impartial was their welcome on shore. To the trusting there was no special favour ; to the doubting no separate severity. All were massacred alike ; and in one brief half-hour a loose scattering of soil rose as a winding-sheet over the forty-two hundred corpses, that heaved convulsively here and there for a moment, and then all was still."—*Casuistry*, vol. viii. p. 265.

Or if we could have a passage where the writer plainly intends putting forth his strength, let us take this, from the conclusion of the " Joan of Arc " :

" Bishop of Beauvais ! thy victim died in fire upon a scaffold— thou upon a down bed. But for the departing minutes of life, both are oftentimes alike. At the farewell crisis, when the gates of death are opening, and flesh is resting from its struggles, oftentimes the tortured and the torturer have the same truce from carnal torment ; both sink together into sleep ; together both, sometimes, kindle into dreams. When the mortal mists were gathering fast upon you two, bishop and shepherd girl,—when the pavilions of life were closing up their shadowy curtains about you—let us try through the gigantic glooms, to decipher the ﬂ⬛⬛ separate visions."

Humour is confessedly a mu⬛
that have it not are tempte⬛
between wit and humour, ⬛
imagination persist in identify⬛

many of those who lack genius are incapable of distinguishing it from talent. The essence of humour I take
to be the same everywhere, but the ground on which it
springs is different ; there is the humour of inventive,
and there is the humour of analytic minds. There is
the humour of Shakespeare or of Swift, which not only
clothes the characters which they create, but is one of
the precedent motives and ingredients in their creation.
And there is the humour which is shown in the presenta-
tion of given and pre-existing characters and situations,
bringing out whatever humorous quality is already
latent in them ; a kind of humour, be it noted, which is
included in the former as the less in the greater, so that
he who has the first has both, but not *vice versa.* One
thing, however, is clear ; there is no humour without
subtilty, as there is no wit without acuteness. It is
natural that the non-creative humour should move by
anthithesis, by inversion of relations, and generally
by imagining some critical circumstance the reverse of
what it actually is. It depends upon subtility as to its
condition.

This is the usual way in which De Quincey's humour
moves ; he imagines the contrary, the contrast, of what
he is describing, thinks what it might appear to spectators with different interests, or from an opposite point of
view ; as, for instance, when he talks of "the general
fate of travellers that intrude upon the solitude of
robbers," or when he professes to palliate his obscurity
of style by assuring you that, though rather obscure, he
will be "not at all more so than Marinus in his Life of
'us." This at least is the logical or intellectual
  y which becomes the vehicle of that shade of
    and fun which is the chief characteristic of
       humour, as it is also of Charles Lamb's.

The *Murder* papers are instances of this kind of humour sustained from beginning to end, and their central idea of treating murder *as a fine art* is an instance of it. The charm of these papers consists far more in the number and variety of the faces under which this central idea is constantly peeping out, and the unflagging vivacity with which the stream of fun flows on, than in the separate quotability of absurd incident or witty antithesis. Or again, take the description of the state-coach in China, where "it was resolved by acclamation that the box was the imperial throne, and for the scoundrel who drove, he might sit where he could find a perch ; " and who was accordingly kicked into the inside, where "he had all the inside places to himself." Or again, the fishing up the duns from the bath, in the paper entitled "Sortilege and Astrology." Or again, to mention but one more case, the whole description of the nursery party in the "Autobiographic Sketches," particularly the schemes of his eldest brother for walking on the ceiling, like the flies, only much better. "'Pooh!' he said, 'they are impostors ; they pretend to do it, but they can't do it as it ought to be done. Ah! you should see *me* standing upright on the ceiling, with my head downwards, for half an hour together, and meditating profoundly.'" That *meditating profoundly* is exquisite, and quite dramatises the character.

But it is not only in those passages in which, from time to time, he rises aloft upon the wings of humour or pathos, nor even in those where he is consciously putting forth his whole command over the powers of prose, that the main beauty of De Quincey's work consists. Its charm lies chiefly in the sometimes stately, but always natural and equable movement of his style at its ordinary level; a style that diff atmosphere of smiles and gaiety around it, a sunny style,

"Buoyant as morning, and as morning clear."

but a style highly distasteful to the gloomy and morose, and to such as think that prose is the inalienable appanage of pedagogues. If language, to use Wordsworth's fine expression developed by De Quincey, is not the mere dress but rather the incarnation of thought, then, style of some kind being inseparable from language, a good style is the perfection, grace, beauty, health, of that incarnation. It is besides of the greatest importance as an aid to exposition, even in treating ordinary matters. As De Quincey puts it : "Style has two separate functions—first to brighten the *intelligibility* of a subject which is obscure to the understanding ; secondly, to regenerate the normal *power* and impressiveness of a subject which has become dormant to the sensibilities" (vol. ix. p. 94).

But how much more is this the case, when the subject in hand is such as to require and repay the brightest light that can be brought to bear upon it ; when it is evanescent and subtly interwoven moods of mind, hardly to be called thoughts or even imaginations, that have to be arrested and interpreted for others ; moods it may be which even the subject of them finds it difficult to arrest and interpret to himself. He who cultivates style for this purpose and in this way, even though his success be small, deserves the praise of perfecting the power and enlarging the grasp of thought, by increasing the subtilty and keenness of language which is its embodiment. The reader's mental powers are increased by the effort to apprehend, as the writer's are by the effort to communicate, the finer shades of emotion and

of thought which fleet over the dim mirror of consciousness. What one man thus describes as passing in
himself another may have experienced without attempting to describe ; but if in reading he recognises it, he
gains not only himself, he gains also a brother in the
describer.

It is true that the profoundest and most sublime
thoughts are ordinarily beyond the reach of any style of
prose writing to convey, though not perhaps to indicate.
Over and above the finest and most accurate description,
something else is requisite to convey its meaning to the
reader, namely, an effort on his part to apprehend it ;
and to spur the apprehension to this effort is generally
far more beyond the power of prose than of verse.
Prose, however balanced and musical in rhythm and
cadence, or however vivid by abruptness or antithesis it
may be made, cannot so isolate its subjects from common
images as to raise them into the higher and purer parts
of the emotional atmosphere ; it carries them along the
ground, with the narrative or argumentative matter
which is the necessary burden of prose writing. But
the use of metre is of itself an announcement that the
burden of prose is not to be expected, that the reader
must supply the filling in of circumstance for himself,
must place himself by an effort of his own in an attitude to which the feelings that are expressed become
intelligible.

Again, while metre thus calls on the reader to make
an effort of his own, it also at the same time aids and
stimulates it. A raising of the mental key, a solemnity
of tone, is given by the mere use of metre, which it
would be vainly sought to inspire by the most perfect
prose. Not to mention the minor advantage that the
metre directs the emphasis more pointedly, by irresistibly

indicating those words on which the burden of thought is laid. For instance, in Shelley's "Adonais":

> "Oh, dream not that the amorous Deep
> Will yet restore him to the vital air ;
> Death feeds on his mute voice, and laughs at our despair."

In prose the imaginative word *Deep* would need introduction if not apology ; and neither *dream* nor *feeds* would have an emphasis inevitably directed upon them, as it now is by the metre.

Although, then, prose can never be the equivalent of verse as a vehicle for poetic imagination, yet there are functions which it can perform, but has never yet performed fully, beauties and graces which are legitimately its own, but which it has never yet fully developed. Just as architecture, notwithstanding that it is subordinate to *use*, is bound to aim at all the beauty, elegance, and ornament, of which it is capable, in subordination to that use, so the art of prose writing has special capacities of beauty which by the law of perfection it is bound to aim at, while satisfying at the same time the logical uses which are its necessary conditions. Apply these principles to De Quincey's interpretive descriptions of subtil and evanescent moods of mind, and I think it will appear no idle boast that he makes, when, in the Preface to his first volume, he speaks of the "Confessions" and "Suspiria" as "modes of impassioned prose ranging under no precedents that he is aware of in any literature ;" by which of course he does not mean that they are superior to, but merely different from, preceding writings.

To deal fully with De Quincey's style would require a volume, and to do it well would tax the powers of the most accomplished critic. But it would abundantly repay the labour, should any one undertake it, to analyse the motives and methods of De Quincey's style and exhibit its characteristics, by comparing them with those of other recognised masters of prose writing, such for instance as Landor, Arnold of Rugby, Lord Macaulay, Mr. Carlyle, Mr. Ruskin, and (last not least) Cardinal Newman.

But the critical science by the canons of which such an attempt must be guided, the science of style, exists as yet but very imperfectly.   Style is, in fact, one entire but inseparable half of the whole sphere of written and spoken literature ; it is the *manner* of it, as distinguished from the *matter*.   Most interesting it is to observe, in the great founder of literary criticism, Aristotle, in his Rhetoric, how at a certain place in that treatise, Book III. cap. 12, a distinction proper to the larger subject of style cuts in athwart, and even threatens to confuse the distinctions proper to the smaller subject of rhetoric. All public speaking, the subject of rhetoric, Aristotle divides into three heads of consultative, forensic, and exhibitory speaking (συμβουλευτικόν, δικανικόν, ἐπιδεικτικὸν γένος). But public speaking and the speeches composed for it are but one part of literature as a whole, are but one part of that whole, of which style, the manner *how*, is one inseparable half, and with which therefore it is co-extensive.   And accordingly in the third Book which is devoted to style, and at the chapter named, a cardinal distinction applicable to style is introduced, under which the styles proper to the three kinds of public speaking have, somehow or other, to be reduced.   This distinction is into style proper to *writing* which is to be read or recited, and style prop̲e̲r̲ ̲t̲o̲ ̲s̲p̲e̲a̲k̲i̲n̲g̲ ̲a̲g̲a̲i̲nst competitors which is to be heard▓▓▓▓▓▓▓▓▓▓▓▓▓γραφ▓▓ ἀγωνιστικὴ λέξις).▓▓▓▓▓▓▓▓the by bringing the▓▓▓▓▓▓▓▓▓▓spea▓

under the head of style proper to *writings*, and leaving the consultative and forensic styles under that of style proper to speaking against competitors in public.

Aristotle thus adumbrates the treatment of style as one inseparable half of the whole field of literature, the manner being inseparable from the matter of every phrase, every transition, every turn of thought however minute ; inseparable, as the members of all distinctions of strictly philosophical analysis are. But the theory of Style so understood has, so far at least as I am aware, remained where Aristotle left it, down not indeed to our own days, but to the days of De Quincey. He added a further distinction, which seems to me as important in the theory of the subject as his own example in the practice of it. Language we have seen him hold with Wordsworth to be the incarnation of thought ; that is, it is the expression externally of the motions of the mind in dealing with its objects, whatever they may be ; it *is* the mind visibly and audibly at work ; its *manner* or mode of dealing with the things that occupy it. Starting from this basis, the distinction which he draws is this. Style, he says, may be treated either as an *organic* or as a *mechanic* thing ; organic so far as it expresses the living motions of the mind, mechanic so far as those motions are subject to rules of art which may be acquired, transmitted and learnt. There are accordingly two branches of the subject, the *organology* and the *mechanology* of style. (See the paper on *Style*, vol. xi. p. 194, Hogg's edit.)

This distinction sets the whole subject of style in a new and I think a true light ; it is at once philosophical and profound ; philosophical because its members are inseparables as well as opposites, and profound because it refers the nature and power of style to their deepest source, namely the character and power of the mind. Most of the distinctions given in treatises of Rhetoric are distinctions of the mechanology, laying down negative rules, precepts, what to avoid, illustrated by examples of faults. The *positive* part of the art of style is included chiefly in the organology, and this, so far as it can be learnt at all, must be learnt by studying the great masters, and by imbibing if possible their spirit.

When for instance, Shakespeare speaks of "taking *arms* against a *sea* of troubles," this is an offence against the mechanology. But when he makes Prospero say to Miranda (*Tempest*, act i. sc. 2) :

> "The fringed curtains of thine eye advance,
> And say what thou seest yond,"

this is a beauty of the organology, and of the highest kind. The fanciful expression is the natural outcome of the peculiar mood of Prospero. He had laid a plan the development of which he is watching with heightened and pleasurable expectation, and the first critical moment is at hand,—Ferdinand is coming into sight. The image of his daughter, too, in her morn of youth and loveliness, is present to him, and for her sake his plan has been laid. The exalted expression is not only *natural* to this state of mind, but also, being so, contributes to make the spectators aware that this *is* Prospero's state. It is a trait in the dramatic delineation of Prospero. That is Shakespeare's *style ;* that is his living *mind.*

But to return from De Quincey's theory to his practice, or rather to De Quincey himself. It is a characteristic, and indeed almost singular circumstance, that the greater portion of the Autobiographic Writings, and considerably the larger half even of the "Confessions of an English Opium-Eater," are occupied with the feelings and events of childhood and boyhood. How few are the writers who have thought it worth their while to go back upon their early days and minutely depict the scenes of their childhood and early youth step by step, as they unrolled themselves, with all their accompaniment of hope and fear, doubting and debate, and the changing yet all-important colouring of momentary feeling. Introspection is common, but not the record of an introspection into the moods of boyhood, recalled in later life, as if for the purpose of exhibiting an actual example of the child being father of the man.

Yet if we would have a true, an intimately true, picture of character in manhood, it is to the springs of character in childhood that we must trace it back, for there lies the succession of turning points which have given it its lasting ply. There, too, in the acts and events of childhood, the springs of character lie bare ; there they are not enveloped in a network of *reasons*, which being the products of experience, are known only to the man, but they appear what they are ; they appear as feelings and motives derived from feelings. Whoever gives us the introspection of his childhood admits us to a far more intimate acquaintance than he who begins only with his manhood.

In one sense De Quincey's manhood came early, even prematurely. He was a self-conscious, self-dependent, actor in the scene of life, and that from motives which are not common at any age, being of an intellectual and imaginative order, when in the judgment of those about him he was an ordinary child, an ordinary schoolboy. On the other hand, while in one sense he too prematurely a man, in another sense he never, at any age, be a child. His loyalty, his response to kind-interestedness, his intellectual equity, never

2 A

left him ; and it was because he would not count on others being different, that he continued a child to the end. Such characters may be led into errors and actions which are deeply blamable, but they are also and in themselves deeply lovable, and their record will be read with gratitude by thousands, for, in a sense truer perhaps and deeper than that in which it can be said of poets, they hold the mirror up to nature.

It is into a non-worldly atmosphere that De Quincey rises when he is depicting himself : it is into that same atmosphere that he raises others about whom he writes, I mean when he describes them from personal observation. In the future, those whom he thus describes will be immeasurably the gainers ; but in the immediate present, as denizens of the world, actors in every-day life, where, by some one or other, handles of disparagement are daily sought against every man, such a description is felt as an unwarranted violation of privacy. A man may violate his own privacy if he chooses ; that of others he has no right to violate, This De Quincey did not always see. He spoke of others as he spoke of himself, freely and openly, occasionally too with a certain recklessness of satirical expression which jars upon the ear, as if the public at large, to whom he spoke, were to a man not only an intelligent but an equitable audience, and would discount what was due to his extravagances. But not one reader in a thousand, of any present audience, can be reckoned on as truly intelligent and equitable. It is only in the future that the voice of the *units* prevails. To *these* it is that De Quincey is really speaking, as much when he writes of others as when he writes of himself : and in *their* judgment it is that those whom he describes will gain from having been described by De Quincey.

Do I then reckon on a long-lived popularity for De Quincey's writings? I certainly do. And why? To say it in one word, because of the total absence from them of the *sophistry* of their period. The sophistry of any period is whatever is written up to the mark of the views and modes of thinking then and there current. These are pre-supposed before the sophistry can succeed. The prevailing tone is caught, and then success is assured. But De Quincey's writings came straight from himself; were not moulded on the tone of the day. How should they have been; he who being most originally as well as richly endowed, had besides enjoyed in large measure one mode of education not often bestowed, especially in these crowded times,—the education of solitude, than which there is no microscope in this world more powerful, if the eye can but endure to use it, nor any instrument more effectual for enforcing on the memory and on the will whatever is steadily contemplated through it. Whatever was original, whatever was peculiar, in De Quincey's organisation, we may be sure was greatly developed and intensified by his escape from school, his four months of lonely wandering over the Welsh hills, and that wandering, perhaps more lonely still, along the " never-ending terraces of Oxford Street." Whatever he wrote was sure to bear the impress of himself, not the impress of the current mode. Right or wrong, feeble or powerful, it was sure to be genuine, an outcome of the writer, not a reflex of the public.

Yet De Quincey was no seeker of solitude in order to escape from society, as a cynic or a misanthrope. Perhaps there never was a nature that more imperatively needed society. His interests were all of the *quicquid agunt homines* type, from "grandeurs that measured

2 A 2

themselves against centuries," or the majesty of the
" *Consul Romanus,*" down to the most trivial anecdote,
the nursery rhyme, or the nursery superstition. He was
a born Conservative, if I may use the expression, a
Conservative by natural constitution, just such a Conservative as Pindar the Greek Lyrist was, having eyes to
see and admire whatever of great or good was already
achieved, birth, wealth, courage, culture, nobility in all
its shapes ; but without that sense, which is the keynote
of Liberalism, of a burden and a task imposed on all
men of striving for a common far-off goal, of aiding in
an arduous development, of realising a hardly to be
gained ideal, in the elevation of mankind as a whole.
History was to him a series of scenes, not a continuous
progress in which the present generation has a practical
part to play.

His own mind, too, is stationary ; there is no growth,
no enlargement, of his intellectual basis, as he advances
in life. He speaks in his later essays from the same
platform of ideas as in his earlier ones ; it is only the
occasion, the application, that is different. He has
acquired much, but he has learnt little. His style on
the other hand, when he applies himself in good earnest,
becomes more perfect, and possibly, too, his artistic
power of exposition. At least both are at their best in
the enlarged edition of the ' Confessions,' published three
years before his death. Comparing this, either in single
passages or as a whole, with the brief and rapidly
written first edition, its superiority is unmistakable. He
lived to make a perfect work of art out of that sketch,
with which his literary career may be said to have
begun, and in which the basis of his reputation was
laid.

These are points which it is essential to remark, in

endeavouring to form a just estimate of De Quincey as a man of letters. Here is the weak side of his mind, here the darkness and narrowness, so at least it seems to me, of the otherwise large and luminous grasp of his intellect. Fragmentary indeed it was not; but it seems as if one whole aspect of human affairs, all that is summed up in the idea of Progress subject to laws which *science* can discover, was to him a blank. The nexus of individuals with one another, of class with class, and the secret but profound relations which connect man with an unseen world,—these were familiar ideas to him; but the nexus between earlier and later generations, between earlier and later races, in order of time, was an idea which he had not grasped, or at least full significance of which he had not realised.

Nor would I be thought blind to the defects which sometimes disfigure his style, the instances here and there of misplaced colloquialism, jokes not worth making, repetitions of himself, repetitions of favourite quotations, which are obvious on the surface. In fact, the necessity of writing on the spur of the moment, and for different audiences, tempted him to ride with too loose a rein, and to repeat too often what, being no more than a groove of his thought, the household furniture of his mind, should strictly have been said but once, if even that. All this comes out but too conspicuously, when scattered essays are assembled in republication.

But why do I bring forward all these deficiencies? To mention them is necessary, in order to a just estimation of his powers; but it would be superfluous to dwell on them, so long as justice is not done to his peculiar merits. Men, and therefore their works when taken as a whole, which is equivalent, are to be judged primarily, not like chains of argument by their weakest parts, but

like poems or pictures by their strongest. Appreciate
these first ; *then* count and weigh the defects. The
defects can only be understood by first knowing the aim
of the writer and the methods which he takes to realise it.
The rule is different for separate works, when these belong
to the literature of knowledge ; for there, the aim and
method being known, a standard for the defects is at
hand. But in judging men, in judging their works as a
whole, and in judging works of the power literature even
separately, to judge by the weakest parts is not only an
injustice, it is a fatal blunder in criticism.

Apart from some brilliant exceptions, such for instance
as the admirable critique in the *New Quarterly Magazine* for July 1875, the want of appreciation shown
towards De Quincey by his literary countrymen is
remarkable. It seems as if we sometimes do our thinking by deputy, wilfully put our eyes in our pockets and
try spectacles instead. A man of great originality
necessarily stands much more alone than men of more
ordinary powers ; he has to dispense with one whole
stratum, so to speak, from which the water-supply of
genial appreciation should be derived. Critics in the
mass naturally, and quite excusably, praise ability and
success in doing that which they themselves are
attempting to do. Not only do they understand it
better, not only do they find it easier to explain to the
public, but they have this direct, though unconsciously
operating, interest in doing so, that they are enforcing
principles of criticism which, in case of their own success,
will redound to their benefit. They praise what they
admire, what they would like to imitate. The original
writer, differing much from his critics, is apt to get scant
justice from them, unless his merits lie very much on the
surface, and his faults be tolerably withdrawn from

observation. Where the reverse is the case, merits, however great, will pass unnoticed, for it is no one's business to unearth them. That De Quincey's writings should, in spite of this, have won and hitherto kept a high place in popular estimation is a circumstance which augurs well for their obtaining in the end a more solid and lasting renown.

INDEX.

+7/

LONDON: PRINTED BY WILLIAM CLOWES AND SONS, LIMITED,
STAMFORD STREET AND CHARING CROSS.

www.ingramcontent.com/pod-product-compliance
Lightning Source LLC
Chambersburg PA
CBHW030906270326
41929CB00008B/591